Freedom and Purpose

Freedom and Purpose

An Introduction to Christian Ethics

Robert Gascoigne

Paulist Press
New York/Mahwah, N.J.

Cover design by Trudi Gershenov
Book design by Lynn Else

Library of Congress Cataloging-in-Publication Data

Gascoigne, Robert.
    Freedom and purpose : an introduction to Christian ethics / Robert Gascoigne.
        p.   cm.
    Includes bibliographical references and index.
    ISBN 0-8091-4221-X (alk. paper)
    1. Christian ethics—Catholic authors. I. Title.

BJ1249.G32 2004
241'.042—dc22

                                                                2004002203

Published by Paulist Press
997 Macarthur Boulevard
Mahwah, New Jersey 07430

www.paulistpress.com

Printed and bound in the
United States of America

Contents

The Structure of This Book

Part One: Foundations

This is made up of two chapters, "Ethics in a Pluralist Society" and "Christian Faith and Ethics." These chapters consider the foundational questions of the nature of morality and ethics, the challenge of contemporary ethical pluralism, and the roles of reason and Christian faith in ethics.

Part Two: What Sort of Person Should I Be?

This part is made up of the chapters "The Moral Person" and "Sin and the Fundamental Option." It considers the nature of the moral person, characterized by freedom, responsibility, and conscience, and the abuse of human freedom in sin.

Part Three: What Is the Good?

The chapter "A Good World" considers the goodness of creation, with particular emphasis on the dignity of the human person as seen through biblical faith.

Part Four: What Should I Do?

The chapters "Love, Rights, and Moral Norms," "The Task of Moral Reasoning," and "Christian Ethics and the Teaching Authority of the Church" consider the nature and development of moral norms in light of a Christian process of moral reasoning.

Appendix: Scriptural Sources for Select Ethical Issues

The appendix examines lengthier scriptural sources regarding human dignity, and love and moral norms.

PART ONE

FOUNDATIONS

Part One is made up of two chapters, "Ethics in a Pluralist Society" and "Christian Faith and Ethics." These chapters consider the foundational questions of the nature of morality and ethics, the challenge of contemporary ethical pluralism, and the roles of reason and Christian faith in ethics.

1

Ethics in a Pluralist Society

What Is the Subject Matter of Ethics?

A schoolchild standing up for another child in the playground who is made fun of because he has a speech defect.

A young couple who love each other faithfully and strive to respect each other's true needs and individuality.

A father and mother patiently and lovingly caring for their children.

A public servant refusing to take a bribe.

A prisoner of conscience who refuses to sign an undertaking that she will desist from criticizing government abuses of human rights.

A busy adult who regularly takes time to visit and care for an aged parent.

A politician who tries to serve the common good.

A businessman who is honest in his dealings and fair to his employees.

All of these are examples of moral action. Some are a part of everyday experience, and some arise in more critical and urgent situations. In a sense, some of them are "ordinary." Yet in a truer sense they are all extraordinary, sometimes even heroic, because they express something that is uniquely precious to human beings: our moral capacity.

What is morality? What are we doing when we act morally? In an initial attempt to answer these questions, let us distinguish morality from what it is not. First of all we can distinguish morality from legality, from obedience to laws. Obedience to a law may well be

3

moral, but it also may not be. There are bad laws, obedience to which may be immoral. (Think of the prisoner of conscience.) Second, we can distinguish morality from self-interest. It is true that if we act morally, if we cooperate with others, for example, we are more likely to achieve some of our goals. It is clear, however, that at least some of the time being moral may be contrary to our immediate self-interest, in the sense that the requirement to cooperate with others or to respect their needs may limit our opportunities to achieve our own goals. (Something parents or couples struggle with, and those in business as well!) Finally, we can distinguish morality from acting in ways that please others, people whom we care about or who are important in our lives. Moral action may well please others, and we are usually glad when acting morally and pleasing others coincide, but sometimes we feel a moral obligation to do something that finds a lot of disfavor among those whom we would like to please. How popular will the schoolchild or politician be?

Acting morally, then, may coincide with any or all of the above reasons for acting, but the reason why we call an action "moral" is different from any of those reasons. What is it that characterizes moral action? When we act morally, we respond to the intrinsic value of the world around us in ways that show respect for that intrinsic value. When we act morally, we do not make self-interest the sole and overriding concern of action, but rather ask ourselves whether or not what we are doing implies respect for the value of the things and living beings that constitute our world. In particular, moral actions reveal that we acknowledge that other human beings have the same fundamental value as ourselves. By being moral we recognize that we live in a world that has its own value, a world that cannot be reduced to a mere instrument for the satisfaction of our own needs and desires.

What motivates us to act morally, if it is not simply obedience to law, self-interest, or the desire to please? If the essence of morality is respect for the inherent value of the world around us, then the motivation to act morally must spring from our experience of the value of the world. We are moral because we have a sense that other things and living beings have value, and this value implies an obligation for us to respect it. Most of all, we have an experience of the value of other persons. We experience that other persons have a value inherent in them *as* persons, a value that obliges us to act in ways that respect their own rights and desire for happiness. So whether through love and fidelity, through commitment to human rights, through compassion for the oppressed, through integrity and justice, all of the moral actions we have considered show a commitment to the value of persons.

Morality has its wellspring in the experience of the value of the world, and especially of human persons. This experience is a fusion of insight and response. We know the value of other persons, but this knowledge is not knowledge of a fact like any other fact. It is a knowledge that calls for a response in action that shows respect for that value. Yet this experience is not one we are forced to have. We can suppress and ignore it. We can live our lives without acting from moral motives. We may obey the law, we may cooperate with others, but our actions may be dictated purely by fear of unpleasant consequences if we break the law, or by fear of others withdrawing their cooperation from us. Yet if we do not live in ways that are motivated by respect for the value of the world and the persons in it, we remain cut off from the experience of community. We deprive ourselves of the experience of creating our own selves in a community of mutual respect with other selves. In this deeper sense, morality is truly in our self-interest.

Morality, then, involves two crucial aspects of our humanity. It involves our awareness of value, our capacity to experience and respond to the inherent goodness of the world, and the things, beings, and persons that make it up. Together with this, it involves our freedom: the freedom to open ourselves to this experience or to suppress and ignore it. *Human beings are moral beings because they have the capacity to experience and know the good and to freely respond to it.* The way we use these moral capacities is fundamental to our quality as persons. Irrespective of whatever other

5

talents we may have or not have, it is our free response to value, our respect for what is good, that expresses our quality as persons.

The moral life is a life freely lived in response to goodness. It is a matter of practice, rather than theory. The quality of persons lies in their moral responses and actions, rather than in their ability to reflect theoretically about the meaning of goodness. Yet reflection about our practice, thinking about why we do what we do, has a very important place in human life. It has intellectual significance, in terms of our human desire to understand ourselves and our world. It can also have moral significance, in terms of our desire to improve our moral practice by reflecting on the meaning, consistency, and consequences of the way we act. The discipline of *ethics* is a systematic and critical reflection on the moral life. *Christian ethics* is the discipline of ethics studied in light of the Christian gospel.

Since ethics is a discipline that reflects on what is of fundamental importance to our existence, it has a long and controversial history. Different ethical theories have understood the meaning and purpose of the moral life in different ways. In order to gain some appreciation of the crucial issues of debate in ethics, we will now turn to consider the three most influential ethical theories in the history of Western thought: *Aristotelianism, Kantianism,* and *Utilitarianism.* In chapter 2, we will begin to consider the relationship between ethics and Christian faith.

Three Ethical Theories

Aristotelianism

The oldest ethical theory that is still a major contender in philosophical debate derives from the ancient Greek philosopher Aristotle (384–322 BC). For Aristotle, the purpose of human action was to achieve *eudaimonia,* "happiness," or better, "flourishing." Human moral action should be oriented toward that which allows human beings to flourish, to fulfill their purpose. For Aristotle, human beings achieve happiness when they live by certain *virtues,* habitual ways of acting which together make up a way of life conducive to happiness. In common with other Greek thinkers, Aristotle identified four virtues, which came to be called the "cardinal virtues" from the Latin *cardo* or "hinge": prudence, justice, courage, and temperance (moderation). Someone who lived by the virtues was a person of good character, a person who had integrated the different aspects of life into a harmonious whole. For Aristotelian ethics, then, morality is about achieving human fulfillment by living a virtuous way of life. As such, it gives morality a rich and satisfying content, emphasizing human fulfillment rather than rules or laws.

In the medieval period, Aristotle's ethical system was adapted to the Christian faith by the great theologian and philosopher Thomas Aquinas (c. 1225–74). Using Aristotle's ethical theory, Aquinas developed an understanding of the Christian life as a life lived by the virtues. He adopted Aristotle's list of the virtues and added the Christian "theological virtues" of faith, hope, and charity.

If the Aristotelian approach sees morality as achieving fulfillment by living out the virtues, then the obvious questions are "What makes up human fulfillment?" and "By what virtues should we live?" Aristotle's answer was to consider a model Athenian citizen and to note the virtues that were characteristic of him. By reflecting on an ideal example of a fulfilled human being, we too can gain a good understanding of how we should live in order to be fulfilled. When we ask what human fulfillment consists of, the answer lies in a lifestyle that has been developed by a moral tradition. A moral tradition is a combination of beliefs and practices, a more or less integrated way of life that offers individual and social fulfillment, developed by experience and passed on from generation to generation in the history of a community.

As we have seen, Aristotle's answer to the question "What virtues should we live by?" was in terms of the moral tradition of elite members of his own society. This raises the question of the relevance of this tradition to other societies. How normative is it? Is it an attractive model of human flourishing for other ages and peoples? Is it possible to adapt Aristotle's ethics so that we no longer think in terms of a model Athenian citizen, but simply "fill in" his general approach with whatever model of fulfilled human life seems appropriate to us? (Clearly, this model will reject Aristotle's view that women and slaves had an inferior status.)

The problem becomes particularly acute when society no longer has any one tradition of values to live by. In Aristotle's time and during the long period of European culture when the Christian worldview was culturally dominant, it was accepted that human life was lived in the context of a divinely created order; all aspects of nature were part of the order of creation, and the moral life consisted of living out this order for the glory of God and the fulfillment of the person. From this point of view, the moral life was part of a unified tradition of values. Ask "Why should we be moral?" and the answer would be in terms of the created order and purpose of things. The point of morality was to fulfill the purpose of human life as created by God.

Kantianism

During the period of thought known as the Enlightenment, the conviction that there was a divinely created order and purpose in things received severe criticism. Some philosophers drew the conclusion that, if there was no such order and purpose, then morality was essentially a matter of convention, a way of maintaining social stability. The Scottish philosopher David Hume argued that, since there existed no overarching purpose to nature or to human existence, we could never prove that we "ought" to do anything, in the moral sense of the word.

It was the German philosopher Immanuel Kant (1724–1804) who attempted to develop a new framework for ethics in the wake of these fundamental challenges to the traditional concepts of order and purpose. Kant accepted many of the critiques of the traditional perspective; he agreed that we could not base morality on a prior belief that there is a moral order in nature, since the sciences could

8

not prove such an order; and he agreed that morality could not be based on the existence of God, since he believed that philosophy could not prove the existence of God. Yet Kant was also convinced that morality was a great deal more than mere convention or simply a matter of fulfilling desires.

Kant did not believe that we could base ethics on a pattern of virtues, given to us by a moral tradition, since there was no longer any agreement about what this tradition should be, nor could anyone show why we should adopt one tradition rather than another. His concern was to find values that could provide a universal foundation for ethics in an age where traditional philosophical and religious views of life were no longer universally accepted. These values were freedom and reason. Freedom and reason were the two characteristics of human beings that gave them the noble status of moral beings (characteristics shared by God, if he existed, which Kant believed, and by the angels, if they existed, which Kant was inclined to doubt).

Many of the skeptical philosophers of the Enlightenment had argued that we could not prove the existence of human freedom. They supposed we could be completely determined by past events, by society, by our genetic inheritance, and so on. Kant agreed that we cannot prove in theoretical terms that we are free, but we sense our freedom through our experience of moral obligation; I experience a call on me to act rightly, a call that I can resist and refuse. If this is so, then I am free in the most fundamental moral sense of the word. This freedom is something crucial about me as a human being. Kant argued that we should begin from freedom and develop morality from it. We should be free to do whatever we wish, whatever we will to do. Our premise is that we are free, and there must be good reason to show why freedom is to be restricted in any way.

This is where Kant's second crucial value—reason—enters into his argument. We are free to act as we wish, but reason tells us that if anyone else acts in the same way, he or she is free also. What if the actions of free people are incompatible? What if my free wish is to rob someone else's house, and his wish is to rob mine? We can see that this results in contradiction: I wish to rob someone else's belongings in order to gain wealth, but others are free to enact a similar wish in order to deprive me of wealth. If we combine freedom and reason, we recognize that I am free to do anything so long as it is something that everyone else is free to do without contradicting the purpose of what we all wish for. Kant's way of formulating this is called the *categorical imperative:* we must always act in such a way that what we wish for, or the "maxim" of our action, could be a universal law. In other words, we act on the premise that we are all free and rational human beings and that whatever we do must be compatible with our free life in common.

The fact that every human being is free and rational was expressed by Kant through the concept of *autonomy,* from the Greek words for "self" and "law." We are autonomous, not because we are "a law unto ourselves" in the anarchic sense of the phrase, but because all moral laws are based on the freedom and reason of human beings. For Kant, this autonomy was what gave human beings their moral dignity, their worth as persons. Since all persons are autonomous, all are fundamentally equal in a moral sense.

This worth or dignity was what led him to the formulation of a second great moral principle: a moral action is an action that respects human beings as autonomous, as free and rational, in short, as *persons.* Kant expressed this in the following dictum: In all your actions, whether in relation to others or yourself, treat every person as an end, and never purely as a means to an end. That is, a person should never be treated purely as a means of achieving someone else's goals. A person's own wishes and interests must be considered or taken into account in actions that will affect him or her. Persons, as ends in themselves, are the goals of action, rather than the means of achieving someone else's goals. For Kant, this could be best expressed in a society where all persons have an opportunity to contribute to the making of laws that would affect all members of society, so that persons are not reduced to the passive instruments of the will of others.

As we have just seen, Kant expressed the foundational values of freedom and reason through two key principles: the categorical imperative and a respect for persons as ends rather than only as means to an end. It follows from his approach that these principles must be respected whatever the consequences. If human persons have a dignity based on reason and freedom, then no action could be morally right that disregards this dignity, however much we are convinced that better consequences might result from doing so. Kant's ethic is based emphatically on the duty we have to respect fundamental principles, rather than on giving consequences the crucial role in indicating what we should do. Because of this, his ethical theory is called *deontological,* from the Greek word for "duty." There is an age-old dictum that expresses the ultimate stance of this approach to ethics: *fiat justitia, et ruant coeli* ("let justice be done, though the heavens fall"). For Kant, the fundamental goal of ethics is not achieving happiness, but respecting the reason and freedom of persons. In this life, such respect and the achievement of happiness may very well not coincide, which led Kant to the hope that there did exist a God whose benevolence and almighty power would reconcile the commitment to justice and the achievement of happiness.

Utilitarianism

During the eighteenth and nineteenth centuries, a very different ethical theory was developed, primarily in England, which was oriented toward the achievement of happiness as the prime purpose of ethics. The thinkers who developed this theory were convinced that there was no good reason to believe in God and that the human race would only achieve happiness, if at all, in this world. These thinkers were called *utilitarians* and their ethical theory was and is known as utilitarianism, from the Latin word *utilis,* meaning "useful." The greatest of the utilitarians was the philosopher and social reformer John Stuart Mill (1806–73).

The utilitarians agreed with Aristotle that the purpose of ethics was happiness, but the way in which this happiness could be achieved

11

was understood very differently. Aristotle had understood happiness as the goal of morality, but the life of the virtues was crucial to what happiness consisted in. We achieve happiness in and through the life of virtue, and we know what the life of virtue is through studying virtuous "models" or fulfilled human beings. The utilitarians, however, argued that there was no such model. Human beings have very different ideas of what happiness consists of, and so it is pointless to prescribe a list of virtues. What we must concentrate on is the achievement of happiness as the result of our actions. What *kinds* of action we perform is not crucial to morality; what is crucial is that the result of this action is greater happiness for human beings.

The earlier utilitarians tended to define happiness in terms of the maximization of pleasure and the minimization of pain. This was later understood in more and more sophisticated ways, so that pleasure could refer to enjoying higher cultural pursuits, for example, and not simply instinctual gratification. But the utilitarians did insist that we have no right to prescribe what are "higher" or "lower" pleasures. A free society, based on critical thinking and the natural sciences, does not accept any traditional picture of human life that includes a hierarchy of pleasures or a model of human fulfillment. What is important is that society is oriented toward maximizing those activities that human beings do, as a matter of fact, find pleasurable and minimizing those that are painful.

For utilitarianism, it is the *consequences* of our actions that are crucial. The fundamental moral disposition is *benevolence*, wishing well to other humans and other sentient beings (higher animals) and acting well on their behalf. From this perspective, Kant's moral philosophy is misguided and potentially fanatical. Kant was right to treat persons as possessed of reason and freedom, but this did not mean that we must abide by certain principles whatever the consequences.

Let us consider a hypothetical situation, in which a Kantian and a utilitarian are likely to disagree about the right course of action. Imagine that a dying millionaire confides to us how to gain access to his wealth, provided that we promise him to transfer it to his spendthrift son. We make the promise and then proceed to spend the money on famine relief. The son was not aware of the promise and was undeserving in any case; the father is dead and is unaware that we have broken our promise; no one else knows about the promise, and so the important and useful social convention of keeping promises is not harmed by our breach of it; and many suffering human beings benefit greatly by the allocation of the wealth to the relief of their hunger.

From a utilitarian point of view, provided these conditions can be met, the right course of action is clear: we should act in such a way that will have the consequences of increasing the happiness of the greatest number of people. From this perspective, there can be no doubt that many more people will be happy if we break our promise, than if we had proceeded to transfer the wealth to the spendthrift son, who—we have every reason to believe—will immediately squander it in ways that may give him pleasure but add nothing else to the sum of human happiness.

From a Kantian perspective, by contrast, breaking our promise to a dying man would be a clear case of using someone merely as a means to an end. The dying millionaire has freely entrusted a secret to us on the basis of our freely given promise to respect his wishes. In breaking this promise for the sake of our own purposes—however benevolent these may be—we are using the millionaire as a means or instrument of our own purposes, flouting his rational autonomy. The only courses of action compatible with rational freedom are either not to make the promise in the first place, thereby freely renouncing the opportunity to gain access to this great wealth, or, once made, to keep it.

For the utilitarian, promising is a useful and important convention rather than a principle that must be adhered to because of the imperatives flowing from the free and rational character of the person. This notion of moral principles as crucial conventions brings us to an important distinction within utilitarian thought. The most radical version of utilitarianism—called *act utilitarianism*—argues that we should consider every act we perform in light of the consequences for human happiness that are likely to result from it. Thus, every time we make a promise, we can subsequently ask ourselves whether keeping the promise will lead to the best possible consequences for human happiness. However, utilitarians soon acknowledged that this kind of reflection or calculation would be impossible to make every time we make a promise. The notion of *rule utilitarianism* was developed to do justice to the fact that acting by certain moral rules does in fact result in the maximization of human happiness in most cases. If I keep my promises, and if others know that I will keep my promises, then we are usually all better off. However, it is crucial that this is a social convention or rule and not a principle in the Kantian sense. When the occasion demands, I may break a promise if the results of my doing so will be much better than the results of keeping it, given that I have taken into account the possible harm done to the useful institution of promise keeping.

Philosophical Pluralism about Ethics

These three great theories of ethics are still the subject of intense philosophical debate and controversy—none of them can be considered to be outmoded or purely of historical interest. From this brief presentation of them, we can see that a study of the history of philosophy does not give us any agreed-upon approach to the solution of ethical problems or any one answer to the question "What is the good life for a human being?" Rather, three dominant answers have emerged: For Aristotle, the good life is the life lived by the virtues in fulfillment of a moral tradition; for Kant, the good life is the life lived on the basis of reason and freedom, respecting the autonomy of persons; for the utilitarians, the good life is the life dedicated to benevolence and to bringing about the greatest happiness of the greatest number. Philosophical debate about ethics shows a very significant *pluralism* about what ethics is, a pluralism that reflects different conceptions of the nature and purpose of human existence. Since none of these ethical theories has been able conclusively to supersede the others, this pluralism remains a part of ethical debate today.

Ethics in a Pluralist Society

This pluralism is not only characteristic of philosophical debate about ethics, it is also a feature of contemporary societies. It is becoming increasingly clear that we live in societies characterized by a pluralism of ethical values. The word *pluralism,* in this context, means that there is no one set of moral values and practices accepted by all members of society and given the force of law. A range of different moral attitudes and lifestyles is present in society and is accepted, more or less tolerantly, by those living their lives in different ways. Since this ethical pluralism is such a widespread and influential characteristic of modern life, we must briefly consider its origins and reflect on its implications and significance.

To understand the nature of a pluralist society, it is helpful to compare a typical Western industrial democracy with other societies that are not pluralist, that is, societies where one worldview and one approach to life is legally and socially mandatory. In medieval Western Europe, the Catholic Church was the dominant cultural, ethical, and religious institution. At least in public, Catholic morality was accepted as the one lifestyle that conformed with the truth about human nature and was capable of bringing about human fulfillment. In traditional Islamic societies, the Islamic law is understood to be the religious and ethical bond linking all members of society together in a community that worships and praises God and that respects the roles and capacities of different social groups. Similarly, in traditional tribal societies, the wisdom of the elders and the age-old social and religious traditions embodied a lifestyle that was accepted by all as the true path to union with the spirits and to oneness with nature. All of these different societies shared a unified body of religious and ethical values, values that enabled a very high degree of social cohesion. Such societies can be defined as *traditional societies,* that is, societies not characterized by a pluralism of ethical values, but rather by a single and dominant tradition of accepted values and practices.

15

Some of the Causes of Pluralism

The first experiments in ethical pluralism were made in ancient Greece, when philosophers known as Sophists began to challenge accepted social values by critical questioning. The experience of foreign cultures and ways of living, brought about by trade and colonization, encouraged a critical attitude to received and accepted values. Later in the Hellenistic period (the time from about 300 BC to 200 AD when Greek, Roman, Egyptian, and Near Eastern cultures intermingled in the Eastern Mediterranean world), there were many experiments in religious and ethical pluralism. However, the most widespread and long-lasting form of ethical pluralism began in modern Western Europe and exercised enormous influence over the rest of the world. For our purposes, this is the crucial source of ethical pluralism.

From about the late-seventeenth century in Western Europe, the age-old links between ethics and religion began to be challenged and, as these critical currents of thought gained in impetus, different aspects of traditional morality were also subjected to scrutiny. The movement of ideas known as the Enlightenment, which had its heyday in the eighteenth and nineteenth centuries, challenged the traditional place of Christianity as the chief source of ethical values and guidance, and argued for various ethical stances based on reason and nature rather than on religion. We have already seen the ethical implications of this in the development of Kantianism and utilitarianism. This intellectual critique of traditional Christianity was reinforced by the economic and social changes brought about by the Industrial Revolution and the political changes resulting from the French Revolution. By the mid-nineteenth century, although most parts of Western Europe and America still lived according to traditional Catholic or Protestant morality, the intellectual and social foundations of ethical pluralism had been laid. Later ideas and social movements were to intensify this process.

Some of the crucial factors in the development of pluralism were the following.

Secularization

The sixteenth and seventeenth centuries had been marred by savage conflict between different religious groups. One very important result of this, as far as ethics was concerned, was criticism of the long-held conviction that ethics, politics, and religion belonged together and were mutually reinforcing. The thinkers of the early Enlightenment argued that, if differences between Christians led to religious war, then the unity of a nation should not be based on allegiance to a particular religion, but must rather be developed from secular—or nonreligious—premises. Different attempts were therefore made to find another basis for the unity of the state or nation—for example, the need for survival and protection from anarchy; the understanding of the institutions of government as a "social contract" based on free consent; or, later, the emotional fulfillment of belonging to a national group and culture.

This secularization of politics also led to the secularization of ethics. Instead of grounding our moral laws in God and the teaching of the churches, philosophers looked for a foundation in human reason or human nature. One striking example of the secularization of the moral life was the institution of civil marriage during the French Revolution; for the first time in history, a couple could be married in a purely secular ceremony, rather than in a religious context.

Religious and Ethical Toleration

The reaction to religious war also encouraged the growth of the idea of religious toleration, which was strongly advocated by some of the smaller "nonconformist" Protestant churches— churches that were to play a crucial role in the early history of the United States and its emphasis on freedom of religion. The emphasis on the importance of toleration in religious matters was eventually extended to toleration for differing political and ethical views as well.

Individualism

One effect of the rejection of traditional forms of social union was a growing emphasis on individuality and individual freedom. This was expressed particularly strongly during the Romantic movement, a movement of literature, art, and ideas that followed the French Revolution. For many exponents of Romanticism, individual feelings and individual self-expression were sacred values that could not be judged by social or religious laws. The understanding of love and marriage, for example, began to be based more and more on the romantic bonds between individuals than on traditional social arrangements.

Breakup of Traditional Communities

Finally, ethical pluralism was encouraged and intensified by the breakup of traditional cultures and communities and exposure to many different cultures and social practices through industrialization and immigration. The effect of industrialization on traditional rural societies was to draw off of great numbers of people to rapidly growing industrial cities; there the social supports for traditional values and ways of life were conspicuously absent. New patterns of life were formed in these huge urban contexts where different social groups and lifestyles clashed or intermingled. Immigration resulted in societies where various ethical and religious traditions were forced to come to terms with each other. Even though these groups often attempted to preserve their traditional lifestyles by forming self-contained communities within a mixed society, exposure to other traditions meant that one's own tradition could no longer be simply taken for granted as the only way of life. Examples of very different ways could be observed as an everyday reality.

The Scope of Ethical Pluralism

The above factors were and are some of the causes of the development of pluralist societies. If these historical developments have resulted in societies that accept a pluralism of ethical values, what is the scope of this pluralism? How much disagreement and difference can a pluralist society typically contain? What values are held in common, despite many differences?

First of all, it follows from the nature of pluralism itself that we cannot be pluralist about the importance of *individual freedom* and *mutual tolerance*. The importance of these values is something we need to agree on, if we are to have a pluralist society at all. These values are supported by the law, since they are the basis of a pluralist society itself. The law expresses a social consensus that individual freedom and mutual tolerance form the best basis for a society where many different worldviews and lifestyles exist.

Social Justice

The more difficult question is whether, apart from freedom and tolerance, there are any other values on which a strong consensus exists in contemporary pluralist societies. Arguably there is some consensus that a certain degree of social justice should be fostered by the law and by the governing institutions of society and that society is united in agreement about the truly needy receiving public assistance. The scope of the principle of social justice is, however, hotly disputed between the main political parties of democratic societies. Political and social theorists, not to mention voters, are in strong disagreement about the extent to which public wealth should be expended in the cause of social justice. Nevertheless, pluralist democratic societies are often capable of sustained commitment to practical programs of social welfare, demonstrating a significant degree of moral consensus in this regard.

If individual freedom and mutual tolerance are the foundational values of pluralist societies, and if they are capable of significant, albeit limited, agreement about social justice, what are the areas where pluralist societies characteristically experience conflict and disagreement? Consider the following.

Sexual Morality

Here pluralism is characterized by controversy over the rights and wrongs of various forms of sexual relations, over the nature and importance of marriage and the family, over the role of divorce, and over the question of homosexuality.

The Scope of Individual Freedom

Although pluralist societies are based on the priority of the value of individual freedom, members of pluralist societies disagree about what the legitimate scope of this individual freedom is and how it relates to social priorities. Controversy about the penal code, for example, often centers on the degree to which individual freedom should be limited as a punishment for crime or for the protection of society. Debates on such topics as the legitimacy of censorship of pornography or of restriction of access to politically sensitive records and information focus on the relationship between the rights of individual freedom and social morality and stability.

The Scope of the Sanctity of Life as an Ethical Concept

While the right to life of the free individual is accepted as a foundational value, the right of the individual to end his or her own life and the right of the mother to terminate the life of the fetus in her womb are matters of intense controversy in pluralist societies. Questions associated with abortion, euthanasia, and suicide are all subject to massive disagreement.

The Hierarchy of Values

What order of importance will be given to different values? In particular, what is the importance of economic values in relation to aesthetic, intellectual, and cultural values? In traditional societies, various aspects of culture, such as the artistic or intellectual life, had a particular role to play that was generally agreed on by the dominant groups. Since pluralist societies have resulted from the transformation or intermingling of traditional societies, however, and since they are based on the importance of individual freedom of choice, they have no uncontroversial way of judging the relative importance of different values, particularly in relation to economic values. An important example of this has been the political controversies associated with the relationship between the spiritual values of indigenous peoples in relation to sacred sites and the economic values associated with mining and pastoral interests.

Pluralism: A Description or an Ethical Attitude?

In any discussion of pluralism, it is important to distinguish between pluralism as a statement of social fact and pluralism as an ethical or philosophical attitude. As a statement of fact, to say that a society is ethically pluralist is simply to say that its members hold different ethical beliefs. This statement of fact need not take up any position about whether or not that is a good thing. In this sense, the word pluralism indicates simply that there is a "plurality" of ethical beliefs and practices in a society.

"Pluralism" can also, however, be an ethical attitude, which holds—to varying degrees—that it is a good thing to have a variety of ethical beliefs and practices in a society. Some people argue that this is a good thing because it affirms individual freedom and encourages diversity of human behavior and lifestyle. Others argue that *diversity* is just another word for "disagreement" and point to the lack of community and the moral confusion that disagreement about ethical matters can cause.

Pluralism and Relativism

Perhaps the most significant development of ethical pluralism, in the sense of an ethical attitude, is *ethical relativism,* the standpoint that, since there are many and varied ethical stances on a particular question, they must all be equally valid or equally false. For the relativist, there is no one set of ethical truths that society holds

21

in common; therefore, there must be no such thing as universal ethical truth at all. Ethics must be purely a matter of individual perspective or of the perspective of certain groups of people. Ethical stances are relative to individual preferences or social contexts, and therefore no particular individual stance can claim the status of ethical truth as such. The relativist argues that if someone says "democracy is good," then this is no more than an expression of that person's own upbringing, social position, or interests. It has nothing to do with whether democracy is good in itself and everything to do with the way that individual sees the world.

There are a number of reasons for the prevalence of relativism in pluralist societies. Most obviously, if there are many different ethical stances coexisting in one society, members of that society are often confronted by people who think very differently from themselves. Thus they have come to the conclusion that ethical judgments are purely relative, that there is no such thing as "true" and "false" in ethics. The individualism prevalent in pluralist societies can also encourage a relativist perspective. If individual freedom is thought to be the highest value, then it is inferred from this that there is no such thing as universal truth in ethics. The individual's own preferences and perspectives, "what's right for me," are the ultimate criteria. Who has a right to tell the individual what is good, and on the basis of what claim to truth?

This argument implies that relativism is the only stance that truly respects individual freedom. Anything other than relativism, it is argued, must be essentially intolerant, since it implies imposing other people's beliefs on the individual and denying his or her unique morality. From this perspective, those who argue for objective morality must also argue for the eradication of individual rights in favor of a morality of abstract and impersonal laws that do not take individual differences into account. Relativism, it is argued, is the only stance appropriate to the tolerance necessary for a pluralist society.

Yet this argument fails to recognize that tolerance itself is an ethical principle, and one that is crucial to a pluralist society. If we are consistently relativist, then we must be relativist about tolerance as well. Is it true that tolerance is good, or is this merely relative to individual stances? If tolerance seems unattractive from the perspective of the one who has the power to impose his or her views on society, does that mean that, for that person, tolerance is not a good thing? If so, then we have no grounds at all for arguing that *that* person should be tolerant, since, on relativist premises, we have already abandoned any objective or universal reason for arguing about ethical values. A pluralist society is based on the value of individual freedom. Once again we could ask whether this value is something good in itself or something that is purely relative to one's standpoint. Does individual freedom cease being a good thing if a majority of people stop believing in it? Far from being the only attitude compatible with a pluralist society consistent relativism actually undermines the very values that are crucial to it, especially the commitment to *respect for persons* that is the basis of tolerance and freedom.

There are a number of possible reactions to relativist arguments. One would be to yearn for the revival of the traditional societies of the past, or even for less pluralist stages in the development of modern society. Apart from being impossible in practical terms, this would not end relativism in any case, since reimposing a traditional lifestyle would not destroy people's awareness that there are other possible lifestyles. Another reaction would be to form a tightly knit group that cuts itself off from pluralist society and attempts to preserve a particular lifestyle. This would allow *this* lifestyle to be developed and passed on within that group, but it would minimize any contribution that the group might make to the ethical life of society as a whole; there is a great danger that it could become self-absorbed and self-centered. Another reaction would be to accept relativism and to argue that there are no moral grounds for preferring one type of behavior to another; all we can do is rely on the laws that are in force in society to preserve social stability. Yet this ignores the fact that laws are framed and passed by people who are themselves members of a pluralist society; laws are expressions of moral attitudes and are subject to the same influences as other moral attitudes.

The final and most positive reaction is to counter relativism by *rational argument*. Rational argument will point out the self-contradictions and inadequacies inherent in relativism and argue that human beings are capable of achieving an important and valuable degree of consensus about the moral life. The refutation of relativism is not intended to deny the validity of a pluralist society, but rather to show that tolerance of different ways of life is quite a different thing from abandoning the search for truth altogether. The search for truth can be engaged in through *civil discourse,* that is, a debate about issues affecting our society characterized both by a sense of the seriousness of what is at stake and by respect for the good will of all participants.

Sources of Moral Truth

Since relativism denies that there can be any such thing as moral truth, then the argument with relativism must proceed by considering what sources of moral truth there are, and what each of them contributes to our understanding of the moral life.

Logic

The most basic answer to relativism is a *logical* one, pointing out its self-contradictions. In the most general terms, total relativism is not a consistent position because it relativizes itself. If I argue that "everything is relative," and if I am a consistent relativist, then my own argument must be relative to my own standpoint. It is no more than an expression of how I happen to perceive the world. If it is no more than this, then there is no reason why it should have any relevance for anyone else. That my upbringing, social position, economic status, personal passions and prejudices, and so on lead me to say that "everything is relative" has no bearing on whether anyone else should believe me. And since I am a relativist, I cannot claim that my statement "everything is relative" is a true statement; I can only claim that this is how I see things. But we believe statements because they make a claim to truth, not because someone says, "This is how I see things." If the relativist were then to change tack and claim that "everything is relative" is a true statement, he would of course be abandoning relativism, since he would be arguing not only that this is the way he sees things, but that it is true. If it is a true statement, however, then it is true independently of him or anyone else, and therefore not relative to any particular standpoint. For example, if it is a true statement that the torture of children is wrong, then it is true for the torturer—who is blind to or ignores its truth—as well as for those who oppose him. Consistent relativism is either self-defeating or self-contradictory.

This logical argument can show that total relativism, like any form of universal skepticism, is self-defeating. It may well be that some human values are relative to particular societies and traditions, but this recognition of the link between values and particular societies is very different from relativism as a total attitude to truth. The logical refutation of this total relativist attitude shows that we have to carefully consider which human values are universal, which make a claim on all of us, and which may have relevance only in particular social contexts. This is particularly important for a pluralist society, since it rests on the distinction between the values that all respect and the values that characterize different groups within it.

Nature

Logical arguments can perform the critical task of undermining the total claims of relativism, but to answer relativism about specifically ethical matters, we must go beyond logic to experience, to reflect on our experience of our own needs and on our nature as human beings. Such reflection will show there are common needs that we seek to satisfy and desires that we seek to fulfill. Some of these needs are shared with higher animals—such as bonding, caring for the young, and being aggressive against marauders—and these form the most elementary forms of morality, such as the protection

25

of the young. Human beings also have a range of needs that are unique to the human species itself. Moral reflection will seek to identify those needs and to enquire into the best means of satisfying them.

Different cultures will interpret some of these needs differently, according to their circumstances. To that extent, a morality based on the fulfillment of needs will have some elements that are relative to different cultures, but there are basic human needs common to all cultures. One of the most basic, as pointed out by the utilitarians, is the desire to seek pleasure and avoid pain. Equally basic, but perhaps subtly different, is the desire for happiness. A powerful argument against relativism in morality, then, is simply to explore the consequences of different moral stances and to show that some are much more conducive to the fulfillment of human needs than others.

Reason and Experience

Rational reflection on experience is a further source of arguments against relativism in the search for moral truth. Relativism argues that our actions are relative to our own feelings and desires and that there is no objective standard for judging actions as "right" or "wrong." Rational reflection on experience, however, gives us good grounds for thinking that right actions are those actions that respect the needs of others. Our starting point might be the natural affections we feel for our family or for our own group; we respect the needs of members of our group because mutual respect within the group is crucial to the fulfillment of our own needs. By reflection on our experience of life, however, we see that other human beings have similar needs, and that their needs are as important to them as mine are to me. We gradually broaden the scope of our experience of the value of persons. If we are open to this experience, then the scope of our respect can broaden, and we begin to grant respect to human beings simply because they *are* human beings and have similar fundamental characteristics to myself. We come to see that the "moral point of view," which respects the needs of each human being, is a superior point of view to egoism, which asserts that the needs of a particular individual or a particular group are somehow more valuable than the needs of others. For the moral point of view, the statement "I have needs" does not override the statement "Mary Jones has needs," since I and Mary Jones are both human beings deserving of respect.

What we have been calling the moral point of view was expressed in a classical form in ancient times as the *Golden Rule,* a moral principle coined by great teachers of moral wisdom in a number of different cultures—notably in Greece, China, India, and Israel. It also finds its place in the Christian gospels in the form "Do to others as you would have them do to you" (Luke 6:31). The Golden Rule expresses the insight, born of reflection on human experience, that others like and dislike having things done to them in essentially the same ways we like and dislike. It also expresses an act of moral imagination in its empathy: if I put myself in someone else's shoes, I can imagine how he or she would feel if I were to treat that person in a particular way. Since I would not want that to be done to me, then I should not do it to that person. The Golden Rule answers relativism by pointing out that human beings experience things in essentially similar ways and that there is no reason why my experiences should be deemed to be more important than someone else's. As we have seen, Kant's moral philosophy of the categorical imperative is related to the essential insights of the Golden Rule: If I do something, then I must also accept that whatever I do could also be done by everyone else, because we are all free and equal rational agents. If I wish to do something to another person, I must also assent to his or her doing it to me.

On the basis of the moral insights contained in the Golden Rule, moral philosophers developed the idea of a *social contract*. According to this idea, the best society is a society of mutual respect. Every member of that society is free to do anything so long as all others are also free to do it. Thus the laws governing a free society have to be worked out in common, so that every member of society has maximum freedom compatible with the freedom of others. Society is based on the agreement of individuals to give up unlimited, anarchic rights and to accept a mutual arrangement that gives freedom within the context of mutual respect and obligation.

Tradition

Logic, nature, reason, and experience are all important sources of moral truth. They do not, however, give us a complete picture of the moral life. We may be able to discern some basic natural needs that are common to humanity, but that will not tell us how these needs should be integrated and harmonized to make up a satisfying and fulfilling human life. For example, we might agree that the values of freedom and justice relate to basic human needs, but disagree about the right balance between economic freedom and social justice in society. Further, the Golden Rule tells us to do unto others as we would have them do unto us, but it does not tell us what we should actually do.

How should we live? What constitutes human fulfillment? These questions ask about the detailed content of morality. What actions, what lifestyle will best fulfill human needs and enable the full flourishing of human capacities? The answers to such questions are found in *moral traditions*.

Moral traditions are combinations of beliefs and practices, more or less integrated ways of life that offer individual or social fulfillment. Such traditions are formed in the history of particular cultures. They have developed through historical experience of what fulfills human needs and enables human flourishing. The word *tradition* derives from the Latin word *tradere,* meaning "to hand on." Traditions are particular ways of life that have developed through the history of a particular culture and are handed on to each new generation. In Western thought, the German philosopher G. W. F. Hegel (1770–1831) was the greatest interpreter of the role of historical tradition in forming our ethical perspectives. Hegel's particular emphasis was on the role of Christian tradition in developing the idea of the subjectivity, or unique worth, of the person and the ways in which this could shape political and social life in the modern world.

Many basic moral questions can be answered by a reasonably straightforward appeal to basic human needs or to the Golden Rule. To inflict needless pain on others, for example, is a clear violation of the Golden Rule (except for the aberrant case of the masochist) and a violation of our biological need to avoid pain wherever possible. Most moral traditions recognize these basic needs, and the Golden Rule, as we have seen, originated in many different cultures. Different moral traditions do, however, express common human needs in different ways, giving priority to different values in their picture of the meaning and purpose of life and action. Modern Western society, for example, puts a high priority on activism and efficiency—on getting the job done, whatever it happens to be. Traditional Indian society puts a great deal more emphasis on meditation and contemplation. Many commentators remark that Japanese society is characterized by a high degree of social solidarity, while Western societies place much more emphasis on freedom of individual action and self-expression. It is also evident that traditional and contemporary Western societies are at variance over the importance of the family in relation to individual freedom. These different societies will give us different answers if we ask what human life is all about and what is conducive to the full flourishing of human capacities. These examples also show us that it is difficult to make simple comparative judgments or evaluations of moral traditions. Different traditions have different strengths and weaknesses, and the decline of a moral tradition in favor of a newly ascendant one is usually a matter of both gain and loss.

The importance of moral traditions is that they give the moral life a much greater content and richness than either a consideration of basic needs or the Golden Rule alone; they paint a picture of a lifestyle for us, rather than simply prescribing a few basic rules. This strength, of course, can become a fatal weakness if a tradition begins to stifle new possibilities for human development that emerge in new social situations; traditions must be subject to critique, in order to test their capacity to guide us to human fulfillment in the situations in which we find ourselves. The relationship of different traditions to each other is also a difficult question for any pluralist society, that is, a society made up of different traditions that must live together in conditions of mutual tolerance and respect.

For the relativist, the existence of different traditions shows that morality is relative to different societies and histories and has no truth to it. This ignores the fact that different traditions do have a great deal in common and do respect fundamental human values. The world religions, for example, show a remarkable degree of consensus about fundamental moral values. Where traditions disagree over important moral questions, the relativist response would be that there is no such thing as objective moral truth, since it is relative to the viewpoints of different traditions. For those who take moral truth seriously, however, the response to such a situation is to pursue the difficult task of *moral dialogue*, for each tradition to learn from the other in conditions of mutual respect in the hope that a common answer can be found.

Moral Philosophies and the Sources of Moral Truth

The sources of moral truth that we have been discussing correspond in an interesting way with the three great moral philosophies briefly described earlier in this chapter. The philosophy of *utilitarianism* emphasizes basic human needs, such as the pursuit of happiness or pleasure and the avoidance of pain; it puts emphasis on the fundamental biological characteristics of human nature. *Kantianism* emphasizes reason, by understanding morality as the point of view that ascribes equal worth to all human beings, since all human beings have reason and freedom, and that describes a moral action as an action conforming to universal rules of fairness. Finally, *Aristotelianism* emphasizes moral traditions by arguing that the good life is a life lived in accordance with the virtues characteristic of a moral lifestyle, a lifestyle conducive to human fulfillment.

Natural Law

The concept of *natural law*, which derives ultimately from ancient Greece, emphasizes the foundations of ethics in the nature of things, in the reality of the world which we inhabit. To say that there is a "natural law" means that things do have a nature and that we can know it. Greek and Roman philosophy, and subsequently the Catholic Church, put great emphasis on the fact that ethics could be based on our knowledge of the true nature of things, a knowledge that human beings could achieve in common since it was open to the rational mind. The Catholic Church was hospitable to the notion of natural law since it was a part of the classical heritage that recognized the moral character of the world imparted to it by the creator.

The great strength of the idea of natural law is that it emphasizes the commonality of the moral life. In response to all forms of relativism, the idea of natural law affirms that there are fundamental needs and purposes of human existence, that we can know them, and that we can know them in common through our shared humanity. Without something akin to a concept of natural law, human beings cannot speak of human ethics, but only of the ethics of different cultures. This would mean that such documents as the Universal Declaration of Human Rights, which affirm the common rights of all humanity, are fictions. This would also have the logical conclusion that moral protest about the degradation of human rights within one's own or another society is groundless, since this moral protest would be appealing to a common human ethics that does not exist.

The concept of natural law expresses something that is crucial to any antirelativist ethical perspective and to any moral concern for the global human community. Yet the notion of a natural law does have serious difficulties. It implies that human beings have a common and unchanging nature that can be used as a basis for ethical thinking. Therefore, by observing human nature, we can note which actions fulfill human needs and purposes, and which actions do not.

Traditional moral teaching, for example, argued that drunkenness was wrong because it deprived someone of the faculty of reason, an important part of our nature; it was therefore against natural law. This argument rightly pointed to the fact that some actions could destroy or degrade fundamental human faculties or characteristics.

The difficulty with this kind of argument, however, was in distinguishing between those characteristics that were truly permanent characteristics of human existence and those that were characteristic of particular cultures and epochs and open to change. The concept of the "nature of things" was used, for example, to justify social inequalities: it was "natural" that there was a social hierarchy, a difference between master and servant; it was "natural" that the husband was head of the family and that the woman's role was restricted to that of wife and mother. The notion of "nature" as a basis of ethics had the strength of pointing out basic and universal human characteristics, but the weakness of confusing these basic characteristics with certain historically conditioned social relationships. It greatly underestimated the extent to which human beings can change the conditions of their lives through their freedom, and fulfill themselves in new ways.

We have also seen that there are different ways in which basic and universal human characteristics can be fulfilled by different moral traditions. These moral traditions do have very significant common elements, but their existence shows that we cannot simply reason from "nature," in order to know what we should do, because the meaning of human "nature" is expressed differently by different moral traditions.

These difficulties with the notion of basing ethics on nature are heightened if we link "nature" and "law." The notion of a natural *law* emphasized that we are *obliged* to respect our fundamental natural characteristics. We put our own humanity at risk if we do not cherish and fulfill those characteristics that make us human— our fundamental biological, moral, and spiritual endowments. The ancient notion of natural law expresses the idea that these characteristics are given to us—whether by God, the gods, or nature—for our stewardship and are not at our own disposal. Yet the idea that our nature brings moral obligation with it can easily degenerate into a rigid and stifling legalism. Human nature does not prescribe a set of laws to be followed; it is rather a potential to be fulfilled, and the ways in which human potential can be fulfilled vary enormously. Respecting the gifts that make us human is not a matter of obeying a set of laws but rather of fulfilling our potential in freedom and responsibility.

How, then, can we preserve what is of value in the concept of natural law while freeing ourselves of its limitations? The crucial value of this concept is its emphasis on the *relationship of ethical reasoning to our universal humanity*. An ethics worthy of the name must be an ethics that attempts to communicate between human beings of different cultures and traditions and to enable action that affirms and fulfills our common humanity. In our discussion of the sources of moral truth, we have seen that this is both a possible and a difficult task. It is a possible task because human beings do have fundamental sources of moral truth in common, as, for example, the concept of the Golden Rule shows. It is a difficult task because our understanding of what fulfills us as human beings is deeply affected by our different visions of human existence, which are formed by the tradition or traditions of our culture.

The existence of different traditions, however, does not prevent human beings from reasoning with each other about their common human existence. We bring different understandings of the world to ethical debate, but we are all called to communicate with each other by explaining why we do the things that we do. In this way, different traditions can engage in a dialogue that, despite its difficulties and tensions, enables them both to give and to receive. Members of a particular tradition can remind others of aspects of human existence that they may have neglected, while accepting that some aspects of their own tradition need to be changed. While recognizing that they differ about how human potential can be fulfilled, different traditions can together affirm the basic human characteristics and potential on which human rights are based. The meaning of natural law today is not a set of obligations that can be read by everyone in the open book of an unchanging human nature, but rather a common and communicative search for insight into what way of life will fulfill the fundamental characteristics and potential of the human person.

Summary of Chapter 1

1. Human beings are moral beings because they have the capacity to experience and know the good and to freely respond to it. The discipline of ethics is a systematic and critical reflection on the moral life.

2. There are three highly influential philosophical theories of ethics: Aristotelianism, which sees the good life as a life oriented to happiness through living the virtues; Kantianism, which understands good action to be action performed out of duty to universal principles based on reason and freedom; and utilitarianism, for which the moral life is based on a benevolent commitment to maximizing pleasure or happiness and minimizing pain.

3. Many contemporary societies are ethically pluralist, that is, there is no one set of moral values and practices accepted by all members of society and given the force of law. Some of the causes of pluralism are secularization, the development of religious and ethical toleration, individualism, and the breakup of traditional communities. Pluralist societies are based on individual freedom and mutual tolerance, but are characterized by disagreement about many other ethical questions.

4. Ethical relativism is the standpoint that there is no objective truth in ethical matters since all ethical beliefs are relative to and determined by the particular standpoint of the person holding those beliefs.

5. The existence of ethical pluralism does not justify relativism, and consistent relativism undermines the values of individual freedom and tolerance, which are crucial to pluralist societies.

6. The falsity of total ethical relativism can be shown by rational argument, drawing on the sources of moral truth: logic, nature, reason, experience, and tradition.

7. The continuing value of the concept of natural law is its emphasis on the commonality and rationality of the human search for ethical insight.

Questions for Discussion

1. Why do you think that the moral quality of a person is so often thought to be the most important thing about that person?

2. If a fulfilled human life is a life lived according to the virtues, what virtues should be preeminent? Would you accept the classical list of the four cardinal virtues or propose others as equally important?

3. Imagine you have promised a dying man to ensure that all his wealth goes to his spendthrift son. No one else knows of the promise, so no one will know that you have broken it and given the money to famine relief. What is your judgment on this situation? Does the situation highlight two different understandings of the moral life? Are such situations so rare that such differences are insignificant?

4. To what extent does ethical pluralism in fact exist in our society? What do you think the significant areas of consensus are? What are areas where you are particularly aware of disagreement?

5. Do you think the logical argument against total relativism succeeds?

6. What are areas of life where you think relativism is justified and areas where it is not?

7. Consider a situation where two people are arguing over human rights. One person argues that human rights are universal and can be appealed to in any country, no matter what local conventions and practices are; the other person argues that human rights are notions characteristic of some Western societies and should not be imposed on very different societies. Who do you think is right? What sources of moral truth could be appealed to in order to argue that human rights are universal? Are there some rights that are universal and some that are dependent on or relative to local conditions?

8. Consider the adequacy of the Golden Rule as a summation of moral action.

9. Consider the following values (and others that you can think of): patriotism, courage, discipline, spontaneity, diligence, hospitality, individuality, solidarity, loyalty, efficiency, incorruptibility, self-sacrifice, tolerance. What moral traditions—associated with particular nations, cultures, or social groups—are you aware of that might incorporate them in different ways?

10. Discuss the contemporary viability of the concept of natural law. Do you think we need to be able to appeal to something akin to natural law in order to justify moral protest about international breaches of human rights?

2

Christian Faith and Ethics

We engage in ethics as a search for what will fulfill the person. Different visions of human life, expressed in different traditions, can contribute to that search and encourage us to persevere with it. This is what makes sense of the notion of a *Christian ethics.* Christian ethics, like all ethics, is a search for what fulfills the person. What qualifies it as "Christian" is that it enters on the search in light of the Christian faith, the Christian vision of life. Christian ethics affirms both the commonality of the human ethical enterprise and the contribution that can be made to it by the Christian faith tradition. Christian ethics does not propose a separate ethical system uniquely its own; rather, the history of Christian ethics shows the attempt of Christians to appraise the value of different ethical philosophies, especially the three we have discussed, to learn from them, and to enrich them from the resources of Christian faith.

If traditions can have an influence on ethics, then those traditions that are based on an experience of God, the creator of all life, must have particular relevance. These experiences of God are expressed in religion, the attempt to express the meaning and purpose of all reality and especially of human existence. A religious faith is a tradition. It is made up of symbols, rituals, scriptures, and beliefs that are passed on from generation to generation as the life-giving bond between each new generation of believers and the founding events of the faith. This tradition carries with it a distinctive vision of the meaning and purpose of human existence.

For Christians, the founding events of their tradition expressed the self-communication of God to ancient Israel, culminating in the life, death, and resurrection of Jesus of Nazareth. Christians believe that the life of this human being revealed the mystery of God in a unique and unsurpassable way, showing God as he really is: as infinite love, irrevocably committed to a reconciling relationship with his human creatures. In Jesus of Nazareth, the mystery of God is revealed. But since Jesus is fully divine and fully human, then his life also reveals the ultimate meaning of human existence. The union of God and humanity in Jesus reveals to us not only the mystery of God but also the mystery of humanity. It is in this life that we find a true and inspiring image of what we are really destined to be. The life and teaching of Jesus gives Christian ethics its distinctive character since it is an approach to ethics that takes his life and teaching as an unsurpassable guide to human fulfillment.

This is of central importance for Christian ethics, but it is a matter that needs to be clarified in relation to some of the critical issues already discussed. We have considered the nature of a pluralist society and the relativism that can be engendered by it. We also considered the historical origins of pluralist societies, origins that had much to do with the after-effects of religious conflict and decisions about the role of religion in political institutions and in ethical practices in general. So a discussion of the Christian character of Christian ethics will need to consider how ethics can be related to religion and how a specifically Christian ethics will relate to a pluralist society.

Religion and Ethics

Any discussion of the relationship between religion and ethics has to come to terms with misunderstandings that have developed over the centuries, which Christians themselves are often responsible for because of a fundamentalist use of the Bible or because of other aspects of Christian tradition. A typical secular response to the notion of a "Christian" ethics is that it is based on the arbitrary decrees of a totalitarian God, since this is the image of God that is associated with crudely literalist presentations of the Ten Commandments. For example, a television debate on ethical questions in contemporary society included a minister of religion commenting that certain practices were not envisaged as permissible in the Bible. A secular member of the panel retorted that pop-up toasters are not conceived of in the Bible, but that had nothing to do with their efficacy or relevance. This sort of exchange emphasizes the extent of the disagreements and misunderstandings associated with this question.

The relevance of religion to ethics has been a matter of debate for thousands of years. The Greek thinker Socrates (469–399 BC) was the great pioneer of ethical debate in Western history. One of Socrates' pupils posed him this question: Are things good because God commands them or does he rather command them because they are good? If we say that things are good because God commands them, then we encourage an image of God as an arbitrary lawgiver, declaring things to be good or bad not because of their intrinsic qualities, but simply as an act of will. An implication of this is that God might make trivial things supremely important in terms of his own commandments (one of the misunderstandings arising from a literalist interpretation of the "forbidden fruit" of Genesis 3), or even that God might command his creatures to do evil things as a test of obedience (a misunderstanding of the story of the sacrifice of Isaac in Genesis 22). On the other hand, if we say God commands things because they are good, then that would seem to imply that religion is quite superfluous to morality: if things are commanded by God because they are good, their goodness is independent of God, and our knowledge of their goodness will be quite independent of our knowledge about God through any religious tradition. The dilemma we are considering seems to imply either an arbitrary God or an ethics for which any religious tradition is irrelevant.

The Harmony of Creation and Revelation

The problem with the question, in the form we have considered it so far, is that it separates *creation* and *revelation:* the will of God as expressed in the nature of the things he has made, that is, creation, and as expressed in the religious traditions based on the revelation of God in Jesus. If we believe that God is the creator, then the goodness of things proceeds from God. God has made them good, as Genesis 1 affirms, and it is his gracious will that they flourish in their goodness. God is not a tyrant imposing arbitrary decrees, but the creator who guides his creatures toward their own fulfillment. If the creator has also revealed himself to his human creatures and invited them to share in his own life, then this revelation cannot be superfluous to knowing what human fulfillment really means. This revelation does not supplant or reject the purposes of God for human life as expressed in creation, since the God of creation and the God of revelation are the same. Rather, it intensifies, confirms, and enriches the knowledge of God's purpose that we have from rational reflection on creation.

The Catholic tradition's answer to this apparent dilemma is to affirm that God commands things because they are good, but that the revelation of God in Jesus Christ can guide us toward the knowledge of what is good. The guidance we find in the person of Jesus is not a denial of the guidance we receive from nature, reason, and experience, since this would be a denial of gifts and abilities that the human creature has as the image of God, the free use of reason to know God's creation and to flourish within it. The guidance that the Christian tradition gives on ethical questions takes very seriously what we know of ethical matters on the basis of an observation of human nature, of human needs and goods, of reasoning about human goals and purposes.

In his Epistle to the Romans, St. Paul emphasizes how all human beings can know the difference between right and wrong on the basis of their own reason and experience. For Paul, whether one has shared in the privilege of the special revelation of God to the Jews, or whether one has worshipped God through the various images and deities of the other religions of the Hellenistic world, all human beings can know God's fundamental purposes for human life from reflection on the nature of things, on creation itself (Rom 1—2). No one can claim to have no sources of moral knowledge, even without the benefit of guidance of the Christian or some other great religious tradition.

To put the problem another way, let us consider two questions. First, "Can someone be moral without being religious?" Clearly, this is so. Explicit religious faith or religious worship is not an essential aspect of a morally good life. Second, "Do religious traditions contribute to ethics?" Without denying the tragic facts of interreligious conflict and violence, it's the basic premise of this book that religious traditions do indeed make an enormously valuable contribution to the moral life of humanity. How then do we reconcile these two statements: that we can be moral without being religious, and, at the same time, that religion can make a critical contribution to morality? As we have seen, someone can be moral without being religious because they can know the goodness of creation through the gift of reason. In this sense *God as creator remains "background"* and is known in and through the goodness of creation. *In revelation, God becomes "foreground,"* and the traditions that develop from this revelation enrich our moral sense through the intimate experience of God that they pass on.

Church, Community, and Tradition

Traditions are passed on by communities, and it is the community of the Church that passes on the witness to Jesus Christ distinctive of the Christian tradition. The Christian sense of life's meaning and purpose, which can so deeply influence morality, is not a matter of merely abstract ideas we can acquire on an individual basis. They are learned through life in a community of faith, and they take on practical meaning and credibility through the experience of that community.

There are many and varied ways in which Christian faith can become part of a person's formative experience: through the life of a Christian family, through Christian education, through participation in a worshipping community, or through the unpredictable ways in which witness to the gospel can be passed on in human encounters. For the Catholic tradition, this experience of Christian community has its most intense focus and source of life in the celebration of the Eucharist, in the memorial of the one who celebrated the coming of the kingdom and who gave himself for the life of others. By sharing in Christ's presence in the Eucharist, members of the Church experience communion with God and with each other, the living basis of their commitment to a Christian vision of the meaning of life.

Christian Faith and Human Dignity

The most important way in which Christian revelation can enrich the ethical insights we have from reflecting on our experience is in reference to the worth of persons themselves. If persons are at the center of ethics, then the worth of persons, often called human dignity, is the fundamental ethical value. Through its teaching that God became a human being, Christian tradition can intensify and enrich the sense of the value of persons that we have from reflection on our experience. We have already seen that the wisdom of the ancient world developed the Golden Rule: Do unto others as you would have them do unto you. The Golden Rule encapsulates the insight that the basis of ethical thinking is to perceive that there is no reason why others should be treated any differently than I myself would wish to be treated. This great insight was developed by Kant in his concept of the categorical imperative: that whatever we wish to do should also be a universal law, compatible with everyone enjoying equality and freedom. Kant saw the value of persons as based on their rationality and freedom. Because human persons could freely choose their own goals and reason about them, then they must be treated as having a special dignity that no state or society has a right to disregard or abolish.

Our rational capacity and our freedom, then, can be considered foundational to human worth. There are other related considerations relevant to human worth and dignity—one would be our experience that every person is unique, has a unique perspective on the world, and brings a unique contribution to the human community. Further, every person has a consciousness of himself or herself. Human beings can stand back and reflect on themselves and their actions; they are reflexively aware of their own existence. These characteristics, and others, are all relevant to the estimation of human persons as possessing a worth that ethics must focus on as its key value.

Christian ethics by no means rejects this understanding of human worth as based on human freedom and reason, but it does argue that religious traditions can enrich it. When we consider the great variations in the power of the rational faculty, the question might arise whether or not this has the implication of differing human value. If a human being is not a self-conscious and free adult, capable of acting on rational decisions, is he or she of less value? Is our value something that flows from the contribution that we can make to a network of social relationships, or is it independent of the status that we have as a result of these relationships? From the perspective of Christian faith, the actual differences between persons make no difference to their value, because their personal value is grounded in their relationship to God, the infinite source of all value. Since all persons are created by God for the purpose of enjoying a uniquely personal relationship with him, then all persons have a unique value. Whatever particular characteristics persons have do not lessen this value, since it is grounded in their creaturely relationship with God. For Christian faith, whether or not we are aware of this relationship and whether we foster or neglect it, it is freely offered by the God of infinite love.

For Christians, it is the story of Jesus that gives humanity this ultimate context for appreciating the worth of persons. It is Jesus who reveals to humanity that God is a loving and providential Father and who invites us to share in his relationship with the Father. The Christian story can evoke in us a greater appreciation of the worth of persons by telling us of Jesus' own sense of God and the ways in which he was able to express God's loving care in his relationships with the range of people that he encountered. Whether friend or enemy, child or adult, in full health or disabled, Jew or Gentile, those who encountered Jesus encountered someone who expressed the love of the Father in word and action, and who respected their unique worth and dignity. The Father's love for Jesus was finally expressed in raising him from the dead for eternal life, and this resurrection, the ultimate expression of human value, is something that God has offered to all who share Jesus' humanity. The ultimate basis of human dignity is that God himself has become human.

Christian Teachings and the Meaning of the Moral Life

The Christian faith can illuminate and enrich our sense of the value of persons. Yet it is not only relevant to ethics in this way; it also presents a picture of the meaning and purpose of human life, which has an important bearing on how we understanding morality. This picture of the meaning of human life can be presented in terms of some of the most fundamental Christian teachings. These teachings, while not specifically ethical in themselves, can deeply affect our understanding of the meaning of life, which is the context within which we think, value, and act. Their significance will be seen as we consider different aspects of ethics in the course of this book.

God as Trinity

The foundation of Christian faith is belief in God as a communion of three divine persons: Father, Son, and Spirit. Bringing the religious heritage of his people to a culmination, Jesus of Nazareth addressed God as "Father." After his resurrection from the dead, his disciples knew him to be the Son of God, the Word made flesh. The experience of the Spirit at Pentecost became the sustaining source of Christian life. Early councils of the Church, especially in the fourth century AD, expressed this experience of faith as the doctrine of the Trinity, that God is three persons in one nature. The Christian belief that God is a communion of persons, sharing an infinite life of love, emphasizes that community, a oneness that affirms and celebrates diversity, is the true destiny of human beings created in the "image of God."

The World as God's Creation

The first two chapters of the book of Genesis portray the world as the good creation of God, created not out of God's need but out of the superabundance of divine freedom and love. Because creation is an expression of God's freedom, it has been given its own autonomy, its own nature, and human beings are free to develop that nature in accordance with their own reason and imagination, in ways that will respect the fundamental purposes that they discern in it. Because the world is God's creation, it exists for all humanity. No human group can claim exclusive possession of the fruits of the earth, depriving others of their share in God's creation.

Humanity as the "Image of God"

The first chapter of the book of Genesis emphasizes that man and woman were created "in the image of God" (Gen 1:27). The meaning of this phrase in its original context was probably connected with the self-images that ancient rulers set up in conquered territories; the image represented the ruler and reminded his subjects of his power. The man and the woman were stewards or "images" of God. They had a unique role in creation as representatives of the creator. The Jewish and Christian traditions put great emphasis on the uniqueness of the human species and the value of the person. This uniqueness is best expressed in the freedom of the person, especially the freedom to choose between good and evil and the responsibility for that choice.

The Human Person as Embodied Spirit

For the Jewish, Christian, and Islamic traditions, the human person is a unique union of spiritual and physical dimensions. This is in contrast to many Indian religious traditions, which understand human individuals to be formed by the reincarnation of the soul in a sequence of different physical forms. The relevance of this for the Christian understanding of human life is that a truly fulfilling lifestyle must be one that does justice to both the spiritual and the physical character of the person. The body is important because our bodies are uniquely ourselves: bodily action expresses the person. This has great significance for the importance of sexuality and sexual relations as expressions of personal life, as well as for the importance of satisfying the basic physical needs of human beings through the just distribution of wealth in society.

Human Sinfulness

Chapters 3—11 of the book of Genesis reflect on the consequences of the exercise of human freedom in choosing evil rather than good. They bear witness to the insight of ancient Judaism, which Christianity inherited, that human beings are created for goodness but are deeply affected by evil choices, both their own and those of others, whether past or present. For the Christian tradition, the freedom of human beings cannot be completely purged of the consequences of these evil choices, whether in the life of an individual or of a society.

The Incarnation

Christian faith is based on the conviction that in Jesus of Nazareth, the Word of God, the second person of the Trinity, became human. God's revelation of himself to humanity reached its culmination in becoming one with the human race in a historical human being, who shared in the human condition in all things except sin (Heb 4:15). The doctrine of the incarnation affirms the intimacy of God with humanity, an intimacy that became a sharing of life. In the incarnation, God affirms the goodness and value of creation to the greatest possible degree, by living the life of a human being and participating in the material universe.

The Paschal Mystery

The life of Jesus reached its climax in his paschal mystery. Christians believe that in the life, death, and resurrection of Jesus God "was reconciling the world to himself" (2 Cor 5:19). The relevance of this for our consideration of Christian ethics is that it encapsulates the realities of forgiveness, redemption, and hope and affirms that these are gifts of God to his human creatures. Christian ethics knows no sin or crime that cannot be forgiven. It is not an ethics that gives each individual one and only one chance in life, but an ethics that recognizes and forgives human sinfulness. It is an ethics of redemption, which holds out hope that evil can be overcome by the power of good, both in the divided human heart and in the conflicts of the world.

The Kingdom of God

Christian ethics is based on the faith that human beings, and indeed the whole cosmos, were created for a good purpose and are not the result of an accidental conjunction of impersonal forces. For the gospels, this purpose is summed up in the image of the kingdom of God: a realm of peace and justice in community, a world within which the goodness of God shines out in the mutual love and respect of persons who are enabled to develop their gifts to the full.

Christian Faith and the Motivation for the Moral Life

While the Christian story can enrich our sense of the value of persons and can give a vision of life that is the background of our moral choices, many moral questions can receive the same answers from Christians as from others, since the human needs and purposes that are involved in them can be identified apart from any religious perspectives. People of different religious traditions or of none, for example, can agree that it is wrong to steal, since stealing is in violation of another's right to own property, a right that receives virtually universal assent.

It is in the *motivation* for morality that we see another influence of religious faith that can affect the *whole* of the moral life. The motivation for our moral lives does depend on what we think the purpose and meaning of life is. If we believe that human life is no more than a particular form of animal life that happened to evolve on this planet in a purposeless universe, then our motivation for morality will clearly not include a relationship to God. It will be focused on respecting and fostering human values for the sake of the human happiness that it is possible to achieve in this life. If, however, we believe that this world is the creation of a good God, who created human beings through the natural processes of evolution as free creatures capable of a relationship with him, then our response to the values of this world will be at the same time a response to God. The moral life will have the significance of deeply affecting our relationship with God, since we know and relate to the creator through his creation, and the purpose of the moral life is to value that creation and to develop it in ways that respect its potential and dynamism. Behind the values of creation lies the authority of God, not as an arbitrary lawgiver, but as the source of all value and the ultimate goal of all human striving. In living the moral life, then, the Christian is not trying to preserve some semblance of order and value in the face of a bleak and ultimately meaningless universe, but is cooperating with God in developing the potential of persons and the other living beings with whom we share our lives.

Christian Ethics in a Pluralist Society

We have been considering the character of Christianity as a moral tradition and the influence that it can have on the way a person sees the moral life and is motivated to live it. Earlier we discussed the fundamental characteristics of a pluralist society and their significance for ethics. We must now turn to the question of the role of Christian ethics within a pluralist society. First of all, we must emphasize that, although Christian ethics is formed by a distinctive tradition, it also shares fundamental sources of moral truth with other ethical traditions, whether secular or religious. Christian ethics, like other approaches to ethics, must consider the importance of fundamental natural needs; it must reflect on human experience, consult the specialized sciences, and reason about the moral principles that will best embody justice and fairness. The relationship of Christian ethics to the great moral philosophies of Aristotelianism, Kantianism, and utilitarianism will be considered at various points in later chapters, but it has been affected by all of them to varying degrees. Philosophical debate about ethics is of continuing importance to Christian ethics.

All of this means that there is a very significant basis for attempting to achieve consensus between Christians and other members of society about moral questions. Formation in a Christian community is, as we have seen, a very important part of the transmission of a Christian vision of the moral life. At the same time, the content of Christian ethics is an attempt to understand the meaning of creation in light of the gospel; it concerns our created humanity as such. Because of this, Christian ethics is not simply a matter of reflecting on the lifestyle of a particular religious community. Rather it is a matter of engaging in the ethical life and reflection of society as a whole, sharing in common moral knowledge and insight, and telling the story of Jesus as an inspiration to the achievement of a common humanity. *Christian ethics is human ethics, addressed in the light of Christian faith in Jesus as the revelation of God, the creator of humanity.*

If Christian ethics is understood in this way, what is its mission in a pluralist society? We have seen above that one of the historical sources of pluralist societies was the rejection of the domination of society by any one religious group. Pluralist societies respect freedom of religious worship, but do not base their laws on the precepts or vision of any particular religion or worldview. If the Christian tradition can make a difference to ethics, what is its role within a pluralist society?

In the Catholic tradition, this has been a very vexed question. After the French Revolution, the papacy tended to support the traditional monarchies of Europe and argued that Catholic monarchs should extend special privileges to Catholicism since it was the true religion. The papal teaching of the nineteenth century was premised on the primacy of truth over error; traditional political systems were deemed best suited to protecting the true Church and to preventing the spread of erroneous doctrines. The practical effect of this stance was that Catholic teaching was often associated with state repression and with backward and authoritarian regimes. Many Catholics argued that the Church would benefit by playing a full part in a democratic society where religious teachings were accepted through free conviction, rather than because they were backed by the authority of the state.

During the first half of the twentieth century, papal teaching began to endorse democratic and pluralist societies—not because it regarded all religious or ethical ideas as equally valid, but because it was gradually being recognized that Catholicism benefited more from free commitment in democratic societies than from state authority in repressive ones. The writings of John Courtney Murray, an American Jesuit, took the argument a step further: by recognizing and respecting democratic and pluralist societies, the Catholic Church would be recognizing the foundational ethical value of freedom of conscience, the heart of human dignity.

From this point of view, respect for free societies was not indifference to truth but rather respect for a fundamental moral value. In two key documents, *Dignitatis Humanae,* the Declaration on Religious Freedom, and *Gaudium et Spes,* the Pastoral Constitution on the Church in the Modern World, the Second Vatican Council (1962–65) endorsed the principle of pluralist societies, while at the same time affirming the Catholic tradition's commitment to hold and teach what it believes to be a true understanding of the meaning and purpose of human life. The opening sentences of *Gaudium* et *Spes* (which means, literally, "Joy and Hope") express the spirit of the document as a whole:

The joys and hopes, griefs and anxieties of the human beings of this age, especially of those who are poor and afflicted—these are also the joys and hopes, griefs and anxieties, of the disciples of Christ, and there is nothing genuinely human which does not raise an echo in their hearts. For their community is made up of human beings, who, united in Christ, are led by the Holy Spirit in their pilgrimage to the Kingdom of the Father, and they have received the news of salvation which is meant for all. For this reason this community feels itself intimately connected with the human race and its history. (§1)

In light of this affirmation, the role of Christian ethics in a pluralist society is a matter both of *witness* to the truth of fulfilled human life that Christians find in Jesus and of *service* to humanity in imitation of Jesus, the "Son of Man," who "came not to be served but to serve, and to give his life a ransom for many" (Mark 10:45).

Discussion of Christian Faith and Ethics in This Book

This chapter has discussed the principal ways in which Christian faith relates to ethics. These will be considered in more detail in subsequent chapters. In order to emphasize the relationship of Christian faith to ethics as the enrichment of a common human enterprise, the discussion of the contribution of Christian faith to insight into particular ethical issues will be incorporated into the chapters that deal with those issues in general terms:

Chapter 3, "The Moral Person," will consider the covenantal character of Christian ethics in relation to our human experience of freedom and responsibility, as well as the meaning of a Christian conscience and character.

Chapter 4, "Sin and the Fundamental Option," will discuss the meaning of evil choices in the context of a covenantal relationship to God and neighbor.

Chapter 5, "A Good World," will consider the contribution of Christian faith to our sense of the worth of persons.

Chapter 6, "Love, Rights, and Moral Norms," will discuss the relationship between law and love in the Bible.

Chapter 7, "The Task of Moral Reasoning," will reflect on the contribution of Christian tradition to the process of moral reasoning.

Chapter 8, "Christian Ethics and the Teaching Authority of the Church," will consider the relationship among Church teaching, moral norms, and the individual conscience in the Catholic tradition.

Summary of Chapter 2

1. Christian ethics is a moral tradition within pluralist society, a tradition whose distinctive character is based on the faith that God the creator is revealed in the life and teaching of Jesus of Nazareth.

2. The relationship between ethics and religion accords with the relationship between creation and revelation. Things are not made good by God's arbitrary decree, nor is knowledge of God's revelation in Jesus superfluous to knowledge of the good. Rather, the world is good because it was created by a good God, and the revelation of that good God to humanity guides and enriches our sense of the goodness of creation.

3. Christian faith can give Christian ethics a distinctive character through the following ways:
   (a) heightening and intensifying awareness of the value of human persons, on the basis of the Christian belief that God became human;

(b) giving a background to the moral life in terms of the meaning and purpose of life as a whole;

(c) setting the motivation for the moral life in the context of a relationship to God.

4. Christian ethics shares fundamental sources of moral truth—logic, nature, reason, and experience—with other ethical traditions, both religious and secular. Christian ethics is human ethics, addressed in the light of Christian faith in Jesus as the revelation of God, the creator of humanity.

5. The teaching of the Second Vatican Council affirmed the Catholic Church's respect for the fundamental principles of pluralist societies, as well as the Church's commitment to seeking and teaching moral truth.

6. The role of Christian ethics in a pluralist society is witness to the truth of fulfilled human life in the person of Jesus and service to humanity in imitation of Jesus.

Questions for Discussion

1. Is it right to do something because God commands it, or does God command it because it is good? What is your response to this ancient problem? What is your evaluation of the solution proposed in the text?

2. To what extent do you think Christian faith influences morality, in terms of—
   (a) the content of morality (what we think is morally important/obligatory)?
   (b) the motivation to be moral (why we make the effort to act morally)?

3. Consider the following Christian teachings: the Trinity, the world as God's creation, humanity as the "image of God,"

the human person as embodied spirit, human sinfulness, the incarnation, the paschal mystery, the kingdom of God. Choose one of them and reflect on its implications for the moral life and for one or more specific moral questions.

4. What do you think Christians have to offer to the moral life of a pluralist society? What is one moral issue where you think Christians share in a broad social consensus, and one issue where Christians tend to have a distinctive point of view?

PART TWO

WHAT SORT OF PERSON SHOULD I BE?

After exploring the foundations of Christian ethics in reason and faith, we now focus on the content of ethics. Part Two is concerned with the *subjective* dimension of ethics, with the *moral subject,* the unique individual who believes, thinks, feels, and acts. Chapter 3 will focus on the moral person, characterized by freedom, responsibility, and conscience. Chapter 4 will consider the meaning of sin, the deliberate rejection or distortion of conscience, in light of the concept of fundamental option.

3

The Moral Person

At the beginning of chapter 1, it was argued that morality involves two crucial aspects of our humanity: our freedom and our capacity to experience and know the good. Whatever talents we happen to be gifted with, whatever opportunities or lack of them are our lot in life, we all have the potential for freedom and the capacity to experience and to affirm the value of our world and the persons within it. It is these attributes which are crucial to our status as persons, and it is in the development and realization of this fundamental potential that someone's personal quality ultimately consists.

The purpose of this chapter is to focus on these fundamental moral characteristics of persons, to consider the nature and interrelationship of freedom, responsibility, and conscience. The field of ethics can be divided into two parts: *subjective* and *objective*. Subjective ethics reflects on the *subject* of moral action, that is, the human person, characterized by freedom, responsibility, and conscience. A moral—or immoral—action is an action performed by a *moral subject,* someone who freely chooses between good and evil, and who has responsibility for that choice. The word *subjective* is often used pejoratively, in the sense of "merely subjective," yet our character as moral subjects is crucial to our humanity. Each person is a unique subject, a unique center of consciousness and freedom, shaping and responding to the world around him or her in unique ways.

Objective ethics, on the other hand, focuses not on the subject of the action but on the action itself—not, for example, on the question "Was this person sincere in acting that way?" but rather on the question "Was this the right thing to do?" These are distinct questions, because a sincere subject does not always choose what is, objectively speaking, the right thing to do, or the right thing may be done for bad subjective reasons. Objective ethics considers the nature of the good and the right, attempting to discover the fundamental goods of human life and the best ways of realizing them. Later chapters will be devoted to the key areas of objective ethics.

Human Freedom

Biologists inform us that living things are adapted to their particular environments. During the course of evolution, different species have evolved detailed patterns of behavior suited to these particular environments. These patterns of behavior are governed by instinct, an unreflective behavioral response to the environment, dictated by the particular species' genetic code. Because of this, virtually all plants and animals are highly specialized. Their evolution—along with the instincts that this has developed—has adapted them to a specialized environment within which they function very effectively. The study of biology provides us with countless examples of remarkable adaptation to particular physical environments, some of them extremely harsh and inhospitable. It is the specialized character of individual species that enables them to live, for example, in the coldest oceans or the driest deserts.

It is evident that the human species is not specialized in this way. Human beings are not as fast as cheetahs, as well-insulated against cold as seals, nor as drought-resistant as eucalyptus trees! The evolution of the human species has resulted in a being that lacks the specialized characteristics of other species, but that has the power to adapt itself to a broad spectrum of different environments, to make tools, and to develop technology, so that this range of possible environments constantly increases. Together with this nonspecialized but highly adaptive character goes a lack of the highly specialized instincts characteristic of other species. Any parent can observe the residual and short-lived instinctual responses in a newborn baby (such as the "grasping reflex"), and some instinctual responses do remain strong throughout life, but a human being's relationship to the environment is dictated by instinct only to a limited and general degree.

This absence of instinct means that *freedom* plays a fundamental role in the life of a human being. Rather than being encapsulated in a specific environment by a highly specialized adaptive evolution and being controlled by a complex pattern of genetically determined instincts, a human being is free to choose different environments and to adapt to those environments in different ways. Whereas the behavior of all other living beings follows certain patterns characteristic of all members of a given species, the behavior of human beings shows extraordinary variation. Different human groups develop particular cultures as part of the process of adapting to and shaping their environment, and individual human beings use the resources of those particular cultures, for example, language, with virtually infinite variation.

If human beings have, to a unique degree, the freedom to relate to their environment in different ways and to use their own skills and resources with great variation, what is this freedom for? What is its meaning? How should we define it?

At one level, we could define freedom as being free from constraints, free to do what we wish, whatever that may be. From this point of view, freedom has no particular aim or purpose, but is simply the characteristic of human beings to be able to choose from a variety of possible courses of action. The fewer constraints there are on our actions, the freer we are. From this point of view, if we remove external constraints—for example, laws imposed by governments and enforced by the police—or if we remove internal constraints—for example, moral norms inculcated in our upbringing—then we become more free, because there is now a greater range of actions that we can do without restriction, whether those restrictions come in the shape of the police force or of strong feelings of guilt. The greater the number of things we are free to do, the freer we are. So, from this perspective, to say that our freedom has any purpose would be to limit freedom, since it would be to channel our freedom in one way rather than in another. This understanding of freedom as the maximization of possible choices by removing constraints can be called *"freedom from."* "Freedom from" can also be called *"negative freedom,"* not in the sense that it is necessarily negative in itself, since freedom from constraints can be a very valuable thing, but rather in the sense that it is a negation of constraints.

The strength of this understanding of freedom is in the critical challenge it poses to any restriction on freedom. It asks what grounds we have for declaring what the purpose of human life is and for restricting freedom to actions that are in harmony with that purpose. In a liberal and pluralist society, there are many understandings of the purpose of human life, and it is often difficult to achieve consensus in ethical matters. Such a society, then, emphasizes individual freedom and tolerance and does not, in general, attempt to lay down what the purpose of human freedom is. At a *political* or *legal* level, this has the advantage of respecting the tolerance and diversity important to a liberal and pluralist society. The institutions of government do not, in general, claim to know what the purpose of human life is and to enact laws accordingly. The purpose of most laws is simply to guarantee that all members of society have roughly equal fundamental rights and freedoms.

At a political level this understanding of freedom as "freedom from" is important since it emphasizes that the state must always carry the burden of proof if it intends to limit the freedom of any individual. It needs to give good reasons, in terms of the common good or of individual rights, for restricting any individual's freedom.

At a *moral* level, however, to define freedom *only* as "freedom from constraint" is much more problematic. Am I really more free when I am freed from all constraints, whether external or internal, on my actions? Am I really more free simply because I have a greater number of choices? Or is it rather the case that, if I choose to constrain my own actions in certain ways, to restrict my choices, I can become more free? If, for example, I choose not to lie and I constrain myself to tell the truth, I have limited my possible courses of action, but have I really become less free? Generally speaking, the person who constantly tells the truth develops an environment of trust around him or herself. It is our experience that an environment of trust enables a whole range of actions and relationships that could not otherwise develop.

To cite a folktale, the boy "who cried wolf" discovered that his own untrustworthiness severely limited his range of possible action! To see the purpose of my freedom to speak in terms of telling the truth is not to lessen freedom, but to increase it, insofar as it increases the realm of trust within which I become free to develop a range of human relationships. By giving my freedom a specific purpose, I can increase its scope and power.

If we consider the case of education, a similar pattern emerges. For a child to submit to the process of schooling is clearly a limitation on freedom—a form of constraint. But is a parent who sends the child to school thereby making that child less free? If the education in question is good education, it will develop the powers of the child and that child's knowledge of his or her society and culture, to the extent that the child's freedom to think and act within that society will be enormously increased. In this case, the constraint on our possible choices of action by the discipline of education develops the realm of knowledge and understanding within which we can freely act.

This understanding of freedom as related to the fulfillment of a purpose that heightens and enriches our human potential is known as *"freedom for."* "Freedom for" is also called "positive freedom" in that it refers to the shaping of freedom for the fulfillment of a positive purpose. While an understanding of freedom as "freedom from" emphasizes the presumption, at a political level, in favor of individual freedom crucial for a liberal society, an insight into the moral implications of human freedom demands an appreciation of freedom as "freedom for." When we are conscious of our freedom, we are conscious that we have it *for* something, that there are good and bad ways of using that freedom. We are aware that it can be used for developing what we believe to be the true purpose of life or for wasting and destroying human potential. Together with the consciousness and experience of freedom comes the consciousness that freedom is not aimless. Its purpose is to develop a world of truth, beauty, and goodness, in all the varied, spontaneous, and unpredictable ways of which human beings are capable.

The fundamental point about "freedom for" is its relationship to morality. If morality is about the fulfillment of the person, then it is about fulfilling rather than restricting our freedom. Superficially, morality involves restrictions on freedom of action: in one sense sexual fidelity is more restrictive than sexual promiscuity. A faithful spouse, for example, has accepted a freely-chosen restriction of sexual relations to his or her spouse. Yet the commitment to fidelity that this involves can make possible a relationship of love, trust, and intimacy that is commonly agreed to be much more fulfilling than sexual promiscuity. It is in this sense of "freedom for" that *morality is not a restriction on freedom, but rather makes a fulfillment of freedom possible,* enabling a depth of human relationships that can only be achieved with the voluntary acceptance of meaningful restraint.[1]

Freedom and Responsibility

The concept of freedom goes hand in hand with the concept of responsibility. If I am free to choose and aware of what I am choosing, then I am responsible for my choice. Because I am free

---

1. The relationship between freedom and morality is brought out very strongly in chapter 1 of John Paul II's encyclical *Veritatis Splendor* (Vatican website, www.vatican.va). The encyclical first quotes from Matthew (beginning 19:16) the dialogue between Jesus and the rich young man: "Then someone came to him and said, 'Teacher, what good must I do to have eternal life?' And he said to him, 'Why do you ask me about what is good? There is only one who is good. If you wish to enter into life, keep the commandments.'" *Veritatis Splendor* then goes on to say, "Jesus points out to the young man that the commandments are the first and indispensable condition for having eternal life; on the other hand, for the young man to give up all he possesses and to follow the Lord is presented as an invitation: 'If you wish...' These words of Jesus reveal the particular dynamic of freedom's growth towards maturity, and at the same time *they bear witness to the fundamental relationship between freedom and divine law.* Human freedom and God's law are not in opposition; on the contrary, they appeal one to the other. The follower of Christ knows that his vocation is to freedom" (§17).

not to do something, I am responsible for doing it. In contrast to other animals, whose instincts dictate behavior patterns, human beings are both free to choose courses of action and at the same time responsible for those choices. Freedom and responsibility are bound together in such a way that whenever freedom is increased, responsibility is also increased, and when freedom is restricted, so also is responsibility lessened.

The concept of responsibility is linked to the way we use praise and blame, particularly in the distinctive ways we use it in relation to human beings. When we use words or actions to praise or blame an animal, we do so not because we attribute moral responsibility to it, but rather in order to train it to do or not do similar things in the future. Praise or blame for a human being can also have the effect of training, of encouraging or discouraging similar future actions. Yet, with a human being, that praise or blame is expressed because of our conviction that it is *deserved*, that the individual in question was to some degree responsible for that action and did something either morally good or morally bad, because the individual's own freedom was expressed in it. An animal can act in a way which is good or bad in the sense of pleasing its master, but only a human being can act in a way which is *morally* good or bad.

The word *responsibility* derives from the Latin word *respondere* meaning "to answer" or "to respond." At the most basic level, responsibility simply means that I am answerable or accountable for my actions. Even if I think that human freedom has no particular purpose, if I define freedom exclusively as "freedom from," I am still responsible or answerable for my actions since I was free not to do them. It was I myself, not some external force, who willed these actions. I am answerable to others for the way my expression of my freedom affects their freedom.

If, however, I do believe that my freedom has a purpose, that it also includes the dimension of "freedom for," then responsibility has the deeper sense of *responding* to that purpose. Then freedom is the great gift that enables us not only to fulfill what is good in the innocent way that an animal fulfills its own nature, but to do what is good out of a free response to the inherent value of goodness. Even more, freedom allows us to respond to what is good by developing its goodness in creative and individual ways. When, for example, a human being responds freely to the good inherent in another person, there are countless individual ways in which that response can be shown, all of which will express the fundamental values of respect and love.

A Covenantal Understanding of Freedom and Responsibility

We are conscious of our freedom and of the responsibility that this brings with it, but we differ in our interpretations of the meaning and purpose of this freedom. We are conscious that moral freedom is a fundamental attribute of the human race, that our freedom gives us a power and dignity that other species do not have. It is one of the "givens" of our existence, but we debate about the meaning of this "givenness." Is our freedom simply an accidental result of impersonal forces, a chance characteristic of the evolution of planet Earth, or is it indeed a gift given to us by the creative mystery at the heart of things? Is it purely a matter of chance that we experience moral freedom, or is it part of the destiny and purpose of our humanity? Whatever our answer to this question may be, we can live out our freedom in honesty and justice. What is crucial to our moral quality as persons is not how we interpret our freedom, but how we use it! Yet our answer will deeply affect our understanding of the significance of our freedom and, therefore, our understanding of the meaning of the moral life as a whole.

Christian ethics interprets our experience of freedom, and the sense of purpose and responsibility that come with it, in terms of a personal relationship with God. The "givenness" of freedom is not the "givenness" of mere accident, nor of impersonal forces and powers, but the gift of the creator. The mystery at the heart of things shows itself to be personal and communicates with its human creatures, inviting them into a relationship of love. For Christian ethics, the life of freedom is a life lived in relationship with a personal God of love. The deepest meaning of our own freedom is that it gives us the power to develop a personal relationship with the God who is freedom, for the human creature to freely come to know and love its creator. For the Christian tradition, human freedom and responsibility are *covenantal,* expressing the response of love for the creator's gift of freedom.

The biblical concept of covenant expresses the meaning of our freedom and responsibility in terms of a relationship with God. The biblical story is, in a fundamental sense, a story of covenant, of a developing and deepening relationship with God, a developing understanding of the divine gift of freedom. Because we are free creatures, God's relationship with us is in our freedom, that is, in history—the story of the lives of free creatures. The biblical covenants between God and his human creatures begin with his relationship with the patriarchs and tribes of Israel and culminating in the life of Jesus of Nazareth.

The biblical concept of covenant had its origin in the secular context of treaty relationships. To this day, the word *covenant* is used in formal legal language to refer to binding contracts or agreements between parties. In the ancient world, the relationship between an overlord and a subject people was often formalized in a covenant, a formal statement of the relationship in terms of dominance and submission. Such covenants marked the turbulent history of the ancient Near East and the succession of empires that attempted to impose systems of rule on subject territories. Covenants were also made at a more everyday level to formalize agreements or contracts between parties about business and other matters. Since the language and formal structure of secular or political covenantal relationships was highly developed, the ancient Israelites turned to it in order to express their relationship with Yahweh, the Lord. They employed the secular language of treaty relationships between a lord and his subjects, but gradually transformed it into a language of freedom and love.

Freedom and Purpose

The history of ancient Israel is a history of the development of the covenantal relationship between Yahweh, the Lord, and his chosen people. This covenantal relationship has its roots in the exodus experience of being liberated from slavery and brought to freedom in a promised land. The liberation of the children of Israel from slavery in Egypt culminates in the covenant of Mount Sinai, the symbol of the Israelite faith's unique character as a union of freedom and responsibility. The Sinai covenant is based on the free initiative of Yahweh, the liberating Lord. The children of Israel had experienced their freedom from slavery as a gift, a wondrous liberation from powerful and ruthless captors. Through this gift of freedom, Yahweh had invited them into relationship with him, to share in his own freedom. The Sinai covenant then solemnizes their response to this gift of freedom, their awareness that they have been freed to live in response to the love of Yahweh (Exod 19—20). The covenant symbolizes an awareness of responsibility, an awareness that the gift of freedom must be worthily accepted.

The covenant of Mount Sinai makes clear that, for the faith of Israel, we do not need to earn or justify our freedom as human beings. We have it by right because we have it as a gift of a free creator who desires to share it with his creatures. The moral life is a life lived in freedom, a life which responds to the gift of freedom by doing good. For the ancient Israelites, this was understood in terms of law, in terms of following the will of God. The Ark of the Covenant, the earliest symbol of the Israelite people's relationship with God, contained the scroll of the Law. By obeying the law of God, the Israelite gave practical and visible testimony to his or her gratitude for the gift of freedom and of the promised land. To live by the Law was to live a life of responsibility before God. In the sense of "freedom for," the Law enabled the fulfillment of freedom, giving a code of life which could lead to long life and prosperity in "the land that the LORD your God is giving you" (Deut 5:16).

The uniqueness of the faith of ancient Israel can be summed up in the phrase *ethical monotheism:* a faith in one God who is himself goodness and can only be worshipped in goodness and truth. The Law was the codified moral and religious tradition of Israel, but it also became the symbol for a grateful and responsive relationship to God.

For the faith of Israel, then, the covenantal relationship was a relationship of gift and response. The teaching of Jesus affirms this relationship on the basis of his profound sense of the nearness and graciousness of the Father. Jesus' teaching does not begin with a list of moral demands, but rather with an affirmation of the blessings of the kingdom of God. The structure of the Sermon on the Mount (or the sermon on the plain, as it is in Luke's Gospel) is one of gift and response (Matt 5—7; Luke 6). Jesus proclaims the blessings of God as free, indiscriminate, and unearned. God's gifts are prior to any effort on our part; our lives are a gift rather than an achievement. The good news of Jesus is that his Father constantly and indiscriminately extends his love to his human creatures. It is the Father who takes the initiative and gives us the blessings of freedom.

In the teaching of Jesus, human freedom is regarded with radical seriousness. Mark's Gospel begins its account of the ministry of Jesus with Jesus' proclamation of the gospel: "The time is fulfilled, and the kingdom of God has come near; repent, and believe in the good news" (Mark 1:15). The English phrase "reform your lives" is an attempt to translate the Greek verb based on the noun *metanoia*, a word that expresses a change or reversal of heart and mind, a conversion of life. Jesus' appeal to his hearers presumes that such conversion is possible and that we have the freedom to bring it about. We are capable of repenting, of turning our lives around, because we have been given the gift of freedom. We bear the burden of responsibility for our own lives since we have the freedom to recognize or ignore the call of goodness. Yet the exercise of this freedom is not an all-or-nothing task. It is not a matter of sheer unaided willpower battering against the stubborn perversities of our character, but rather a capacity to be open to the aid of the Spirit of God. For Jesus, human freedom is exercised in response to grace, to the ceaseless gifts of God, gifts that can be received by the one who is open to them in prayer and hope (Luke 11:1–13).

The one who lives by love of God and love of neighbor fulfills the gift of freedom by responding to the blessings of the kingdom of God. For the Christian, this is the meaning of a *covenantal existence*, an existence sustained by a free relationship with God and neighbor. The covenantal character of existence means that, in our response to the neighbor, we are also responding to God. A covenantal understanding of ethics can inform our sense of the value and importance of the moral life by reminding us that it is ultimately not a matter of obedience to laws, nor even of allegiance to noble principles, but rather a fidelity to persons, to the three-personed God and to the person of our neighbor. If we can enrich our moral life with this awareness, then our obedience to sound and useful laws, as well as our allegiance to noble principles, will be given a subtle and distinctive focus, since the character of our obedience and allegiance will be shaped by our understanding of the moral life as a free response to the value of persons.

In chapter 2, it was noted that the Christian doctrine of the Trinity emphasizes that God is a communion of persons. The fulfillment of human persons, created in the image of God, is to make a communion or community of life possible, in many different forms and contexts. *A covenantal understanding of ethics is an ethics oriented toward community, toward personal fulfillment through faithful relationships to God and neighbor.*

Freedom or Determinism?

This discussion of freedom and responsibility is based on the premise that human beings really are free in a significant moral sense of the word. The discussion of covenant makes clear that this premise is a crucial aspect of the understanding of human existence characteristic of the Jewish and Christian traditions. Yet this is not a premise that everyone would accept; it has, in fact, been a subject for philosophical dispute for thousands of years. This dispute has the shorthand title "free will versus determinism" and focuses on the question whether our will, or volition, is free and therefore responsible, or whether we are in fact determined by the circumstances of heredity and environment.

If our choices are fully determined by these circumstances, then moral responsibility is an illusion. There is no difference of effect, and there should be no difference of intent, between the praise or blame given to animals and that applied to human beings. The purpose of such praise and blame would be purely and simply to modify behavior, not to attribute moral desert. Further, the lack of biological specialization of human beings would be seen as nothing more than an accidental product of evolution, rather than as the result of a divine intention, realized through the processes of evolution, to create a being that is itself creative and responsible.

The determinist argument can take different forms, but the most influential ones are *social* and *psychological* determinism. Social determinists argue that human freedom is illusory since the study of society gives us evidence that individual action is determined by social forces. People have the values they do, and act in the ways they do, because they are members of particular societies; they have no freedom to choose their own values or act in ways that are expressions of individual freedom. Clearly, different societies do have different values and ways of acting, and the moral sense of individuals is formed differently by these different social environments. It can be very difficult for an individual to develop and live by a system of values that is at variance with his or her society. The difficulty and the anguish of the vocation of a prophet, in the true sense of the word, is to do this very thing in a way which can provide inspiration and example for others. Yet the prophetic vocation has been fulfilled by many outstanding figures, both religious and secular, who have shown that it is possible to resist the pressures of social conformism and to challenge a society to reform its values.

A crucial weakness of social determinism lies in its failure to take account of the developments in a society's moral beliefs that are closely associated with the prophetic example and commitment of individuals. If we consider some of the progress made in moral awareness in modern times, then the failure of social determinism to understand social change becomes evident. Much of this progress is associated with the committed initiative of individuals who reacted against dominant social values. Rather than internalizing these dominant values, they criticized them in light of their insight into the true meaning of human fulfillment. The African American leader Martin Luther King Jr. did not internalize the dominant image of blacks characteristic of his own society, but criticized it in light of ideals of human fulfillment derived from Christian tradition and from the traditions of American democracy. Mahatma Gandhi did not internalize the image of India characteristic of the dominant colonial ethos, but criticized it in light of Hindu, Christian, and democratic ideas of human dignity and nationhood.

Most people are not prophets, and their actions are based on an acceptance of the prevailing values of their culture. Yet this does not show that they have no moral freedom or responsibility. Different cultures can understand the difference between good and evil very differently, but moral choice does remain an exercise of personal freedom.

Let us take the example of a Western officer and a Japanese officer in World War II, each trained in the military code characteristic of his own culture at that time. For the Westerner, to surrender was a highly regrettable but completely honorable course of action in a militarily hopeless situation. For the Japanese, surrender was a dishonorable action, demonstrating a lack of dedication to the Emperor and the nation. Each officer identifies "good" and "evil" in different ways; their values have been formed by their respective cultures. Yet this does not mean that they have no moral freedom. Within the world of values that each inhabits, each must choose whether to act well or badly, to exercise freedom for good or for evil. The Westerner can act well by surrendering with honor, or badly by abandoning his soldiers or committing suicide. The Japanese can act well by fighting to the death, or badly by surrendering out of cowardice. Each is free to do good or evil in the way that his own culture understands it. Personal freedom and responsibility are exercised within the realm of value that we are aware of because of our social environment. Therefore, the fact that we share the values of a particular culture (to varying degrees of exclusiveness), does not mean that we have no moral freedom. It simply means that our freedom is exercised within the "space" formed by that particular culture.

Psychological determinism would argue, in turn, that each officer did what he did because of the circumstances of individual upbringing. If every effect has a cause, if all that we are and do is an effect of previous occurrences, then the appearance of freedom in our actions is an illusion. All that we do is the result of an unbroken chain of causality that stretches back to earliest childhood; our actions are determined by our past actions and experiences. The laws of cause and effect mean that there can be no free actions, since—for this argument—a free action is an action without a cause.

The answer to this rejection of the reality of moral freedom is not to deny that causality is part of our lives. If our actions had no relationship to previous actions, then they would be arbitrary and unpredictable. One of the purposes of moral education is to help individuals to develop *character*, that is, a moral personality characterized by a consistent pattern of good action. This is, as we saw in chapter 1, one of the ideals of the Aristotelian tradition in ethics. To deny causality in our actions, to argue that we are not affected by our past actions, would be to reject this notion of moral character, which is based precisely on the cumulative effect of good action on the personality.

To argue for the reality of moral freedom is not to deny causality, but rather to affirm that the influence of causality does not preclude the reality of choice in our lives. The circumstances of our lives constantly present us with choices, and we experience the freedom to make these choices—to decide for one course of action or the other. When we decide, we are aware that "I could have done otherwise"; we are aware that our own freedom can give a chain of events two different outcomes; we are aware that we have the power to choose between two outcomes, rather than being simply determined by the circumstances of our lives to act in a particular way. Our own freedom, based on our judgment of what is the right thing to do, has the power to influence the course of our lives.

Determinism and Reductionism

Both social and psychological determinism are forms of *reductionism*. Reductionism, as the name suggests, claims to be able to reduce what it judges to be illusory claims and entities to the forces that are really operating in a situation. In the case of freedom, the reductionist reduces human action, which others believe to spring from freedom, to social and psychological determinants. The fundamental problem with any total reductionism in relation to human freedom is the same as that which we encountered with total relativism: total reductionism reduces its own claims together with all other claims.

If, for example, the social reductionist claims that all actions and statements are simply the result of social forces, without any role for human freedom, then his or her own claim must also be simply the expression of social forces. As such, it can make no claim to truth, since a true statement claims to be true independently of what has caused someone to make it. It claims to be a statement about reality as such, not simply the determined outcome of particular social forces. If the reductionist is asked what the grounds are for accepting his statement as true, then he cannot simply point to the social forces that have caused him to make it. He must rather provide us with some evidence that is credible independently of such social forces, inviting our free assent through insight into the truth of his claims. But in attempting to provide such evidence, the reductionist destroys his own case since he thereby admits that there is such a thing as a truth independent of social forces. At the same time he admits our freedom to know this truth and to accept it as true because we have insight into its truth, rather than because we are constrained to do so by social forces.

Let us consider the example of two people arguing which political party is best to govern a country. Both of them are reductionists. Each is attempting to persuade the other of the truth of his views, yet at the same time each holds that the reason they hold those views is purely because of the influence of social forces on their lives. Each must then respond to the other: "You are not advocating your views because they are true, but because you have been determined to hold them by your social environment. But I have been determined by different forces, so I hold different views. If you gave me reasons why your views were true, reasons independent of the forces determining your beliefs, I could, if I were not determined by different forces, consider the truth of your views. But you cannot give me any reasons that you could claim to be true—true independently of your or my conditioning—but only reasons that express your own social conditioning." Such an argument would be a pointless exercise and a denial of the human capacity to transcend, to a significant and crucial degree, the real influence of our social environment and engage in a common search for truth.

Total reductionism destroys its own case. If we deny freedom, then we deny our ability to find the truth and to recognize it when we find it. If we deny this, then we are incapable of saying anything worth believing at all. We cannot prove with the force of geometrical logic that we have freedom, but we can show that an understanding of human life without freedom is not recognizably human since it denies so many dimensions of what we experience and value as human existence.

To reject total reductionism, however, is not to deny the influence of society and of my own psychological biography on my actions. Our freedom consists in choosing between good and evil within the world of values and experience of life characteristic of our own situation. When we reflect on our lives, we quickly become aware how much social and psychological circumstances have led to our having a life of one kind rather than another. A middle-class white male, for example, usually has a very different set of life circumstances than a member of a racial minority. He will not, as a rule, experience racial prejudice and is far more likely to have a range of choices of career, living conditions, and leisure. He is not likely to experience the strong bonds of an extended family often characteristic of members of racial minorities. He is more likely to understand the meaning of life in terms of individual achievement rather than group solidarity. These different life circumstances clearly provide a context for individual life that is largely beyond individual choice. Individual choice, and the responsibility for it, take place within this context.

An individual whose circumstances of life offer little chance of free choice and action is clearly less responsible for the shape and development of his or her life than one whose circumstances offer a wide field of choice and opportunity. The more free we are, the more responsible, and vice versa. An appreciation of the social and psychological constraints on the life of an individual enables us to see how restricted the scope of freedom can be. This must be a factor in considering the degree of people's responsibility for the course of their lives. It is crucial, however, that this does not become a general denial of their moral freedom, since this would also mean a denial of their freedom to transcend and reform the circumstances of their lives. This is a question we will return to in the next chapter.

Conscience

Our freedom, then, is deeply associated with ourselves. Within the constraints and opportunities of life, we make ourselves through the exercise of our own freedom. But this freedom does not exist in a purposeless void: our freedom experiences a real difference between good and evil in the world. We are aware of our freedom in relation to the world, but at the same time we are aware of values within the world that demand our respect. We are free, but at the same time we are called. We experience a sense of obligation to exercise our freedom for the development of what is good and the overcoming of evil. While other living things live out their lives by instinct, expressing in countless individual existences the behavior unique to their species, human beings experience a calling to shape the world by the exercise of freedom. They are uniquely aware that they have the power to develop the goods and values of this world or to distort and destroy them.

This human experience of the call of goodness is called *conscience,* and it is intimately bound up with freedom and responsibility. Conscience is at the core of the moral person since it is our free response to the good. When we act freely according to conscience, we fulfill something of crucial value to the person. Conscience is our awareness of the difference between good and evil, and of the crucial importance of this difference for our decisions and actions. The quality of conscience can be understood in terms of the sensitivity with which we are aware of that difference, and of the response we make to it. A conscience that is sensitive to the call of goodness seeks to discover what will serve the good and avoid evil. It seeks to translate its fundamental sensitivity to what is good into a practical knowledge of how to act. Its search for moral knowledge is motivated by its sense of how important this knowledge is for our lives. This search culminates in the use of the knowledge it has gained as the basis for a moral judgment, a judgment expressed in action.

Conscience is a form of knowledge, but a form of knowledge with unique characteristics. The knowledge of conscience is based not on theoretical speculation or factual observation, but rather on our response to what is good. The talents, or lack of them, that we have as thinkers or observers are distinct from the fundamental sensitivity of our response to goodness. We know the goodness of this world through the response that opens our hearts to it. Yet this response to what is good must be expressed in action, and action can only be based on factual knowledge of the world. The knowledge of response must be united with factual knowledge in order for conscience to have practical effect. I may, for example, respond to the call of goodness by wishing to do something for my poverty-stricken neighbors. But unless I have well-grounded factual knowledge of what will in fact assist them, my attempts to help may be frustrated and ineffectual.

The knowledge of conscience, then, is a knowledge that is both more profound than factual knowledge and dependent on it for action. It is for this reason that conscience can be both good and mistaken: good in its response to goodness, mistaken in the factual knowledge used to make a practical judgment. The knowledge of the heart motivates the search for factual knowledge but cannot guarantee that it will find it.

Conscience and the Moral Subject

Our conscience is expressed in our judgment of what is good and what is evil in the world around us. This judgment seeks to judge the world as it is and not merely as we would like it to be. Yet the judgment of conscience has a uniquely personal dimension, since the result of a judgment of conscience is a decision. And a decision—together with its resulting actions—is the expression of my freedom and responsibility. Nothing is more personal than this. Only my own judgment of right and wrong can guide my own freedom, since the actions of my own freedom involve my own responsibility. Because conscience involves my judgment of *moral* truth, and this judgment has immediate relevance to the *practice* of my decisions and actions, then only my own conscience can guide my own practice.

Let us consider a case in which someone is asked to defer to someone else's judgment of a situation with moral implications. A junior officer in a large finance company is instructed by a superior to make entries into the computer that the junior officer believes involve defrauding another company. When questioned, the superior says that, although these entries seem to result in fraud, they in fact do not, because certain corrections will be made at a higher level. When the junior officer asks for more details, she receives none and is told to defer to the greater knowledge of her superior. She is then directed to make the computer entries and to take the normal responsibility for doing so. As far as she can understand, what she is doing will be fraud, and she is being asked to defer to someone else's judgment of a moral situation, based on the claim that facts unknown to her make a crucial difference.

In what circumstances would it be right to defer to the superior's judgment? A crucial factor will be the superior's general trustworthiness. A generally trustworthy supervisor may not—in the situation we are considering—have the time to provide the relevant explanatory information, or it may be too complex. But his or her earlier trustworthiness may be good-enough grounds for the junior officer to defer to her superior's judgment.

In the case of a supervisor who isn't trustworthy, deferring to the judgment of that person does compromise conscience, because the junior officer will be using her own freedom to do an act she knows may be possibly wrong.

Conscience as a Subjective Relationship to Objective Truth

I cannot defer to the judgment of others against my own conscience because my own responsibility is at stake. This essential characteristic of conscience highlights its *subjective* character: conscience is at the core of our existence as moral subjects. My conscience cannot be exchanged for someone else's any more than I, a unique individual, can be exchanged for someone else. Since my conscience guides my freedom, and my free actions make me who I am as a moral subject, to abandon my own conscience is to abandon my moral selfhood.

Conscience is subjective since it is *my* search for truth, and its judgment uniquely binds my responsibility. It is my own, but at the same time it is a search for *objective* truth. Conscience searches for the truth of the matter—not a truth that is unique to me, nor to anyone else, but a truth that will apply to anyone faced with the same moral question in the same situation. Conscience is the moral subject's commitment to moral truth. This commitment goes outside ourselves to the real world in which we live. If it were not a desire to find what is objectively true, the judgments of conscience would tell us only about our own preferences and prejudices, rather than about the real world of values. This union of subjective and objective is essential to conscience, since conscience is the relationship of the moral subject to objective truth.

It follows from the subjective character of conscience that *sincerity* is the test of a good conscience. But true sincerity is anything but subjective in the pejorative sense of the word; the truly sincere person strives to achieve the greatest possible objectivity in moral matters, to find the truth. A sincerity that is satisfied with a limited truth is not sincerity but insincerity, a flight from the truth. Sincerity to conscience has its real test in the degree of commitment to discovering the truth and removing the barriers to true insight—prejudice, ignorance, and self-centeredness. If conscience is not formed by a committed and sustained search for truth, then it is not truly conscience, but rather a means of preserving one's existing, comfortable view of things.

The character of conscience as a subjective grasp of objective moral truth explains both its crucial importance to our existence as moral persons and the importance of the *formation and development of conscience.* If the subjective character of conscience is ignored, if we set aside our own conscience and simply defer to the moral judgments of others, then we lose something essential to our own character as a moral person. If, on the other hand, we pay no attention to the formation of conscience, then our conscience remains stuck fast in the world of our own passions and prejudices. The dangers of this are evident when we consider the damage caused by people sincerely committed to destructive ideologies.

An appreciation of conscience as a subjective relationship to objective truth can also help to understand the ways in which conscience can be both sincere and wrong. A sincere, or good, conscience is a conscience dedicated to finding the truth, using all the resources that are available to it. A sincere conscience expresses the commitment of the moral subject to having a truthful relationship to the world. This sincerity, however, cannot guarantee that conscience will find the truth—for many reasons, it may elude us. The situations that we need to judge may be too complex, we may not be correctly informed, or our conscience—through no fault of our own—may have been formed in ways that make it very difficult for us to see the truth in this situation. Our conscience is not an infallible guide to what is objectively true. Yet we have no higher guide to action: if we have done all we can to form our own conscience by a sincere search for truth, then setting set aside our own conscience is setting aside what we believe to be the truth.

Conscience in Church Teaching

Because conscience is crucial to the nature of the person as a moral subject, Church teaching emphasizes that conscience, our personal insight into moral truth, is the ultimate norm of personal action:

Deep within their conscience human beings discover a law, which they have not laid upon themselves, but which they must obey. Its voice, always calling them to love and to do what is good and avoid evil, rings in their heart at the right moment with the command: do this, shun that. For human beings have in their heart a law inscribed by God: their dignity lies in obedience to this law and they will be judged by it. Conscience is the most intimate center and sanctuary of a person, in which the person is alone with God, whose voice echoes within. In a wonderful way, conscience makes known that law which is fulfilled in the love of God and of neighbor. By fidelity to conscience Christians are united with other human beings in the search for truth and for the true solutions to the many moral problems which arise in the lives of individuals and in society. The more a correct conscience prevails, so much the more do persons and groups turn away from blind willfulness and strive to conform to the objective norms of morality. It can often happen that conscience errs through ignorance which it is unable to overcome, without thereby losing its dignity. This cannot be said of the person who shows little concern for seeking what is true and good, or when conscience gradually becomes nearly blind through the habit of sin. (*Gaudium et Spes*, §16)

This text takes its inspiration from the insight of the Hebrew prophets that external codes of law can make no appeal to human beings unless they can address our internal sensitivity to goodness. For Jeremiah, the new covenant would be based on a law "written on the heart," an internal and personal response to the Lord (Jer 31:33). Law must reflect our awareness of the difference between good and evil, and it is this awareness that is at the root of human dignity. Conscience is the knowledge of the heart that expresses our response to goodness.

This affirmation of the importance of conscience interprets it in terms of a relationship to God, since conscience is an awareness of goodness and truth, which have their source in God. Further, the knowledge of conscience is the knowledge of response, so that the response to goodness in conscience is a response to God. From a Christian perspective, then, an atheist's or agnostic's sincere commitment to conscience and the overriding importance of truth and goodness is an *implicit form* of commitment to God, a recognition that human life can only be fulfilled by dedication to transcendent values.

The text of *Gaudium et Spes* goes on to emphasize that a common commitment to conscience is what motivates the human search for mutual understanding, the patient dialogue that can lead to cooperative action for human welfare. It notes that conscience as response to goodness can fail, for reasons beyond our control, in its search for true and relevant factual knowledge, and thereby act in misguided ways without losing its dignity. This is to be distinguished from the lack of sincerity which deprives the search for truth of commitment and direction.

Conscience and Guilt

The above passage from the Second Vatican Council emphasizes the priority of conscience as the core of the moral person. Many
great figures have extolled its transcendent importance as the guide
of personal life. When asked to drink a toast to the pope, the great
English churchman John Henry Newman replied that he would
gladly do so, but would drink a toast to conscience first. The human
rights organization Amnesty International is dedicated to liberating
"Prisoners of Conscience"—men and women whose witness to
human rights poses a prophetic challenge to despotic regimes.

Yet conscience also has its counterfeits and surrogates. One of
these is the confusion of the judgment of conscience with feelings of
guilt. It was emphasized above that conscience should be considered
a form of knowledge and a process of judgment; it is the moral subject's attempt to discern, with all the powers of the intellect and all
the commitment of the will, the right thing to do in a particular situation. As such it involves feeling, since it is the response of the
whole person to the moral quality of that situation. But this is quite
different from simply "feeling guilty." A feeling of guilt may or may
not be a sign that we have in fact rejected the judgment of conscience; the presence or strength of that feeling is no indication in
itself that we have done so. Whereas acting against conscience is to
act against what we judge to be wrong, guilt may arise from actions
that transgress various taboos and conventions, but that may not be
morally wrong at all. We feel guilty in doing them, not because we
reflectively and critically judge them to be wrong, but because they
are associated with infringing certain taboos. Someone brought up in
a strongly patriotic home, for example, might "feel guilty" about criticizing his country in the presence of foreigners, yet recognize that
the facts of the matter may demand it.

In many cases, moral growth may be a matter of outgrowing
the guilt associated with certain actions and realizing that they are
not wrong. Tragically, many human relationships are based on
manipulation rather than on frank reciprocity; partners and family

81

members, for example, sometimes seek to gain their ends by exploiting the guilt feelings of others. Such guilt feelings may be associated with expectations that people have of themselves and that they cannot fulfill—expectations that are unfair and unrealistic and, in fact, that may be imposed by others rather than freely accepted as just and reasonable. Guilt may be simply a crippling residue from our psychic past and a means of personal exploitation. Such guilt can only be dispelled by throwing the light of love and reason on personal relationships—the love that seeks to empower and liberate rather than manipulate, and the reason that critically dissolves a false sense of obligation in favor of a fair appreciation of each person's needs and abilities.

This is not to deny the importance of that guilt which is a genuine sign of our having gone against the judgment of conscience. Such guilt, arising from the painful awareness of the dissonance between what we have done and what we sincerely believe to be true, is a sign of moral sensitivity. The disappearance of guilt, in this sense, would be a sign of the disappearance of conscience, since it would mean that this awareness of dissonance had atrophied. We would no longer feel guilty, since we would have lost any sense of the difference between right and wrong. The amoral person, the one who has lost this sense, does not feel guilt and is thus deprived of the spur to set out on the path of moral reform. Guilt, in this sense, is the response of the moral subject to its own insincerity, its own brokenness.

It is crucial that this guilt does not become a fruitless and self-destructive sense of moral hopelessness, but rather an incentive to resolution and renewal. The sense of guilt, which emphasizes our own moral dissonance and insincerity, develops into a feeling of remorse, a sense of loss that seeks to make positive amends. The story of Peter's denial of Jesus is a classic portrayal of sin, guilt, and remorse. Peter's denials escalated in vehemence to the point of cursing. Yet he remained sensitive to his vocation of discipleship, his sense of guilt aroused to a flood of tears of remorse at the sound of the cock crowing, remorse that opened him to the forgiveness of the risen Christ (Mark 14:66–72; John 21:15–19).

Conscience and "Superego"

The confusion of conscience with guilt is closely related to the confusion of conscience with an internalized sense of what external powers demand of us. Often guilt feelings arise because we have gone against the wishes of someone who exerts power over us. Such guilt is not the result of an awareness of having done wrong or gone against the sincere judgment of conscience, but rather of having challenged the powers that give us security. Human beings live in social contexts that give them various degrees of security and recognition. From childhood we grow in self-esteem by receiving the recognition of others. The approval and disapproval of others is crucial to the development of our own sense of self, since that self is formed within the context of relationships with others. During the formative stages of life, our own sense of what is right and what is wrong is strongly associated with what is approved or disapproved of by those whose judgments affect our own self-esteem.

The psychoanalyst Sigmund Freud coined the term *superego* for the internalization of the external powers that confer approval or disapproval on our actions. The superego represents all the structures of power in society, as well as the power that "significant others" have in relation to our personal lives. The superego is our internalization of laws and social conventions, in addition to the wishes of parents, spouses, and friends. The superego claims the power to confer security, to protect us from harm, or to administer punishment; it represents the social context within which we feel secure or insecure. Actions that conform to the expectations of the superego result in approval and an enhancement of self-esteem, while those which flout its expectations result in shame and guilt.

The actions demanded by the superego may, of course, be good or bad. Genuinely loving parents expect and reward constructive and cooperative behavior from their children, since such behavior is for the benefit of the children themselves. A police state, on the other hand, affirms the actions of its secret police by rewards of status and wealth, even though those actions are anything but oriented to general human welfare. Of itself the mere approval of the superego is no indication of the moral quality of the action that evokes this approval; it is simply an indication that we have done what external powers expect of us and will reward.

The Formation of Conscience

The dangers of confusing conscience with superego emphasize the importance and necessity of the formation of conscience. This formation is essentially a matter of a deepening and broadening of moral insight. A crucial aspect of the formation of conscience is that it be distinguished from the superego as soon as the development of the person allows it. It is natural that small children identify right and wrong with the approval and disapproval of parents, since it is their parents who introduce them to the world and its values and disvalues. Yet it is the parents' task to show the developing child that the rightness or wrongness of actions is not directly equivalent to their approval or disapproval, but goes beyond it, and indeed, beyond the approval or disapproval of any other power.

The formation of conscience depends on the realization that the judgment of what is good is quite distinct from the question of whether my actions meet with the approval of those whom I cherish or fear—however often, in practice, these two things may coincide. Therefore, moral education must emphasize the independence of moral judgment from the wishes of others. It will not succeed in educating persons to make moral judgments unless those persons have the confidence to be able to resist the demands of the superego and be motivated by the desire to do good for its own sake. This is why the development of personal self-esteem is also crucial for the formation of conscience. Those truly concerned for the child's development as a moral subject will not only encourage his or her powers of moral reasoning, but also show that they value the child's status as a subject, a person of freedom and responsibility.

From the point of view of Christian ethics, the distinction between conscience and superego is fundamentally linked to the development of a genuinely biblical image of God. The age-old debate discussed in chapter 2 (is something good because God commands it, or does he command it because it is good?) is not merely a philosophical conundrum but goes right to the heart of Christian ethics. Many religious people have been plagued by an image of God as a heavenly lawmaker, a fearsome deity who arbitrarily makes things right and wrong. The implication of this attitude was that the laws of God had no reason we could discern or debate and that they must be blindly and literally followed. This image of God as arbitrary lawgiver provoked anxiety concerning divine approval or disapproval, so that God became a kind of celestial superego whose disapproval would result in eternal loss.

Historically speaking, the reaction to this image was the increasing rejection of any connection between God and morality since this "God" was seen to be less benevolent than many human beings! By contrast, Christians find in the gospels a God who makes men and women inherently good, and who makes them in his own image so that they have the power to know what is good and to cooperate with his purposes in creation. The teaching of Jesus constantly emphasizes that the will of God is that all people should flourish; traditional laws must be interpreted in light of this fundamental creative imperative. In this perspective, God is no longer a celestial superego, but rather the creator of a world of inherent value, encouraging and guiding his human creatures to discover and develop this value.

Law and the Formation of Conscience

A crucial phase of the formation of conscience is development of an understanding of right and wrong that transcends the desire to please external powers. A further phase is that development which can put *law* into its proper context and perspective. Jesus did not end the struggle against religious legalism; many Christians have had to do so within the churches founded in his name. In all walks of life, religious and secular, the tension between morality and law continues. This tension derives from the fact that laws are necessary for the ordered life of any society, but that an elevation of law to the absolute determinant of a society's life runs the grave risk of destroying the moral concerns that originally inspired the law. A law, for example, that forbids driving above a certain speed limit may, when interpreted absolutely, impose a harsh sentence on someone who drove above that speed limit in the well-grounded hope that he or she might thereby save lives without involving any serious risks to third parties.

A conscience dominated by legalism is an undeveloped conscience because it has not yet gone beyond the letter of the law to the spirit of the law, to an understanding of why laws have been enacted and promulgated. The development of conscience includes the realization that laws are made to serve certain goods, and the value of laws depends on how well they serve the enhancement of that good in the life of a society. A developed conscience obeys the law because of the good it serves and because of an appreciation of society's need for a common framework of action, not because laws are seen as absolute. This is particularly important in situations when laws are seen to express inadequate or distorted appreciations of human values—laws, for example, that sanction discrimination or embody unjust economic relationships. A well-formed conscience will be able to appeal above such laws to what is truly good for human beings in community, perhaps contributing to the reform of law in the ways that are open to citizens of democratic societies.

Conscience and Openness to the Truth

We have seen that the formation of conscience involves one's deepening insight into the nature of the good and developing the realization that things are not made good by the approval of particular persons or by being laid down in laws. The confidence to achieve this realization and to make judgments based on it is enhanced by a person's growing self-esteem, the conviction that one is a unique moral subject, capable of moral insight and moral judgment. Conscience, as emphasized above, is our subjective relationship to objective moral truth, and the development of conscience is fundamentally a matter of the moral subject's increasing openness to and desire for the truth. This openness to the truth is the basis for a well-formed conscience, the conscience of a moral subject who does not rest content with a narrow and self-serving view of the world, but is rather intent on knowing what really is good for him or herself and for others.

This openness to the truth must involve a genuine use of our personal intelligence and of all the resources available to us. It will involve respect for all the sources of moral truth discussed in chapter 1: logic, nature, reason, experience, and tradition. By coming to terms with these sources of truth, the subjective conscience affirms its sincerity, its desire to know and do the truth. An appreciation of what experience and tradition have to offer us will involve a respect for the *authority* of that experience and tradition—the authority, for example, of wise and experienced persons, or the insight into the meaning of human life expressed in traditions. Respect for authority, in this sense, is quite other than obedience to the superego. Respect for the authority of experience and tradition is respect based on the recognition that they have something to teach us; they are *authoritative* (in contrast to "authoritarian") and can guide us to insights through the wisdom gained from experience. Such authority is a source of knowledge that we can freely come to share, rather than a power that demands obedience irrespective of moral criteria. Experience and tradition, while providing richer and more complex insights than other sources of moral truth, must be open to reasoned challenge and critique, lest they threaten to become a form of legalism in their own right.

Conscience and Faith in God

Openness to all these sources of truth must be based on the subjective confidence that I am capable of knowing what is good and of making the judgments that form the moral pattern of my life. It is enhanced by self-esteem and by a freedom from fear and compulsion. Such fear is often induced by the insecurity associated with challenging the demands of those who have power over us. This insecurity may be overcome by the security of conscience and self-esteem achieved in a positive upbringing; someone may be able to risk the anger of an employer or figure of public authority in doing what is right, because they can draw on a strong sense of their own integrity and worth derived from earlier life, especially from their family.

Yet the experience of clashing with evil, of attempting to persevere against the power of entrenched corruption or discrimination, raises questions that have troubled people of conscience since ancient times: Is the universe indifferent to the outcome of the struggle of good and evil? Is this struggle a struggle between evenly balanced forces—good and bad gods? Or is it a struggle, which for all its anguish and sorrow, will end in the absolute victory of good—a victory that, because it is the victory of good, will include magnanimity to the defeated forces of evil? Because these questions concern the character of ultimate reality, they can only receive a religious answer. Christian faith responds to them with the proclamation of the paschal mystery. Jesus of Nazareth, in his proclamation of a kingdom of peace, freedom, and justice, challenged the power of political tyranny and religious legalism and was crucified by them. His resurrection is the sign that God, the good creator of the universe, will bring all things to goodness in his kingdom. For the Christian, faith in the paschal mystery as the ultimate meaning of the moral life can be a source of the strength and confidence needed to do what is good, rather than what is approved of. Moral courage and self-esteem can be strengthened by faith in the unconditional love of the God of the covenant. In the words of the Jesus of John's Gospel to his disciples: "In the world you face persecution. But take courage; I have conquered the world!" (16:33).

Conversion

Finally, openness to the truth must involve conversion, the change of life that turns our freedom away from selfish goals and moral blindness toward the truth. In proclaiming the coming of the kingdom of God, Jesus preached *metanoia:* a change of heart, a turning away from sin, a "conversion" of lifestyle from self-centeredness to an orientation to God and neighbor. Conversion changes the subject's life by overcoming the limitations of self-centeredness and opening us to the real world of value around us. It displaces the ego from the center of the universe and sets it in the context of relationships of love and respect for others. Conversion brings the insight that it is only by losing ourselves in commitment to true values that we gain ourselves by the fulfilled life that this commitment makes possible. This conversion may happen through more or less dramatic experiences in a person's life, or it may be a very gradual process.

Whether it happens through one special event or continuous development, the openness to the truth that conversion brings must be constantly renewed. Conversion is not a once-and-for-all transformation of the person, but a commitment of mind and heart to the truth that must be reaffirmed throughout life. The converted conscience is one whose freedom from fear is yet "God-fearing," respecting the authority of truth and goodness; one whose openness to the sources of truth and knowledge is not for the sake of gaining power over our neighbor, but rather for the sake of learning how best to serve those values on which the fulfillment of all of us depends.

Character

In chapter 1 we saw that the most ancient of the great ethical theories put great emphasis on virtue and character. The *virtues* are habits of action that go together to form someone of good *charac-ter.* Character, then, is the quality of the good moral subject, some-one who has integrated moral ways of thinking, feeling, and acting into his or her life. For someone of good character, the relationship between conscience and inclination need not be one of constant tension. If character is developed by a habitual commitment to the virtues, then inclination can be shaped in ways that enable a spon-taneous conformity to conscience. If someone learns, for example, to habitually act in a compassionate way, then the personal effort required to overcome our own feelings of laziness and apathy and to show sympathy with others becomes less onerous and hesitant. It is in the nature of habits that they incline us to certain ways of act-ing; both good and bad habits, by force of repetition and familiarity, shape our lives in a certain way. Just as bad habits set up obstacles to positive growth, good habits pose obstacles to our inclination to assert the needs of our own ego over the call of goodness.

Since character is the shape of the whole of a person's moral life, it cannot be learned from a code of rules, but only by imitation and experience. People develop character by responding to the cir-cumstances of their own lives in imitation of other people of char-acter who, they believe, come to terms with life in a morally successful way. All of us can recall people whose response to life was a model for us, an example of how to live the moral life that we find worthy of imitation. Many cultures have passed down stories of the great men and women of their tradition because they are examples of character, models of courage, justice, compassion, wisdom, or other virtues. These stories define a part of a culture's or nation's moral tradition and are therefore invested with great importance. Some of the most bitter disputes in the life of a nation focus on whether or not a person who has been revered as one of the nation's great moral characters was in fact worthy of this reverence. Historians know that they can expect resistance if they attempt to "debunk" a nation's moral heroes.

As members of many different cultures, Christians add their own voices to both this reverence and these disputes. Yet the primary

90

focus of their own search for a model of character will be in Jesus of Nazareth. A Christian character is a character formed by imitation of the life of Jesus. This imitation is *discipleship,* the attempt to follow Jesus by attending to his words and learning from his actions. By reading the gospels, we can come to an appreciation of the character of Jesus and the virtues that informed his life. By responding to his call to conversion, we can open ourselves to making these virtues the informing principles of our own lives.

Christians can find in Jesus a model of truthfulness, justice, courage, and forgiveness. His unshakeable faith in the love of the Father and sure hope for the coming of the kingdom are the foundations of his disciples' faith and hope. Most of all, the quality of his love is an inexhaustible source of inspiration for Christians and for many members of other traditions. It is part of the faith of Christians that the love of Jesus was not in vain, not an illusory or a naïve response to a world that is really determined by considerations of power and self-interest, but rather that his love is a revelation of the mystery that has created the world and will guide it to fulfillment.

In seeking to imitate the character of Jesus, the Christian must be aware that Christians of different ages have portrayed him in many different ways. When we consider the different images characteristic of past ages, it is apparent how much the needs and preferences of particular cultures have shaped a Jesus in their own image. The Byzantine Church imaged Jesus as the *pantocrator,* the all-powerful Lord whose divine power was mirrored in the earthly power of emperor and patriarch; nineteenth-century paintings of the Good Shepherd portray a Jesus of meekness, gentleness, and sensitivity; some contemporary images of Jesus from Latin America show a revolutionary prophet of justice.

We cannot escape coming to the gospels with our own ethical and cultural concerns, nor need we try to. What is crucial is that we attempt to become critically aware of them, so that they do not prevent us hearing the message of the gospel in ways that can both speak to those concerns and draw us beyond them. We may, for example, seek personal consolation in the gospel and end up finding both words of consolation and words that challenge us to transcend our own concerns through a deeper sense of the meaning of sharing in the lives and concerns of others. Critical biblical studies can also help us to focus on the true meaning of gospel texts. In these ways, we can attempt to open ourselves to the help the gospels can give us in the development of moral character.

Summary of Chapter 3

1. A human being is a moral subject, characterized by freedom, responsibility, and conscience.

2. Freedom is fundamental to human existence, in contrast to the existence of other species, which are confined to specific environments and behaviors.

3. An understanding of freedom as "freedom from" constraint (negative freedom) needs to be supplemented by a "positive" understanding of freedom as "freedom for" the fulfillment of the purpose of human life.

4. Since I am free, I am responsible. This means both that I am answerable for my actions and that my freedom responds to the purposes of life.

5. For Christian ethics, freedom and responsibility are covenantal, understood in the context of a personal relationship with God and neighbor.

6. The concept of covenant has its origins in the experience of the children of Israel, who were liberated by a God to whom they could respond by obedience to his Law. The covenantal character of Christian ethics is expressed in Jesus' proclamation of the blessings of the kingdom and his call for the response of *metanoia* or conversion.

7. Our values are formed within a social environment, but social determinism fails to recognize that individuals can

reform a society's values through insight into what fulfills human beings.

8. Psychological determinism fails to recognize that the influence of causality does not preclude the reality of choice in our lives.

9. Total reductionism, like total relativism, is self-contradictory. Our freedom is exercised in the context of the influences of society and of our personal history, but it cannot be reduced to the determined outcome of these influences.

10. Conscience is our personal awareness of the difference between good and evil. Conscience is a knowledge of response, which must be united with factual knowledge in order to judge and act in specific situations. This means that conscience can be good, but mistaken—good in its response, but mistaken in its specific judgments.

11. Conscience is integrally related to the freedom and responsibility of the moral subject: only my own conscience can guide my freedom.

12. Conscience is a subjective relationship to objective moral truth. A good conscience is a sincere conscience, and a sincere conscience is a conscience that is committed to finding the truth.

13. Catholic teaching affirms that we must follow our conscience, since our relationship to truth in conscience is an implicit expression of our relationship to God, the source of truth.

14. Awareness of conscience should not be identified with feelings of guilt. Such feelings may arise from our awareness of having done wrong, but they can also be caused by morally neutral or morally right actions that breach taboos or conventions.

15. Conscience should not be confused with the superego, the internalized expectations of external powers that confer praise and blame, reward and punishment. What is right is logically quite distinct from what is approved of.

16. The formation of conscience includes these points:
    (a) an appreciation of the role and limits of law;
    (b) subjective self-confidence in moral judgment and action;
    (c) openness to all sources of moral truth, including the authority of tradition and experience;
    (d) faith in the power of goodness;
    (e) conversion.

17. Character is the quality of a moral subject who habitually acts in ways that are described by the virtues. Character is learned by experience and imitation; Christian character is developed by the imitation of Jesus, which is discipleship.

Questions for Discussion

1. Are our freedom and our awareness of the difference between good and evil constitutive of our humanity? What is the difference between a human being's awareness of the difference between good and evil and an animal's awareness of what it should and should not do?

2. Consider the contrast between "freedom from" and "freedom for." Can I become more free by choosing to constrain my actions in certain ways? Is a moral person less free than a person who does not recognize moral constraints?

3. Consider the notions of praise and blame. To what extent do we use them simply as "behavior modifiers," and to what extent do we imply a recognition of freedom and responsibility by using them?

4. What difference do you think a covenantal understanding of the moral life makes?

5. To what extent is it possible to develop and live by values which are different from those of society? Give some examples.

6. Even if we do not question the basic values of our society, do we still have freedom and responsibility?

7. Does total reductionism refute itself? What is the truth in social and psychological reductionism? How much freedom do we have within our circumstances of life?

8. In what ways is conscience linked to freedom and responsibility? To what extent is my own conscience basic to my own individual identity as a person?

9. Consider the case of the junior officer in a finance company described in this chapter. When is it right to defer to judgments of others in matters that involve my own moral responsibility?

10. What is the link between subjectivity and objectivity as far as conscience is concerned? What does it mean to say that someone is genuinely sincere about doing the right thing?

11. Consider the relationship between conscience and feelings of guilt. How should they be distinguished from each other?

12. How should people be educated so that they can distinguish between conscience and superego?

13. What do you think most radically differentiates an ill-developed from a well-developed conscience?

14. What do you think is meant by Christian character? What are the images of Jesus that tend to influence Christians today? How true do you think they are to the gospels?

4

Sin and the Fundamental Option

The Reality of Moral Freedom

It has been argued in earlier chapters that freedom and the capacity to know the good are at the heart of what makes us human. Yet the capacity to know the good and to freely choose it also implies the freedom to reject it. The freedom of human beings to discover what is good in the world and creatively develop it is also a freedom to deny and distort the good, to choose evil.

What Is Evil?

What is it "to choose evil"? Would a human being deliberately choose what is known to be bad? Why? If the good is what gives life and develops and fulfills human potential, then why would anyone ever choose evil? One answer is that evil is only ever chosen out of ignorance: to do evil is a sign of lack of insight. This answer seems to lessen the apparent absurdity of choosing evil; people do not actually choose to do what is bad, but choose it because they do not know that it is bad. Yet this flies in the face of our experience of the freedom to do evil despite our knowledge that it is evil. We make a fundamental distinction in our experience between someone who does wrong out of ignorance and someone who does wrong out of malice or weakness of will—someone who knows that something is wrong but does it anyway. This is the meaning of the experience of guilt—the dissonance between our knowledge of truth in conscience and the decisions and actions that express our freedom in ways which ignore or repress conscience.

96

If the choice of evil is not simply an expression of ignorance, why is it ever made? One possible answer is that we face a choice between good and evil "worlds" and that some people simply find the attractions of the "evil world" more fascinating. For the Christian tradition, however, there is no such "evil world": only the good world created by a good God. What exists is essentially good. Evil cannot exist in any "pure" form; it is always the distortion of something good. From a logical point of view, an "evil world" must be a self-destructive world, a world which could not—in the long run!—compete with a good world. The choice of evil is a choice that distorts the values of this good world, values which it is the responsibility of human beings to discover and develop. Whatever form it takes—whether the distortion of human relationships or the destruction of the natural world to satisfy human greed—evil is the corruption and debasement of what is good.

For the Christian tradition, the meaning of evil is classically expressed in the story of the fall of man and woman in Genesis 3. This story articulates our experience of the goodness of the created world through the beauty of the garden within which the man and woman were created (Gen 2:9). It also articulates our experience of freedom through the invitation of God to the man and woman to eat of the fruit of all the trees except of that which symbolized the "knowledge of good and evil," a knowledge of—in the sense of involvement with—evil that would destroy human innocence and challenge the Creator's good purposes (2:16–17). The story highlights the character of evil as the distortion of good in the way the temptation to eat of the forbidden fruit is portrayed (3:1–6), and it emphasizes the destructive effects of evil on the relationships between the man and woman themselves, between them and God, and between them and nature (3:8–19).

If evil is the distortion of what is good, then the essence of evil is in the human decision to distort the values that we find in the world. If we accept the goodness of this world, we accept that we can find fulfillment within it; if we commit our freedom to developing its values, then this will also bring about our own development.

97

Developing the values of the world does not mean simply carrying out a narrow and pre-scripted role; as we have seen, human beings can freely choose a very wide range of behavior, all of which is good. They are not constrained by instinct to one kind of behavior or one kind of environment. Pursuing the good means to pursue the fundamental values of the world around us, developing them in diverse and creative ways.

The choice of evil is the choice to distort the meaning of these values and their inner relationships. We can see evidence of this in the characteristics of familiar phenomena of human evil. The racist distorts the good of creation by denying the fundamental unity of the human race, affirmed by both science and faith, and asserting the superiority of one race over another. Similarly, a person seeking to dominate others rejects the truth that human beings can be fulfilled only in a community of shared interests and recreates the world as oriented to the satisfaction of his ego alone. The sexually promiscuous person ignores the personal commitment inherent in the physical language of sexual intercourse, thereby reducing the personal values of creation to the selfish pursuit of pleasure.

In each case, we see that the choice of evil is essentially a choice to distort the relationship of the self to the world. Rather than fulfilling itself by realizing the potential of created values, the self seeks to remake the world by distorting those values and their relationship to each other. The logical conclusion of evil choices is therefore idolatry: the worship of the self or of part of creation, instead of the creator. This idolatry is no less real for its lack of explicitly religious ritual, just as genuine devotion to the creator may be implicitly expressed through unselfish devotion to what is good rather than in religious acts.

Freedom and Evil

Yet if evil is not the choice of evil as such, but rather the distortion or abuse of what is good, the question of the free choice of such distortion remains. In ancient times, it was often argued that evil was the result of ignorance of the good, a lack of insight. Today, this argument is expressed in terms of social and psychological conditioning. From this point of view, people do not freely make evil choices—rather, the limitations and deprivations of their upbringing and environment make it impossible for them to have a clear insight into what is good and to choose and act accordingly.

This approach gains a lot of credence for many people, because of the excessive and manipulative use of the Christian language of sin and guilt in the past. Such language often did exaggerate the degree of human freedom and responsibility, to the extent that individuals were morbidly preoccupied with the consequences of eternal torment because of relatively trivial individual actions. Catholics were taught, for example, that deliberately eating meat on Friday was a mortal sin, which could have eternal damnation as its consequence. Reacting against such abuses of the notions of choice and guilt, many people argued for a concept of humanity without guilt, for the essential sinlessness and innocence of human beings. If only the right kinds of environment could be created, then the spontaneous goodness of human beings could flourish, freed from the complexes induced by those who exploited guilt for their own ends.

For the Catholic tradition, human beings are essentially good. They are oriented to and fulfilled by what is good, and their experience of the results of evil choices is that they are self-destructive and unsatisfying. Yet to say that human beings are essentially good is not to say that they are innocent; the freedom of human beings is involved with evil choices, choices of which they are guiltily aware. Manipulation of the language of sin and guilt did much to bring such concepts into disrepute, yet a denial of them results in the denial of the difference between good and evil and of the reality of human freedom. The debate over the reality of evil choices is inextricably combined with the debate over the scope of human freedom and responsibility. These issues arise, for example, when a society confronts the experience of violent crime. Often the debate over the penal policy appropriate to such crimes is expressed in two opposed positions:

One position is that we are free and that the evil we perpetrate is our personal responsibility. We should therefore be punished appropriately. From this point of view, those who argue that certain crimes are the result of socioeconomic deprivation are blind to the reality of human freedom and undermine every individual's sense of personal responsibility for his or her actions.

The opposed position is that the evil we perpetrate is the result of socioeconomic deprivation. Any punishment, then, should have a purely rehabilitatory role. From this point of view, those who argue for the reality of human freedom are dogmatic in theory and harsh in practice.

The Christian tradition emphasizes that we do have the freedom to commit evil, but that we also live in a world characterized by many evils we are not personally responsible for, a world burdened by the evils of history. One aspect of the traditional doctrine of "original sin" is our experience that we live in a world that cannot free itself of evil; as such, an our own choices are constantly affected by the influence of the evil choices of others. We ourselves are not personally responsible for these evils, yet they limit our spontaneous ability to do good. How often, for example, do we hesitate to do good to a stranger for fear that we will be harmed or exploited, especially if we are in situations which we know have led to tragic cases of violence? The evils that we hear of color our relationships with others, and our potential for giving is stunted by a sense of threat and anxiety.

We are free, but our freedom is limited by many *impediments,* factors which lessen our freedom and therefore our responsibility:

- our social environment, which may be one of gross deprivation or brutalization, or which tends to socialize us into an acceptance of certain evils such as racism or dishonesty;
- our genetic inheritance, which may, for example, predispose us to fits of temper or compulsive behavior;

- our particular stresses and influences, which may make it more difficult to make a fully free and responsible choice.

Our legal tradition, in common with the Christian tradition, is based on the notion that human beings are free and responsible and therefore responsible for evil choices, but that responsibility may be lessened by impediments or, in legal language, mitigating circumstances. These impediments must be taken into account, but they do not take away the reality of human freedom. They do not justify the reduction of human action to the determining effects of heredity and environment.

Sin and Conscience

In chapter 3 we considered the covenantal understanding of freedom and responsibility that is fundamental to Christian ethics. The concept of sin is essentially a religious concept: it is the converse of the covenant. Sin is the harming or breaking of the covenantal relationship with God and neighbor. Secular ethics tends to speak of "moral wrong" or "moral evil" rather than of "sin." In a secular perspective, the awareness of subjective "moral evil" is the awareness of going against conscience, without interpreting conscience as a relationship with God. While the believer interprets the experience of conscience in terms of a covenantal relationship with God, the nonbeliever interprets it as the subjective awareness of the real difference between good and evil. The reality of freedom and the choice between good and evil are the same for both. For the believer, however, the difference between doing good and doing evil is the difference between consciously developing and harming our subjective relationship to God, the source of goodness.

Since our conscience is our free and personal awareness of value, which is also our awareness of our relationship with God, *sin is the deliberate rejection or distortion of conscience.* By freely rejecting the judgment of conscience, we reject what we believe to

101

be right. Perhaps more typically, we sin by deliberately distorting our conscience: we attempt to deceive ourselves into believing that something is right by suppressing factors that we know are contrary to what we desire and emphasizing those factors that conform to our immediate desires. Since sin is the deliberate rejection or distortion of conscience, which is at the core of the moral subject, sin is a *subjective* reality. It is the moral subject's free choice to abuse freedom by distorting the created goodness of this world, known to us in conscience.

Sin, Freedom, and the Fundamental Option

Sin is an expression of freedom—the choice to use freedom in a way which reflects the self's attempt to set up a new order of priorities in the world around it, rather than to respect the real relationships of created values. The concept of sin makes no sense without an affirmation of the reality of freedom. Therefore, in order to understand the nature of sin, we must reflect on the meaning and scope of our freedom. It is the use of our freedom, in response to all the opportunities of life, that makes us who we are. In Christian language, the response of our own freedom to the grace of God, expressed through the goodness of this world and the offer of a covenantal relationship with him, makes us who we are. We do not make ourselves out of nothing, but it is our freedom that develops our selves on the basis of all that is given to us in life. We have argued in previous chapters that a fundamental characteristic of a human being is the use of freedom in response to the real difference between good and evil.

The fundamental choice that makes individual human beings who they are is the free choice between good and evil. Of course, we make countless choices in our lives—many of them irrelevant to morality, some of them involving moral choice. Yet persons are characterized by some degree of unity: except in cases of severe mental illness, a person expresses a fundamentally unified response to the circumstances of life and to the real difference between good and evil. Human persons are not made up of a jumble of incoherent and contradictory individual actions, as if their freedom had no purpose or direction to it. Normally the human expression of freedom is in a certain direction, and individual actions make up the texture of a certain pattern of life. What gives this pattern of life its coherence is our *fundamental option*—an option that is truly fundamental in the sense that it deals with the choice between good and evil. Do we respond to the creator God of the covenant (or, in the case of someone without any religious belief, to the call of real values in conscience) by respecting and developing created values, or do we distort those values according to the dictates of the self that sets itself up in opposition to God?

The fundamental option, then, is the essential unity of a person's life, a life lived for or against the love of God and of neighbor.[1] This option can, of course, be changed: response to the love of God can result in a conversion of life away from egoism and toward affirmation of the value of the neighbor. Change can also result in the abandonment of humane values and the choice of a selfish lifestyle. An option can deepen and intensify, while maintaining a consistent direction. A particular action, too, may be the crucial culmination of a pattern of behavior, committing our lives for good or evil. To say that our lives are characterized by a fundamental option is not to deny change and development, but to affirm that our personal character usually develops and expresses itself in a pattern of actions over a period of time and not in individual actions taken in isolation.

---

1. The meaning and importance of the fundamental option is powerfully illustrated in a diary entry of Dag Hammarskjöld, the Swedish Secretary-General of the United Nations from 1953 until his death in a plane crash in the Congo in 1961. On Pentecost Sunday 1961, just a few months before his death, he wrote: "I don't know Who—or what—put the question, I don't know when it was put. I don't even remember answering. But at some moment I did answer *Yes* to Someone—or Something—and from that hour I was certain that existence is meaningful and that, therefore, my life, in self-surrender, has a goal." (D. Hammarskjöld, *Markings*, trans. W. H. Auden and Leif Sjöberg [London: Faber and Faber, 1964], 169.)

The concept of a fundamental option is based on the relationship between freedom and the self. We make ourselves through our freedom and that freedom has a basic consistency of purpose expressed over time. Yet we are not completely consistent or coherent: our freedom does not always express who we really are. Individual acts, when taken in isolation, may not express our fundamental option. We are characterized by inconsistency on a background of more fundamental consistency. An essentially kind person, for example, may act in an unkind way on isolated occasions.

The Fundamental Option and Sin

This concept of the fundamental option is very useful for understanding the meaning of the moral life. It is also useful for understanding sin, especially in ways that are different from the traditional understanding. This difference is particularly evident in understanding the distinction between mortal and venial sin. *Mortal* or deadly sin (from the Latin *mors,* meaning "death") is sin in the full sense of the word, sin which destroys a person's relationship to God. *Venial* sin (from the Latin *venia,* meaning indulgence or pardon) is sin which harms this relationship but does not destroy it; in other words, it is pardonable.

In the traditional understanding, originally derived from the scholastic philosophy and theology of the medieval period, a mortal sin is defined by three characteristics: if someone has a full and deliberate intent to do wrong, if they are fully aware of what they are doing, and if the action itself is intrinsically serious. An intrinsically serious action is one that involves "grave matter," that is, an action that involves the abuse or destruction of a fundamental good. A venial sin lacks one of these three characteristics. Theoretical considerations of the differences between mortal and venial sin usually assume that awareness and intent are present, leaving the difference to be constituted by the difference between "grave" and "light" matter. If knowledge and intent are assumed, then certain kinds of action can be classed as mortal sins because of the objective gravity of the matter involved.

This approach does take serious account of the importance of subjective factors, such as deliberate intent and full awareness. It involves an appreciation of sin as an abuse of human freedom, and therefore an appreciation that freedom is not fully expressed where intent and awareness are absent. However, its focus on the difference between mortal and venial sin in terms of gravity fails to do full justice to the subjective character of sin and to the relationship between freedom and the person. If someone does one action that is objectively seriously wrong, does this mean that their subjectivity is now radically alienated from God, their relationship to God destroyed? Let us consider an example: A man and woman have a strong and immediate physical attraction to each other and engage in a "one night stand." They know what they are doing and are aware that their sexual intimacy is not based on committed love for each other, nor indeed on any personal or emotional bond. It is an untypical action and one that they quickly and sincerely repent of in word and deed. It is not repeated.

From the perspective of the Christian ethical tradition (and virtually all other religious traditions), what this man and woman have done is seriously wrong. They have degraded each other by reducing each other's body to a display of impersonal sexual attraction, rather than the physical presence of a person with all the depths of emotional, moral, and spiritual individuality which that conveys. They have abused the physical language of sexual relations by using it without the commitment of love. They have sinned. Have they, however, sinned mortally? Prior to their repentance, was their relationship to God destroyed? If they were to die without repentance, would they be destined to be cut off from the vision of God for all eternity, regardless of what good they had done prior to this act? According to the logic of the traditional concept of sin, all of this may well be the case, although the necessity of knowledge and intent is emphasized.

Since mortal sins are defined in terms of actions, one action can have this effect.[2]

What is implausible about this traditional account is how one action can totally reverse the character of someone's life. This is what the traditional account claims since it holds that an essentially good person can make him or herself worthy of eternal damnation in one action. This implies that we are totally consistent in the constitution and expression of our selves: when we act, we express the whole self in the most radical way, and one action can radically remake the self. The value of the concept of the fundamental option, in contrast, is to emphasize that this is untypical of human freedom. Usually the nature of our selves can only be judged by the long-term pattern of our actions. We express our fundamental

---

2. The official teaching of the Church acknowledges the value of the concept of the fundamental option as a way of expressing the character of Christian life as a fundamental decision of faith that engages a person's whole life (*Veritatis Splendor*, §66), but is critical of any use of the concept that dissociates the meaning of mortal sin from particular acts involving grave matter. "A person therefore sins mortally not only when his action comes from direct contempt for love of God and neighbor, but also when he consciously and freely, for whatever reason, chooses something which is seriously disordered. For in this choice...there is already included contempt for the Divine commandment: the person turns himself away from God and loses charity. Now according to Christian tradition and the Church's teaching, and as right reason also recognizes, the moral order of sexuality involves such high values of human life that every direct violation of this order is objectively serious. It is true that in sins of the sexual order, in view of their kind and their causes, it more easily happens that free consent is not fully given; this is a fact which calls for caution in all judgment as to the subject's responsibility" (*Declaration on Certain Problems of Sexual Ethics, Personae Humanae* [1975], §10, Vatican website, www.vatican.va). "The *fundamental orientation can be radically changed by particular acts*...The separation of fundamental option from deliberate choices of particular kinds of behaviour, disordered in themselves or in their circumstances, which would not engage that option, thus involves a denial of Catholic doctrine on mortal sin: With the whole tradition of the Church, we call mortal sin the act by which man freely and consciously rejects God, his law, the covenant of love that God offers, preferring to turn in on himself or to some created and finite reality, something contrary to the divine will. This can occur in a direct and formal way, in the sins of idolatry, apostasy and atheism; or in an equivalent way, as in every act of disobedience to God's commandments in a grave matter" (*Veritatis Splendor*, §70).

option for goodness in a pattern of good actions, but this does not necessarily mean that we are totally consistent in this goodness. We can sin by freely doing wrong in individual actions, without these individual actions necessarily reversing the whole thrust and meaning of our lives. This is not to deny that a gravely immoral act can be the culmination of a pattern of action and the sign of a negative fundamental option. Yet an isolated and untypical action, quickly repented of, is unlikely to change someone's fundamental option.

Let us now consider a contrary case. A member of a local community is notorious for the vicious and spiteful way that he speaks about others. His life is a pattern of uncharitable lies and acts of unkindness. He is not guilty of any spectacular acts of wrongdoing; these might, after all, result in unpleasant consequences with the law. Yet his relationships to others are marked either by flattery to superiors or petty vindictiveness to inferiors. In terms of the traditional distinction between mortal and venial sin, this man is guilty of a long and squalid sequence of venial sins. None of these individual acts of spite and pettiness might constitute the "grave matter" defined as characteristic of mortal sin. Taken in isolation, they are trivial. Yet they make up the texture of his life and constitute the meaning—or rather lack of it—of his existence. His fundamental option is an option against love of neighbor, because the consistent direction of the expression of his freedom is against the well-being of his neighbors. Such a person may well be in a state of mortal sin.

The concept of a fundamental option helps us to appreciate more fully that mortal sin is a state of being, a condition of the person, rather than a matter of individual actions taken in isolation. In light of this concept, mortal or deadly sin is a state of personal being that rejects the love of God and neighbor at the deepest and freest core of the person. It is usually a matter of the overall shape and direction of the person's life. To be in a state of mortal sin is to have severed the relationship with God by destroying all sensitivity to the call of created values on our own freedom. The love of God constantly offers the gift of conversion from this state of spiritual suicide, but the freedom that God has given his human creatures is a freedom that includes the possibility of self-destruction. Hell is not a place that God has created, but a state of being that human beings may create for themselves, a state of being with ultimate consequences.[3] Hell is a possibility of human freedom, although we do not know whether any human being has ever realized this frightful possibility. While the Catholic Church has solemnly declared, in its formal acts of canonization of saints, that many individuals are in heaven, it has never declared that anyone is in hell.

In the same light, *venial sin* is an act which is inconsistent with a fundamental option toward goodness. A person making a fundamental option for the covenant may act from time to time in a way that does not reflect that option. A person may consciously and willingly fail to live the covenant in uncharacteristic individual actions. Such actions express only a superficial commitment of the person's subjectivity, a subjectivity which remains fundamentally committed to the love of God and neighbor. Venial sin is the deliberate and culpable inconsistency of the good person. Venial sin is serious, because it is a failure to develop that which is most fundamental to our existence as persons—our relationship to the good and to God who is the source of all good. While venial sin may be the inconsistency of the good person, which is kept in check by an abiding and fundamental commitment to the love of God and neighbor, it can also become a pattern in a person's life, its influence on a person's character deepening through cumulative effect. Such erosion of a fundamental option toward goodness must be resisted by the person's commitment to ever deeper consistency of life, a life which aims to be all of a piece in its active valuing of what is good.

The concept of the fundamental option helps us to take the subjective character of sin with due seriousness. At the same time,

---

3. Some theologians, including this writer, argue that someone who has rejected the love of God in this fundamental sense will not rise again to eternal life and will simply cease to exist after death; this is "hell." The official teaching of the Church is that the immortality of the soul means that all human beings will have eternal life, and those (if any) who have ultimately rejected God's love will experience the eternal and self-chosen deprivation of that love.

the distinction between "grave" and "light" matters points to something very important in the formation of conscience. It alerts us to the goods in our world and the imperative to value them. It reminds us that some goods are more valuable than others, and that actions which attack or destroy those goods are correspondingly serious. Fundamental goods—such as life, sexuality, and our moral and spiritual integrity—do involve our own response in freedom more deeply, especially if our conscience has been formed in a way that leads it to respect what is really central to the moral life. A well-formed conscience, for example, will be aware that to murder someone is a much more serious destruction of value than to steal five dollars. An informed awareness of the objective seriousness of certain actions, as harmful to the goods of creation, is essential to the fulfillment of the most basic objective of the moral life: to do good and avoid evil.

What is of greatest importance is common to both the traditional approach and the "fundamental option" approach: sincere repentance of sin brings complete forgiveness by the infinite love and mercy of God. A part of this repentance, and of the experience of forgiveness, is the resolve to make amends and heal the human consequences of sin, both in ourselves and in others, as much as lies in our power.

Summary of Chapter 4

1. Human freedom includes the freedom to make evil choices. These choices cannot be explained simply as resulting from ignorance, but are rather signs of our culpable rejection of goodness.

2. Evil is the distortion of what is good, resulting from the distortion of the relationship of the self to the world. The logical conclusion of evil is idolatry, the worship of the self or part of creation, instead of the creator.

3. Human beings are good, but they are not innocent. They make evil choices, and they live in a world profoundly affected by evil choices.

4. Our awareness that we are free to choose and do evil must include an awareness of the impediments on freedom that lessen personal responsibility.

5. Sin harms or breaks the covenantal relationship with God and our neighbor; it is the deliberate rejection or distortion of conscience and is therefore a subjective reality.

6. Normally the lives of human beings are characterized by a certain consistency, a fundamental option, for or against the love of God and neighbor.

7. The traditional understanding of mortal sin defines it in terms of full knowledge, full intent, and grave matter. The defect of this understanding is in its tendency to equate the degree of subjective sinfulness with objective gravity of matter, coupled with an understanding of sin in terms of individual actions.

8. In light of the concept of fundamental option, mortal sin is a state of personal being that rejects the love of God and neighbor at the deepest and freest core of the person. Venial sin is an act that is inconsistent with a fundamental option toward goodness.

Questions for Discussion

1. How much truth is there in the proposition that people choose evil purely out of ignorance?

2. Can evil exist in itself, or is it always the distortion of something good?

3. Study the text of Genesis 2 and 3 with the aid of a biblical commentary. For this text, what constitutes sin? How does

it interpret the psychology of temptation? How does it portray the effects of evil on relationships between humanity and God, human beings with each other, human beings and nature?

4. Consider some examples of human evil. To what extent can they be interpreted as the result of a distortion of the relationship of the ego to the world? Which goods are thereby destroyed or distorted? Is it true to say that idolatry is the logical conclusion of evil choices?

5. What does it mean to say that human beings are essentially good? Is it true?

6. Consider the positions cited in the debate over violent crime. What is the truth in each position? Outline what you think is a Christian interpretation of the relationship between recognizing freedom and responsibility and acknowledging the deprived and brutalized circumstances often characteristic of criminals' backgrounds.

7. What does it mean to say that sin is a subjective reality? Why is it so closely related to conscience? Consider examples of the ways in which sin is the result of a deliberate distortion of conscience.

8. To what extent are human beings consistent in their actions? Do their lives show a fundamental option for good or evil?

9. Compare the traditional understanding of mortal sin with an understanding based on the concept of fundamental option. What do you think the strengths and weaknesses of each approach are? Is it possible to commit mortal sin in one action? Is it possible to have a mortally sinful fundamental option which is expressed only in trivial actions?

PART THREE
WHAT IS THE GOOD?

At the beginning of chapter 3, a distinction was made between the *subjective* and *objective* dimensions of ethics. The subjective dimension is concerned with reflection on the nature of the moral subject, characterized by freedom, responsibility, and conscience. Reflection on the subjective dimension of ethics is concerned with the acting person, the one who chooses and acts in freedom. Objective ethics, in turn, is concerned with the world within which the acting person lives, chooses, and acts. Objective ethics seeks to guide the actions of the moral subject, so that a person who sincerely seeks to do good will do so on the basis of knowledge of what is good. We have seen that a truly sincere conscience is one that strives to know the world within which it judges and decides. The first concern of objective ethics, then, is to know what is good, to understand the world, and to discover what is truly valuable in it. To act well we need to interpret our experience so that we have some understanding of the relative importance of the features of the world that claim our attention, desire, and concern. The key question of this section, therefore, is *What is the good?* It considers the goodness of creation, with particular emphasis on the dignity of the human person in the light of biblical faith.

5

A Good World

Two Kinds of Values: Virtues and Goods

In chapter 3, we saw that moral character is made up of certain *virtues* or *moral values*. These values are characteristics of the moral subject—a person who lives and acts by these values is a person of good moral character. Moral values describe the person: we speak of the virtues of justice, compassion, and love; we also speak of a just, compassionate, or loving person. Finally, these values characterize the decisions and actions of the person, and we speak of just, compassionate, or loving actions. Moral values, then, are the values that form the character of the moral person or subject.

In living by these values, the moral person relates to a world of value characterized by inherent goodness, which offers the person the potential to realize him- or herself and flourish. The challenge that faces the moral subject is to discern what the different goods in the world are and what their relationship is. We can only act well within this world if we know it, if we pay attention to it, and if we commit ourselves to developing its inherent goodness. We are aware of many different goods, but we are faced with the task of interpreting their relationships and their relative importance. For example, we are aware of the good of freedom and of all the possibilities for diverse human flourishing that it allows. Yet we are also aware that unlimited freedom of action can result in gross inequality, since some act freely on the basis of much greater talents, opportunities, and advantages than others. We are aware of the good of economic wealth, yet we wonder how much of it is desirable when it seems to come at the cost of the despoliation of nature. We are aware of the good of freedom of information, yet we sympathize with those whose lives have been shattered by the media's invasion of their privacy.

The questions posed by the task of putting different goods in a balanced and just relationship show that there is a difference between these goods and the moral values that should make up the moral person. Goods such as freedom, wealth, nature, and privacy make up the concern and object of moral action. The whole point of morality is to live in ways that do justice to these goods. Yet an action can be moral and at the same time choose to restrict or even eliminate one of these goods. For example, we might argue that it is just to severely restrict freedom of information about people's private lives unless some legitimate and significant public interest can be demonstrated. The action of restricting this freedom is a just action characterized by the moral value of justice, but it is an action that severely restricts a good—freedom of information—because it subordinates it in relevant circumstances to another good—personal privacy.

A moral action expresses moral values. If we are committed to the moral life, we can never be unjust, untruthful, dishonest, or unloving. These moral values are what Aristotle and Aquinas called *virtues*. Yet we can be moral and still limit the scope of certain goods because we believe that it is just to subordinate them to other goods. There are two kinds of value relevant for morality: the moral values or virtues themselves, characterizing the moral person, and those things of objective value that are identified as *goods*. Virtues are such qualities as love, justice, honesty, and truthfulness, and these qualities characterize actions, decisions, or persons; goods are things or states of being of objective and inherent value, and these things include freedom, life, wealth, happiness, and the beauty of nature. A person may or may not be virtuous but is in any case a good, because of the inherent value of human life.

A Good World

The Christian tradition sees this world as good, created by a God who is all-good. God created this world so that it could be fulfilled in the kingdom of God. The belief that our lives have a purpose has a fundamental significance for ethics; it means that ethics has an *objective* and *obligatory* character about it. Ethics relates to what is objectively good, rather than subjective desires and preferences, because it relates to the good that is an inherent part of the created world. Ethics has an obligatory character about it as well: if we can discern the true purpose of our lives in the world, then we are obliged to respond to that purpose because we believe it expresses the creative will of God.

A Hierarchy of Goods

Our experience makes us aware of many different goods, but these goods vary in the value we believe we should give to them. In order to guide our moral action, we need to develop some *hierarchy* of goods. The word *hierarchy* derives from the Greek words for "sacred rule"; it originally referred to persons of sacred power and is used by some Christian churches to refer to the role of bishops. The relevance of the concept of a hierarchy refers to the fact that not all goods are of the same value and that our search for ethical orientation requires some ordering of these goods. A hierarchy of goods is an understanding of goods in a relationship ordered according to their relative value.

From the perspective of religious faith, God is the highest good. If God exists, if there is an infinitely loving and infinitely powerful creator of the universe who has revealed himself to humanity for the sake of happiness, then God must be the highest good. It follows from this that the claims of human beings must be subordinated to the imperative to honor and worship God. Many ancient religions certainly saw things in these terms, even to the point of sacrificing the lives of human beings to the god or gods of their religious traditions. Yet religious traditions gradually came to the insight that true worship of God or authentic communion with the Absolute could not at the same time be destructive of our humanity. For the Buddha, for example, the "noble eightfold path" is a path leading to Nirvana and, at the same time, a path of human compassion.

For Christian ethics love of God and love of neighbor are a unity since love of God must include love for our neighbor, God's creation, and love of neighbor implies love for the creator. If God has become a human being, a human being whose life revealed the love of God through his own loving ministry to human beings, then there can be no dissonance between the love of God and love of neighbor. The prophets of Israel often emphasized that acts of compassion and mercy were a higher form of worship than sacrificial ritual. For Jesus the liturgical worship of God could not be authentically offered by those who have hurt their neighbor: "When you are offering your gift at the altar, if you remember that your brother or sister has something against you, leave your gift there before the altar and go; first be reconciled to your brother or sister, and then come and offer your gift" (Matt 5:23–24). The best of those who fought in the crusades and religious wars of history understood their struggle as a defense of a truth they were prepared to die and, if necessary, to kill for. Yet in doing so, they did mistake the essence of the very truth they fought for: the true worship of God must always go hand in hand with loving respect for our neighbor.

The Good of Nature

Since Christian ethics sees the love of God and love of neighbor as a unity, it recognizes no higher ethical good than the good of human persons. In common with many other ethical traditions, both religious and secular, Christian ethics puts respect for persons at the apex of its hierarchy of goods. The fundamental concern of Christian ethics, then, is the good of human persons, and this good will be the focus of subsequent discussion. Yet if we recall the conviction expressed in Genesis 1, that God saw all creation to be good, we must raise the question of the goodness of nature and of the relationship between its value and the value of persons.

Contemporary Christians are coming to an awareness that their own tradition shares some of the responsibility for the damage done to nature by the development of Western technological civilization.

Christians often interpreted the words of Genesis to "fill the earth and subdue it; and have dominion...over every living thing that moves upon the earth" (1:28) as a justification for a reckless and fateful exploitation of nature. Today Christians are recognizing that they have much to learn from the religions of indigenous peoples, which are informed by a reverence for nature. The example of such peoples can motivate Christians to turn again to the sources of their own tradition, and realize that the intention of the scriptures was not to justify the destruction of nature, but rather to instruct us to be responsible stewards of the goods of nature.

Since it is a part of God's good creation, nature has value in itself and not only in relation to human beings. The wonders and beauty of nature glorify God (Ps 19), and animals experience the goodness and love of God through their experience of the pleasure of life itself. The critical question for Christian ethics is this: What is the relationship between the good of human beings and the good of nature? In general terms, an understanding of this relationship must be informed by the insight that human beings and nature share a common home, planet Earth. As was noted at the beginning of chapter 3, human beings and the higher animals also share some behavioral and instinctual characteristics. Actions that respect the natural world are usually actions that will benefit the future of the human race. Human stewardship of the earth is for the common good of human beings and all the other species that inhabit the planet. For Christian ethics, the unique value of the human species does mean human beings have the right to kill animals, but only in ways which inflict a minimum of pain and for the satisfaction of basic human needs.

Human Dignity

Contemporary ethical language expresses the meaning of respect for persons in terms of human dignity. "Human dignity" refers partly to the human person's possession of basic rights: the essential rights to food, clothing, and shelter; the right to free self-expression within the context of social cooperation; the right to basic equality before the law; and so on. Yet human dignity is a good that implies more than can be expressed in legal concepts. It refers also to the basic respect with which persons are to be treated because they are persons: the respect that will allow them to develop their own potential, to make some personal contribution to common goals, and to feel "at home" in an environment within which they are known and acknowledged. The concept of human dignity emphasizes that every human being has a personal worth and that the task of society is to acknowledge and develop that worth.

The way in which human dignity is expressed will vary greatly from one culture to another. In many traditional societies, where decisions are made by a relatively small group, human dignity may mean allowing every individual to participate fully in the ceremonies and activities that give that society identity and self-respect. In contemporary democratic societies, however, a basic aspect of human dignity is the right to participate in decision making.

The notion of human dignity emphasizes that social or biological handicaps affecting an individual do not lessen his or her personal worth. To put respect for human dignity into practice is to attempt to make it possible for every individual to give to others and to receive from others, that is, to contribute to the common good and to receive the assistance of society.

Christian Faith and Human Dignity

The discussion in chapters 1 and 2 emphasized that Christian faith does not replace other sources of moral truth but seeks rather to enrich them in light of the revelation of God in Jesus. Human dignity is of great importance in much secular ethical thinking, especially in the Kantian ethical tradition. For this tradition, the dignity of human persons is based on their freedom and reason. Together these make up the person's ethical autonomy, that is, the character of the person as a free moral subject, capable of insight into and assent to moral truth. Because each human person is free and rational, persons may not be used simply as a means for the realization of the plans of others, but must be respected as "ends in themselves" who have the right to give or withdraw assent to actions that will affect them.

For Christian faith, however, the dignity of human persons does not ultimately depend on their freedom and rationality, but rather on their relationship to God. All human beings, however handicapped, have been created by God to grow in response to God's love and to share that love with other human beings. Our freedom and rationality are expressions of something even more fundamental: our capacity for a relationship with God. For Christian faith, all human beings have been gifted with the capacity to know and love God. Whether they know God through the call of conscience to follow the good and reject evil, or through the sacred symbols characteristic of different religious traditions, all human beings have received the divine gift that enables them to hear the word of God in their hearts.

Even more than this, because God shared in our existence in the life of an individual human being, because of the incarnation of the Son of God in Jesus of Nazareth, then all human beings are invited into the most intimate relationship with God. Because of the human life of the divine Son, all humanity is invited to become sons and daughters of the Father. It is this which gives human beings their irreducible and inalienable dignity. If the individual human person is a being who lives in a personal and intimate relationship with God, then no earthly authority can have the right to assert total sovereignty over him or her.

Biblical Sources of Human Dignity

The beginnings of the biblical tradition of human dignity are in the exodus story, a story of the liberation of slaves from captivity. The exodus was the great event that gave the faith of Israel its fundamental character—its faith in God as liberator and its conviction that only a free commitment to goodness could be a fitting response to God's gift of freedom.

The context of the exodus was the forced labor of a large number of immigrant workers in Egypt. Their leader, Moses, experienced the call of a liberating God. This call hearkened back to the hopes and experiences of the immigrants' forefathers who had left the land of Canaan in search of food and work in Egypt—forefathers whose stories were told in the ancient sagas of Abraham, Isaac, Jacob, and Joseph. What was so distinctive about Moses' experience of God was that it was addressed to a slave people, calling them out of slavery. While other ancient religions reinforced and sacralized structures of established order—the prestige and power of kings, cities, and emperors—the God who called Moses subverted such structures for the sake of the freedom of those who suffered under them. While the gods and goddesses of other religions identified with particular nations, places, and cultures, the God who called Moses was free to call his chosen people out of a place of slavery into another land, to freely extend his power across the world for the sake of the freedom of human beings.

From the book of Exodus we learn that God is a God who has pity for human suffering, who wishes people to be liberated and to live a life of dignity. All forms of enslavement and oppression are a mockery of God's will as creator of humanity in his own image. Human suffering is not "the will of God" but rather something which must be abolished. God's will is done on earth when the conditions for truly humane existence are created. The faith that the prophet Moses gave the world is a faith that binds the worship of God and compassion for human suffering into an inextricable unity, since it was born in an experience that fused the holiness of God with his pity for oppressed slaves. The words of compassion that God speaks to Moses concerning the suffering Hebrews apply no less to all similar situations in our own time:

God called to him out of the bush, "Moses, Moses!" And he said, "Here I am." Then he said, "Come no closer!

122

Remove the sandals from your feet, for the place on which you are standing is holy ground." He said further, "I am the God of your father, the God of Abraham, the God of Isaac, and the God of Jacob." And Moses hid his face, for he was afraid to look at God.

Then the LORD said, "I have observed the misery of my people who are in Egypt; I have heard their cry on account of their taskmasters. Indeed, I know their sufferings, and I have come down to deliver them from the Egyptians, and to bring them up out of that land to a good and broad land, a land flowing with milk and honey." (Exod 3:4–8)

As we saw in chapter 3, the response to the Lord's gift of liberation was the covenant of Mt. Sinai. By following the Law, the people of Israel remained faithful to the Lord who had freed them from slavery and given them the promised land. It was this covenant which was invoked by later prophets in their attempts to maintain and strengthen respect for human dignity within Israel. Prophecy was one of the most distinctive and powerful phenomena in the religious life of ancient Israel, and the heritage of the prophets is of inestimable value for Christian ethics. A prophet was an individual who experienced a personal call to witness to God, to communicate the word of God to his people. Some prophets communicated great hope for the future, but their major concern was far from being the detailed prediction of future events. The prophets were concerned with the relationship between the Lord and the people of Israel. On the basis of their own intense sense of calling, they inspired and admonished their people and attempted to renew their fidelity to the covenant. They sought to communicate the Lord's purposes by interpreting the crisis-ridden political and social events of their own day.

A crucial feature of prophecy was that it was independent of both secular and religious institutional structures. Just as the exodus faith itself represented a subversion of the sacred order of ancient Egypt, which was based on one man's "divinely" sanctioned domination of the multitudes, so the prophets witnessed to the will of God as sovereign over political power. This became a critical issue when the Israelite tribes committed themselves to the institution of monarchy under the pressure of invasion by highly organized and well-armed enemies. The kings of Israel were the "Lord's anointed," and they might be the political saviors of their people, but they remained subject to the moral law, because this was the law of God. When the great king David took a man's wife and arranged to have him killed in battle, it was the prophet Nathan who confronted the king in the name of God (2 Sam 12). To put it in modern language, Nathan forcefully reminded the king that the human dignity of his subjects could not be abolished by royal whim, and that no political power had the right to abolish the rights conferred on human beings by their creator.

During the reigns of David, Solomon, and their successors, the ancient tribal order of Israel was gradually replaced by a monarchy, governing the land through a centralized bureaucracy. The relative economic equality of the past gave way to an increasing gap between rich and poor, as fortunes were amassed in the large economic projects of the monarchy and more and more people became the laboring poor, subject to the whims of political and economic masters. This situation gave ample opportunity for the abuse of power and privilege and for the elimination of human rights. Religion now centered around the temple cult and its elaborate liturgical and sacrificial rites. A religious and political elite had emerged, smug in the conviction of national prestige, ignoring the moral demands of the covenant and subordinating religious practice to the priorities of the state.

This situation provoked a prophetic response. Isaiah of Jerusalem, who lived during the eighth century BC, was one of the most outstanding of those prophets who in the name of the Sinai covenant attacked the new relationships of power and wealth. One of Isaiah's chief objects of criticism was the illusion that the sacrificial cult was all that was required to be faithful to the covenant with God. He attacked the tendency to emasculate the moral potential of the covenant by interpreting it simply as a divine guarantee to protect and preserve the monarchy and the established religious institutions. For Isaiah, the sacrificial liturgy could only be authentically offered by those who showed their fidelity to the covenant by respecting the dignity of the downtrodden and marginalized. The abuses of human dignity, in the various forms of exploitation characteristic of the Israelite state and society, were a rejection of the covenant and a betrayal of Israel's true identity:

> Hear, O heavens, and listen, O earth; for the LORD has spoken: I reared children and brought them up, but they have rebelled against me. The ox knows its owner, and the donkey its master's crib; but Israel does not know, my people do not understand....What to me is the multitude of your sacrifices? says the LORD; I have had enough of burnt offerings of rams and the fat of fed beasts; I do not delight in the blood of bulls, or of lambs, or of goats....When you stretch out your hands, I will hide my eyes from you; even though you make many prayers, I will not listen; your hands are full of blood.
>
> Wash yourselves; make yourselves clean; remove the evil of your doings from before my eyes; cease to do evil, learn to do good; seek justice, rescue the oppressed, defend the orphan, plead for the widow. (Isa 1:2–3, 11, 15–17)

Isaiah denounced those who amassed wealth and land, buying out small farmers and depriving others of the opportunity of a secure livelihood. By surrounding themselves with their own vast estates, the wealthy had isolated themselves from contact with their fellow human beings and driven others to penury, a denial of the human community that was the ethical meaning of the covenant with the Lord (5:8). Isaiah was critical of the kings of his own day, who sought security in unwise foreign alliances rather than in giving justice to their people. But his hope for the future focused on a kingly figure who would respect and foster human dignity, one who could fittingly embody God's rule over the earth (9:1–6; 11:1–9).

Earlier generations of Israelites had understood justice and mutual respect to be binding on them only in relationships within their own community. The primitive Hebrews had perceived their liberation from Egypt and entry into the promised land as a divine commission to attack and destroy those who opposed them. The prophets, however, were able to interpret God's relationship to humanity in more universal terms. They perceived that Israel's status as the chosen people was not for the sake of exclusive privilege, but rather a means of witnessing to the God who was Lord of all nations. This insight was provoked and deepened by the conquest of Judah, the last remaining Israelite state, by the Babylonians. The destruction in 587 BC of the holy city of Jerusalem and the exile of the elite of Judah to Babylon were associated with a new insight into the universality of God's providence. This new vision was expressed by an anonymous writer whose words were included in the book named after the earlier prophet, Isaiah of Jerusalem:

> He says, "It is too light a thing that you should be my servant to raise up the tribes of Jacob and to restore the survivors of Israel; I will give you as a light to the nations, that my salvation may reach to the end of the earth." (Isa 49:6)

In the sixth century, during their period of captivity in Babylon, Israelite priestly writers expressed this new understanding of God's relationship to the whole world through their story of creation, which became the first chapter of the book of Genesis. A crucial element of their creation story is its expression of the creation of humanity:

> Then God said, "Let us make humankind in our image, according to our likeness; and let them have dominion over the fish of the sea, and over the birds of the air, and over the cattle, and over all the wild animals of the earth, and over every creeping thing that creeps upon the

earth." So God created humankind in his image, in the image of God he created them; male and female he created them. (Gen 1:26–27)

In its original context, the phrase "in the image of God" was probably connected with the self-images that ancient rulers set up in conquered territories; the image represented the ruler and reminded his subjects of his power. The man and the woman, then, were stewards or "images" of God; they had a unique role in creation as representatives of the creator. Because every human being was in some sense an image of the creator, human life had a special status and was deemed to be protected by God. The covenant with Noah in Genesis 9 emphasizes the value of human life because of its special relationship to God:

"From human beings, each one for the blood of another, I will require a reckoning for human life. Whoever sheds the blood of a human, by a human shall that person's blood be shed; for in his own image God made humankind." (Gen 9:5–6)

Significantly the creation story and the covenant with Noah emphasize the value of all human beings, not only of Israelites. All human beings had dignity through their relationship to God, although they may not have been called to the special—and onerous!—role of witness that was Israel's destiny. In later Jewish and Christian history, the creation story's depiction of humanity as created "in the image of God" becomes a touchstone for a moral and religious understanding of the human person, gifted with reason, freedom, and conscience, and open and responsive to the love of God.

The Gospels

In chapter 3, we saw that the central message of Jesus' preaching was the kingdom of God. What did the preaching of the kingdom mean in terms of human dignity? Jesus' preaching drew on the experience of God as creator, liberator, and savior that was characteristic of his own Jewish tradition. It is important to remember that the kingdom of God in the preaching of Jesus is not about a kingdom in an authoritarian or tyrannical sense. For the people of Jesus' time, a just king was the only person who could give the poor and persecuted welfare and redress. The image of "kingdom" draws on the prophetic hopes of a just king who could mediate the justice of God. The image of the kingdom of God implies an environment in which good can flourish and in which every human being can find peace, justice, and freedom. The kingdom of God is a state of things in which human beings can become all that they can be, all that their destiny as God's image enables them to be. It is the fulfillment of our yearning for God and of our search for the meaning of our own lives.

Jesus' sense of the immediacy of the kingdom of God was based on a profound and intense experience of God as Father, an experience summed up in his use of the word *Abba*, a diminutive form of the Aramaic word for father that implied both childlike dependence and intimacy and deep respect and veneration. In addressing God as Abba, Jesus expressed complete trust and confidence in God as a loving providential Father. His own sense of God's nearness and loving care gave Jesus the confidence to proclaim God's love for every individual. The life of every human being was grounded in the providence and compassion of the Father. If God lavishes such beauty on nature, how much more must he be concerned about the fate of human persons, created in his own image:

> "Consider the lilies, how they grow: they neither toil nor spin; yet I tell you, even Solomon in all his glory was not clothed like one of these. But if God so clothes the grass of the field, which is alive today and tomorrow is thrown into the oven, how much more will he clothe you—you of little faith!" (Luke 12:27–28)

The most radical expression of Jesus' faith in the kingdom of God was his proclamation of the blessings of the kingdom as a reversal of the circumstances of this world. In the Beatitudes of Luke's Gospel, Jesus proclaims the reversal of worldly values and the abolition of all affronts to human dignity:

> Then he looked up at his disciples and said:
> "Blessed are you who are poor,
>   for yours is the kingdom of God.
> "Blessed are you who are hungry now,
>   for you will be filled.
> "Blessed are you who weep now,
>   for you will laugh.
> "Blessed are you when people hate you, and when they
>   exclude you, revile you, and defame you on account of
>   the Son of Man." (Luke 6:20–22)

In his works of healing, Jesus communicated the compassion of God and a sense of worth to those whose afflictions had forced them to the margins of a society terrified of infectious diseases and concerned with ritual purity. His cure of the "Gerasene demoniac," a man driven mad by suffering, restores peace and dignity to someone whose wild anguish had cut him off from human community (Mark 5). Jesus refused to accept the common interpretation for the origin of sickness in personal sin or the sin of parents (John 9:1–3). His relationship with the sick is one of compassion, and his healing a restoration of the person's place in society and in the community of their loved ones (for example, the daughter of Jairus, Mark 5:35–43). By associating with sinners, and even sharing meals with them, Jesus proclaimed in symbolic gesture that sinners were not cut off from the love of God.

There were other groups, too, whose humanity was affirmed by Jesus. The children whom his disciples tried to send away were welcomed, and their innocence was portrayed as a symbol of participation in the kingdom of God. A foreign woman's child is healed (Matt 15:21–28) and a Roman officer held up as a model of faith in God's healing mercy (Luke 7:1–10). Jesus' relationships with women give them a dignity usually denied in his culture; many gospel narratives attest to the role of his women disciples and to the respect and warmth that characterized his friendships with women. The dignity of all those he debates with is affirmed in his appeal, through story and argument, to the insight of their own conscience. In the story of the rich young man, we see Jesus' invitation to follow him offered in freedom and respect, without any kind of spiritual blackmail (Matt 19:16–22).

The parables of Jesus were a particularly powerful aspect of his ministry, well-suited to confront and challenge his critics and to expand the horizons of his listeners. The effect of the parables was to deepen and radicalize his listeners' understanding of the love of God and the worth of persons. In the parable of the prodigal son, for example, a repentant son's dignity is restored by a loving father; a sinner is not ostracized, but accepted back into the bosom of the family. In the parable of the Good Samaritan, Jesus overturns his listeners' expectations by describing a hated foreigner as neighbor to a man left for dead by thieves. In so doing Jesus radicalized and universalized the concept of neighbor, making of it anyone who stands in need of our help. The modern concept of the worth of persons owes much to this story: our neighbor is not defined by his social relationship to us, but by his need, just as our own capacity to act and be like a neighbor is independent of anything except our own compassion and sense of justice.

The New Testament

Jesus' ministry ended in his arrest and execution, an end which implied that his own vision of the kingdom had been an illusion. The one who had preached the coming of a reign of compassion and justice had himself become a victim of a very different kind of rule, the rule of power that resorts to terror to achieve its ends. Yet very soon after his death, the disciples of Jesus—the women first— experienced him as risen and glorified. All that he had said and done had been confirmed by the Father. He had overcome death and been invested with the Father's glory (Rev 1:17–20).

For the New Testament, all human beings can share in the resurrection of Jesus—he is the "first fruits of those who have died," the one in whose resurrection God offers hope to the human race (1 Cor 15:20). The ultimate meaning of human dignity is that all human beings are destined for eternal life, since they share their humanity with the One who rose from the dead on Easter morning and who sits at the right hand of the Father.

The degradation of human worth so often characteristic of our world will be overcome in a life that enables the realization of the created potential of every person. For St. Paul, the Christian's union with the risen Christ meant a union of radical equality with other Christians. The differences of power, status, race, and sex cannot obscure or override the fundamental equality that all have in relation to Christ (Gal 3:28).

The Bible and Human Dignity—Conclusion

In the Bible, then, we find a rich testimony to the dignity of human persons. We see the source of human dignity in the creative act of a free and loving God, who has invited human beings into relationship with himself. We hear the prophets witnessing to the value of human dignity in various historical situations, protesting against unjust and degrading images of God and of the human person. We observe how the Israelite tradition conceived the worth of persons in increasingly universal terms. In Jesus, we see the worth of human persons fostered and proclaimed in the context of the kingdom of God, the ultimate environment for human flourishing and fulfillment. We are given insights into human dignity through the power of Jesus' parables, and learn the concrete meaning of human dignity through the ways in which he related to others, removing all barriers to the appreciation of the worth of persons. Jesus' vision of God and of humanity is confirmed in his resurrection, which sets the dignity of all human beings in the context of an eternal relationship to God.

Human Dignity and Rights

We have considered the general meaning of the concept of human dignity and the ways in which it can be enriched by the Christian story. We now need to examine some of its more specific implications. The notion of human dignity can be interpreted in terms of the *inalienable rights* of the human person: the *good* or worth of the person can be expressed as *rights*. To say that these rights are "inalienable" is to say that they are characteristic of human persons as persons. They are prior to the rights of society or of the state and cannot be abolished by society or the state. Human rights are based on human dignity itself, which is rooted in the freedom and reason of persons and, for Christians, in their personal relationship to God.

The notion of rights implies that there are certain characteristics of persons that must be respected by society. Rights have as their corollary the obligation of others to respect them. Society itself must be based on the premise that all its members have these rights. A society is an association of free persons, each having rights and each respecting the rights of others. In this sense, even though persons cannot exist without society, the rights of persons are prior to the rights of society. All the laws of a particular society must be justified in terms of the ways in which they protect and enhance the rights of persons within that society. Laws cannot be justified simply through "reasons of state," that is, because they serve the interest of the state or the government in a way which cannot be expressed in terms of service to the rights of citizens.

This understanding of human rights developed during the seventeenth and eighteenth centuries and influenced the two great revolutions of that time, which, for all the bloodshed and human suffering associated with them, were the context for declarations of human rights that would have a great influence on the modern world. The American Revolution of 1776 and the declaration of independence of the United States of America were associated with an epoch-making declaration of human rights. The French Revolution of 1789 was associated with the *Declaration of the Rights of Man and the Citizen* by the National Assembly.

After the appalling desecration of human rights in World War II, a *Universal Declaration of Human Rights* was formulated by the United Nations Organization and published in 1948. This declaration has, in the postwar period, served as a charter and rallying point for individuals and organizations attempting to further the cause of human rights in different countries. Virtually all members of the United Nations signed the declaration and gave assent to these rights in theory (although they may not respect them in practice), indicating that these basic human rights are largely a matter of consensus among the different ethical traditions of the world. In chapter 1, we indicated that the contemporary meaning of the concept of "natural law" was that human beings can come to some agreement about fundamental ethical truths and can communicate with each other in the search for what fulfils the human person. The contemporary attempt to emphasize respect for universal human rights expresses this notion of "natural law" in a way that is crucial for justice and peace in the world.

Rights and the Human Person

What are the rights of the human person, and how do we identify them? If rights are an expression of human dignity, of the worth of the human person, then an understanding of the meaning and relationship of human rights must be derived from a prior understanding of the person. Since rights reflect the needs, characteristics, and capacities of the human person, they can be best put in context by reflection on the varied and interrelated dimensions of personal existence. If the human person is created for a purpose, then the fundamental characteristics of the person must be respected; they imply rights and consequent obligations. If we know that the human person has the potential to be free and responsible, then this is not simply a fact we can ignore. This knowledge *obliges* us to respect that freedom and responsibility.

Since human rights express the fundamental dimensions of personal existence, we will consider those dimensions and the rights that they imply. We will arrive at a sense of the scope of human rights by considering the person that is the subject of rights. The list below first considers a dimension of personal existence, then the rights that express it, then the prohibitions and obligations that are the corollary of those rights. The questions of whether some rights can override others, and whether there are some rights that are truly inalienable and should never be overridden, will be considered at the end of the discussion and in the next chapter.

Prohibitions forbid acting in ways that show disrespect for human rights; *obligations* are requirements to act in ways that will fulfill human rights. In general, prohibitions are much easier to fulfill than obligations. It is easier, for example, for state and society to prohibit killing and torture than it is to provide the minimum material requirements for physical existence. The obligations associated with human rights call for a much more active role of state and society on behalf of the human person. The fulfillment of these obligations can only be achieved insofar as the wealth and general development of any society permits it. Yet these obligations are not thereby less important than prohibitions. If the human person is to fulfill his or her potential, we are obliged not only to refrain from frustrating that fulfillment, but also actively to assist it.

The distinction between "prohibitions" and "obligations" associated with human rights corresponds to the distinction between "freedom from" (negative freedom) and "freedom for" (positive freedom) discussed in chapter 3. "Freedom from" prohibits unwarranted interference with my freedom. It is directly concerned, for example, with the classical liberal rights of freedom of movement, speech, assembly, and political action. "Freedom for" obliges state and society to provide the means for full human development and motivates the call for such "social rights" as decent welfare provision, universal education, and just working conditions.

Human Rights and the Dimensions of Personal Existence

1. Physical

Humans are physical, embodied beings and have fundamental physical needs. They need protection from bodily injury and threat and require at least a basic minimum of food, clothing, and shelter. The human person's bodily life and health are a presupposition for the exercise of all other human capacities and, in this sense, is fundamental.

Rights

Every person has a right to physical integrity and security, and in the first place the right to life. This right outlaws unjustified killing and torture, and the violation of the person's sexual integrity. Human beings have a right to a basic minimum of the material necessities for the preservation of physical life.

Negatively, this prohibits unjustified killing and all forms of torture and sexual assault.

Positively, it obliges others to strive to provide the basic minimum of the material necessities for the preservation of physical life.

2. Spiritual

Human beings are created by God and gifted by God with the potential to know and love their creator. They are capable of knowing God through their conscience and through religious traditions and of communicating with God in prayer.

The importance of the spiritual capacity of the human person is a matter of great controversy in contemporary culture, but there is good evidence to suggest that its neglect has been the cause of many cultural and psychological ills. For the religious traditions of humanity, the expression of our spiritual capacity is as basic to our health and fulfillment as the fulfillment of our physical needs. The words of the book of Deuteronomy give classical expression to this conviction: "One does not live by bread alone, but by every word that comes from the mouth of the LORD" (8:3, cf. Matt 4:4).

Rights

Human persons have a right to freedom of conscience, belief, and worship, and the right to belong to a religious community of their choice. They have a right to educate their children in their own religious tradition and to communicate their religious beliefs in public.

Negatively, this right prohibits all forms of religious persecution and invalidates all attempts to interfere with the free profession of religious beliefs.

The positive implications of these rights are much more controversial. Some nations, especially the United States of America, put a high value on religious belief, but traditionally prohibit any support for religious groups by the allocation of public resources. This prohibition is made for the sake of the freedom of religion from state interference or favor. It can be argued, however, that recognition of the importance of religious beliefs for a large proportion of citizens entails an allocation of public resources, which derive from the taxes of those citizens, for some activities of those groups related to religion. In Australia, this has been the argument in favor of public funding of Catholic and other religious schools. In Germany, this argument is used in favor of the state's collection and distribution of a special tax, levied on those registered as church members, for the financial upkeep of churches, as well as for the presence of religious education and theology in publicly funded and administered schools and universities.

3. Moral

The human person is a moral subject, characterized by freedom, responsibility, and conscience. Since our moral capacity is our capacity to respond to the good, and since it can never conflict with authentic worship of God, a person's moral quality is of the highest importance. Whatever our personal moral quality, however, we cannot lose the dignity that comes simply from our inherent status as a moral subject.

Rights

The moral rights of the human person apply particularly to the rights of conscience. As we have seen, the dignity of conscience is not based on its necessarily being correct in its beliefs and decisions, since the decisions of conscience are the attempt of the subject to grasp objective moral truth, an attempt which can and often does fail. Its dignity is based rather on its status as the core of the moral subject, the uniquely personal relationship between an individual and the truth. The rights of conscience, then, cannot consist of the right to do whatever an individual decides is right, since this may grossly abuse the rights of others (as in the case of a conscientious racist), but rather in the special respect given to conscience in certain circumstances. These circumstances include the right to conscientious objection to military service, especially to carrying arms—that is, the right not to be forced to kill others—and the right to refuse medical treatment.

The rights of conscience would also include the right to be able to form conscience. This would involve the right to information relevant to the formation of conscience and the right to an education that fostered the development of conscience.

Negatively, the state may not force its citizens to carry arms, nor impose medical treatment on them.

Positively, the state and those responsible for the media are obliged to foster free access to reliable and adequate sources of information, and those responsible for education are obliged to ensure that it enhances the formation of conscience.

4. Personal

The human person is *personal,* a unique individual, who develops through relationships with other individuals. Every human person requires freedom in order to be able to develop this uniqueness and thereby make an irreplaceable contribution to the richness and value of human community.

Rights

The rights to our own individuality include the right to freedom of movement, the right to freedom of choice of employment, the right to marry, and the right to choose a marriage partner or to give consent to a partner chosen by others. In general terms, each person has a right to the opportunity to develop natural capacities to the fullest.

Negatively, the state is obliged to refrain from any restrictions of these rights.

Positively, it is obliged to give as much opportunity as possible for the development of personal capacities, for example, through education.

5. Social

Personal life is by its very nature social, a life lived in community. Human persons are formed by social life and are oriented to a common life with other persons.

Rights

Everyone has the right to a nationality and to the status of a member of society, for example, as a citizen.

Negatively, this prohibits all laws depriving people of citizenship or nationality without just cause.

Positively, it obliges states to foster opportunities for new citizenship for refugees and displaced persons.

6. Sexual

Every human person is characterized by a distinctive sexuality, relating to others through this sexuality. Human beings are oriented to sexual relationships, and the sexual relationship between a man and a woman can bear fruit in new human life. Man and woman are characterized by a fundamental equality.

Rights

The relevant rights include the right to marry and to have children, the right of both sexes to an equality of other relevant rights, and the rights of homosexuals to preserve their own identity free from harassment and persecution.

Negatively, these rights prohibit sexual discrimination, forced marriages, forced restrictions on a couple's right to have children, and laws that legitimate any police interference in the privacy of sexual relationships between consenting adults.

7. Intellectual

Human beings have the capacity to know and reason. They are characterized by a fundamental orientation to the truth, a desire to know.

Rights

Intellectual rights embrace the right of opportunity of access to the truth, and the right to develop intellectual abilities.

Negatively, this prohibits any unjustified censorship and any propaganda.

Positively, it obliges the state and other responsible groups to provide an education which develops intellectual capacities.

8. Economic

Human beings are capable of work, of transforming nature through their own labor. They express their own individuality and fulfill physical needs through ownership of possessions; they seek to satisfy their own needs through the exchange of goods and services with others.

Rights

Economic rights include the right to own property, the right to enter into economic contracts, the right to buy and sell goods subject to appropriate license, the right to withdraw labor, the right to form economic and professional associations or trade unions for the protection of economic rights, and the right to work.

Negatively, these rights prohibit all laws that unjustifiably restrict the exercise of these rights.

Positively, they oblige governments to foster economic policies calculated to provide employment for as many citizens as possible.

9. *Political*

Human societies require government, which involves the exercise of the power to make laws and to direct the use of common resources. The freedom and responsibility of human persons are best recognized through a democratic political system.

Rights

Everyone has the right to vote, to form political parties and interest groups, to publicize one's political views, to engage in political campaigns, to stand for political office, and to take part in government.

Negatively, any unjustified restriction of these rights is prohibited.

Positively, these rights oblige governments to actively foster a political climate and institutional context within which these rights can be exercised.

10. *Cultural*

Human beings are characterized by a cultural identity, especially a particular language, based on a cultural tradition marked out by particular customs, symbols, and practices.

Rights

Every person has the right to use and foster the language of one's cultural group and to foster one's cultural identity without persecution or harassment.

Negatively, any persecution of cultural identity is prohibited.

The positive obligations stemming from cultural rights are more controversial. Some nations, while avoiding any persecution of the identity of cultural minorities, tend to favor the investment of resources for the development of national cultural homogeneity for the sake of national unity and stability. Others commit more resources to fostering distinct and diverse subcultures within the framework of an overarching political and legal culture for the sake of the preservation of these subcultures in their diversity.

11. Artistic

Human beings are creative and seek to express themselves in forms of beauty that have no use value, but which are crucial to human health and fulfillment. Through word, sound, color, and image they express meaning and emotion, and achieve insight into the conditions of their own existence.

Rights

Artistic rights include the right to free artistic expression and the right to an opportunity to develop artistic capacities.

Negatively, this prohibits restriction of artistic expression.

Positively, it obliges the state and other authorities to provide opportunities for the development of artistic capacities.

The Common Good

These rights and mutual obligations together make up the *common good,* "the sum total of social conditions which allow people, either as groups or as individuals, to reach their fulfillment more fully and more easily."[1] The concept of the common good emphasizes the *interdependence of rights and obligations:* my rights imply obligations on others, and vice versa. This interdependence can be preserved and enhanced only by a commitment to the common good, which includes various provisions for the security, education, and welfare of citizens set up by the government from the financial resources derived from taxation.

For the social teaching of the Catholic Church, this notion of the common good is of great importance in emphasizing our mutual

---

1. Vatican II, *Gaudium et Spes,* Pastoral Constitution on the Church in the Modern World, §26.

rights and obligations as an expression of our communal and inter-dependent character as human persons.

Relationships between Rights

Persons should have free exercise of their rights, so long as this does not interfere with the rights of others. This is easy to say, but difficult to interpret! What do we mean by "interfere with the rights of others"? When rights clash, is there any hierarchy of rights that can guide us in deciding which rights should override others? Are there some rights that can never be overridden?

Rights that emphasize our freedom are limited by respect for the fundamental rights of others. Our freedom of speech, for example, is limited by the right of others to privacy. (Private matters can become matters of legitimate public interest when, for example, a person holding public office is engaging in activities in private life that seriously detract from the quality of exercise of that public office.) Rights that give economic freedom are limited by the imperative to respect the fundamental physical needs of others. Rights that emphasize freedom can also be suspended for a limited period of time when this is necessary to protect the most fundamental rights. In time of war, for example, a government may have a right to limit freedom of information in order to protect the safety of citizens.

Are there any rights that may never be overridden or suspended? Are there rights which pertain to personal dignity in such a direct way that to ignore these rights amounts to a direct attack on human dignity itself? These would be rights that express our fundamental physical, moral, and spiritual dignity, of which no person and no institution has any right to deprive us. These rights imply some basic prohibitions, including the following:

- deliberate and direct taking of innocent human life
- judicial murder
- brainwashing
- sexual assault

- torture
- slavery

The question whether or not there are some actions that are wrong in all circumstances, and therefore subject to absolute prohibition, is a matter of fundamental controversy between the Kantian and utilitarian ethical traditions. It will be considered in more detail in the next chapter.

Awareness of Human Rights

We have made an attempt to enumerate human rights on the basis of the constitutive dimensions of the human person. If these are permanent and universal dimensions of the human person, then the above rights are objective and independent of particular situations. They imply obligations, whether particular societies choose to respect or ignore them. (As we have noted, positive obligations do not apply where societies simply do not have the economic resources to fulfill certain rights in adequate ways.) As we argued in chapter 1, contrary to the claims of relativism, there are sources of moral truth that can guide us in perceiving and defining human rights.

Yet, although the permanent validity of human rights is based on the permanent character of the most fundamental dimensions of the human person, our awareness of these rights is profoundly affected by historical change and historical experience. The worth of the human person, the basis of all rights, has been variously perceived and understood in the course of history. Our moral awareness itself has a history—the history of our attempts to understand the full potential of human beings in relation to social, economic, and cultural change. This history shows dramatic and prophetic moments of insight, when the meaning of human dignity is discovered in liberating and exciting ways, as well as moments of tragic and fateful blindness, when past moral achievements are forgotten in a climate of apathy, cynicism, and violence.

In chapter 1, mention was made of the great moral insight of the ancient world, the Golden Rule, which implies a fundamental moral equality. Earlier in this chapter, we discussed the moral awareness and insights characteristic of the faith of Israel, and the proclamation of the depth and universality of human dignity implicit in the words and actions of Jesus of Nazareth. During the course of modern history, cultural developments have led to a new awareness of many rights that today either are matters of consensus or at least enjoy widespread support:

- The right of all to freedom of religious belief and worship was first championed by Protestant writers in England, Holland, and America during the seventeenth and eighteenth centuries.
- The right of voters to elect political representatives and to take part in government was first associated with the English revolution of the seventeenth century. It was spread further by the influence of the American and French revolutions in the eighteenth century.
- The rights of the worker to humane working conditions and to the formation of trade unions were affirmed by the trade unions and socialist parties of the nineteenth century.
- The rights of children to an education and to freedom from onerous labor were affirmed by social reformers of the nineteenth century.
- The right of black people to be free from slavery was affirmed by reformers in Western Europe and America in the nineteenth century, notably by William Wilberforce in England and Abraham Lincoln in the United States.
- The right of women to vote was the subject of a campaign by the suffragette movement in North America and Western Europe in the early twentieth century; the right of women to a role other than that of wife or mother has been affirmed by the women's liberation movement of recent decades.
- The right of non-European nations to self-government was affirmed in the decolonization movement that gathered strength after World War II.

- The rights of indigenous peoples in relation to European colonizers were first affirmed by the Dominican priest and bishop Bartolomeo de las Casas in the context of Spain's conquest of the New World. These rights have recently been affirmed in various ways by land rights and other movements in countries where indigenous peoples were displaced and threatened with extinction by European settlement.

Tragically, this review of historical progress in insight into the meaning and implications of the dignity of the human person must be seen in relation to areas of blindness and decline in moral awareness characteristic of modern times:

- The fall of civilized countries into totalitarianism, of both fascist and communist varieties, has been one of the most disastrous factors in the disregard for human dignity so frighteningly evident in much of twentieth-century history.
- A decline in awareness of the depth and meaning of sexual relations among many groups in Western societies has also been witnessed in recent decades, which is a cheapening of a great human good.
- A decline in the awareness of the right to life of the unborn child is also evident, as social and governmental support for legislation allowing abortion has grown.
- A weakened commitment to social justice in many Western countries has occurred as a highly individualist and materialist social ethos gains in strength.

Human Rights and Ideology

At all times, perception and awareness of human rights must combat the power of *ideology*. Ideology, in the negative sense of the word, is a belief system that purports to justify what is in fact unjustifiable; it hides reality for the benefit of the power and privilege of that group which engenders and propagates the ideology. Ideology

145

may be completely cynical, a system of beliefs produced by people who know that these beliefs are false but who propagate them for reasons of the protection of power. More commonly, ideologies are believed to a considerable degree by the groups whose prejudices, self-interest, and limited perspectives they reflect. The ideology and the positions of power and privilege it protects and justifies are interwoven, so that those holding such positions become unaware of social and moral reality, living in a false world of their own making.

Many of the great examples of moral progress mentioned above were made possible by a critical confrontation with ideology. A practical struggle against injustice was usually complemented by an intellectual struggle to show that the theoretical justifications for existing inequalities or restrictions on freedom were illusory. Those who campaigned against racism, slavery, and the oppression of indigenous peoples, for example, subjected theories of racial superiority to intellectual critique, showing that they had no scientific foundation. Those who fought for the rights of the worker also criticized the theory of laissez-faire capitalism, arguing not only that it caused massive social inequality and hardship, but also great economic instability and inefficiency. The women's liberation movement has argued that the exclusion of women from many walks of life cannot be justified by the biological differences between men and women.

For Christians, the story of Jesus must be the greatest source of inspiration for heightening awareness of human dignity and for combating ideologies of whatever kind. His own life showed a fearless readiness to confront religious ideologies that militated against human dignity. Christians have often been slow to perceive injustice in various areas of life, leaving moral leadership to secular groups; the light of the gospel has often been hidden under a bushel (Matt 5:15), confined within a Church preoccupied by hopes and fears for the next world, rather than shone on the wider human issues of the day. In many other situations, however, Christians have been foremost in protecting and extending the value of human dignity. The story of Jesus will not give present-day Christians ready-made critiques of ideologies or situations of injustice, nor solutions to contemporary moral problems. The task of a distinctively Christian ethics is to reflect on these issues in light of the story of Jesus and to be inspired by him to respect human dignity with depth, intensity, and universality.

Human Dignity and Duties to Myself

We have focused above on the ways in which human dignity can be understood and expressed in terms of rights—rights which imply obligations on the part of others. Yet this discussion of rights and their accompanying obligations does not cover all aspects of human dignity. The moral good of human dignity includes the dignity of my own self and therefore implies duties to myself. If the worth of persons were restricted to rights and obligations between persons, then my actions affecting my own self would be outside the scope of morality.

For some secular understandings of ethics, this is indeed the case: morality is understood to be about relationships between people who have rights. If I act in ways which affect only myself, then moral considerations are not relevant. Since no one can say what the true purpose of life is, then no one has any grounds for calling any action moral or immoral unless it concerns the rights of free and independent persons. Sexual activity between consenting adults, from this point of view, is not really a moral question. Or again, if a person chooses to end his or her life at a particular time, without interfering with the rights of others, this is purely a personal concern. The meaning of our lives is the meaning we ourselves choose to give it, so long as we respect the obligations imposed on us by the rights of others. Other secular perspectives draw, like Christian ethics, on the "natural law" tradition and stress the ethical imperatives for personal life that stem from the meaning and character of our humanity.

As we saw in chapter 1, in a pluralist society lawmakers must respect the fact that there are many different views of morality and the meaning of life within society; the law must in general confine itself to defining rights and obligations between citizens, rather than directing its citizens to behave in particular ways in areas that affect only themselves—or at least affect others only indirectly.

From a *legal* point of view, therefore, in a liberal and pluralist society, the concept of duties purely to myself has little content.

The law is, however, responsible for the *common good,* and a part of this responsibility is to ensure that individual freedom is not exercised in ways which ignore goods and relationships that have great importance for our communal life. This *tension between individual autonomy and moral community* relates, for example, to such matters as the following:

- The community cost of individual behavior; for example, may the law require me to wear a seatbelt when driving?
- Family law; for example, what is the social importance of the bond of marriage?
- Reproductive technology; for example, should unmarried women be entitled to use public in vitro fertilization facilities?
- Euthanasia; for example, should there be legal sanctions against someone assisting someone ending their own life?
- Abortion; for example, is the fetus another human being who has rights that override the mother's autonomous right to terminate her pregnancy?
- Social justice; for example, can limitations be placed on individual economic freedom in order to ensure basic standards of economic welfare for all?

From a *moral* point of view, my own human dignity is as important as that of any other person, and its value obliges my own actions as much as the value of other persons does. I am not free to disregard the good of my own person. I must rather discern the purposes of personal life and live by them. The moral duties that I have to myself are, like rights, based on a respect for what truly fulfils the good of the human person, including:

- Respect for my own life and for my physical health and safety. Someone might fail to respect this by engaging in dangerous sports and pastimes, or by physical self-abuse through consumption of drugs or overindulgence in food and drink.

- Respect for the true meaning and purpose of my sexuality, expressed through the commitment of love and fidelity.
- Respect for my own self-esteem. I have a duty to respect myself as a person who is unique and the object of the love of God. This prohibits self-hatred and actions that degrade and deny my own personal worth. I have an obligation to respect my own talents and potential for contributing something uniquely my own to the human community.

Summary of Chapter 5

1. In ethics, a distinction is made between two kinds of value: virtues, or moral values, which are qualities of decisions, actions, and persons; and goods, which are things, beings, or persons of inherent value. The human person may or may not be virtuous, but he or she is a good because a person has inherent value.

2. This good world is characterized by a hierarchy of goods. The union of love of God and love of neighbor means that devotion to God, the absolute and ultimate good, cannot clash with respect for the good of human persons. The worth of human persons is greater than that of any other goods in nature, but nature itself has a value that is independent of human beings, and human beings cannot fulfill themselves without respecting the good of nature.

3. The concept of human dignity emphasizes that every human being has a personal worth and that others are obliged to acknowledge and develop that worth.

4. Christian ethics understands the ultimate foundations of human dignity in terms of each individual's personal relationship with God. The Bible is a rich source of affirmations of and insight into human dignity, most notably:

- the exodus narrative, which tells the story of God's liberating compassion for slaves;
- the prophetic writings, which witness to personal integrity and social justice in light of faith in God;
- the gospels, which portray Jesus' affirmation of the dignity of all those he encountered;
- other New Testament writings, which affirm the worth of all human beings in terms of their destiny of eternal life in union with Jesus.

5. The good, or worth, of human persons can be expressed as rights, which imply corollary obligations. There have been great statements of human rights in modern history, most notably the Universal Declaration of Human Rights.

6. Human rights are related to the constitutive dimensions of the human person: physical, spiritual, moral, personal, social, sexual, intellectual, economic, political, cultural, and artistic.

7. Our mutual rights and obligations go together to make up the common good, the conditions which can foster the fulfillment of all members of society.

8. Some rights, especially some freedoms, may be temporarily overridden in some circumstances, but other rights, such as the right of an innocent person to life, may never be overridden.

9. Human rights are objective and universal, but our awareness of them has developed historically. History is marked by great milestones in the awareness of human rights, but is also characterized by signs of moral blindness and decline.

10. A critical examination of ideology helps to develop awareness of human rights.

11. The good of persons is expressed not only in terms of rights, which imply duties to others, but also in terms of

my duties to myself, which include respect for my own life and physical well-being, for the meaning and purpose of human sexuality, and for my own self-esteem.

Questions for Discussion

1. In reference to morality, we can distinguish between virtues and goods. Make a list of virtues, which identify moral qualities of decisions, actions and persons, and of goods, which identify the things and beings which have worth and value.

2. Study Exodus 3, and Isaiah 1, 9:1–6, 11:1–9. What do you learn of the relationship between faith in God and concern for justice?

3. Study three incidents from the gospels where Jesus encounters another person, whether as healer, teacher or friend. In what ways do you think his relationship to that person communicates a sense of their worth in the sight of God?

4. Study Genesis 1 with the aid of a biblical commentary and consider the meaning of the phrase "in the image of God" in relation to the creation of man and woman.

5. Obtain a copy of the Universal Declaration of Human Rights. In what ways are the rights listed related to constitutive dimensions of the human person?

6. Consider the dimensions of the human person presented in this chapter. Do you agree with this list? Take three dimensions and consider in more detail what rights and what prohibitions and obligations flow from them.

7. In what ways or through whom do you think awareness of human rights is increasing today? How is it decreasing?

8. What would you identify as contemporary ideologies which hinder an appreciation of human rights?

9. What does respect for human dignity mean, in the circumstances of our society, in relation to marginalized populations? Consider:
—the elderly,
—the disabled,
—criminals,
—children.

10. To what extent and in what situations do you think recognition of the dignity of persons entails their having a role in decision making?

11. How important is a strong sense of the common good for the welfare of all members of society? What kind and level of taxation would be a fair balance between supporting the common good and respecting the freedom of individual property/income?

12. Are my duties to myself as important as my duty to respect the rights of others? Consider in more detail the meaning of two of the duties to myself mentioned in the text.

PART FOUR

WHAT SHOULD I DO?

This part considers the nature and development of moral norms in light of a Christian process of moral reasoning. Chapter 6, "Love, Rights, and Moral Norms," will discuss the nature of moral norms, the rules or standards of moral action that attempt to express how we should act in relation to goods in specific ways and situations. Chapter 7, "The Task of Moral Reasoning," will focus on the process of moral reasoning, the ways in which we develop norms. Chapter 8, "Christian Ethics and the Teaching Authority of the Church," will consider the role of Church teaching in this process.

6

Love, Rights, and Moral Norms

In chapter 3 we considered the moral person in terms of free-dom, responsibility, conscience, and character. These qualities of the moral person or subject make up the answer to the question: *What kind of person should I be?* As we have seen in chapter 5, the question *What is the good?* is a different and equally important question. It is a question focused not on the moral person and the virtues that characterize that person, but rather on the goods in the world. The answer to the first question will tell me what virtues should inform my life; the answer to the second will highlight what is truly of value in the world. Yet neither answer will, of itself, tell me what to do. The question *What should I do?* is a different question and asks for a different kind of answer. The subject of the next three chapters is the role and meaning of such answers, which are called *moral norms*.

We have seen that a fulfilled moral subject has a character made up of virtues. For Christian ethics, the virtue of love sums up the others: to love one's neighbor as oneself is the essence of the ethical way of life. A loving person will deliberate on the best course of action by reflecting on the question *What is the loving thing to do?* Yet our disposition to love others will not by itself tell us what to do in relation to specific ethical situations. We can have models of loving character, which can guide us in our actions; for the Christian, Jesus is the supreme model. By reading and hearing his story, the Christian's insight into the meaning of love can be deep-ened and refined. Yet Jesus faced the specific moral challenges of an ancient culture, his own times. His life is not a code of behavior, nor does it give us a list of things that we should do. Jesus responded with love, freedom, and reason to the moral challenges inherent in his own ministry. The contemporary Christian, like all contemporary human beings, must do the same.

To know what the loving thing to do is, we must know the world. We must know human beings, and we must have reflected on what fulfils their God-given potential. We must have thought about the meaning of human dignity in the context of our own society. We may come to understand love for others as the disposition to value their personal dignity, to act in ways which show respect for that dignity and for the rights that flow from it. But we have seen that there are different rights, and that the relationship between them is not always clear. We do not always know which right has priority. We can know about rights, but this may not tell us what to do here and now. Action usually involves balancing the claims of different rights and understanding their relationship in a given situation. So we can be loving, and we can be aware of the rights of the human person, but we still need to take a further step to have a clear and relevant guide for action in a concrete situation.

Consider the following example: You are invited to become a board member of a public authority that has the power to classify films for audience ratings. The board has to consider the relationship of two rights: on the one hand, the freedom to make and see films and, on the other hand, the right of the public not to be exposed to violence and pornography without some warning, which includes the right of parents to protect their children from such exposure. The difficulty of the task of such a board is to achieve some kind of balance between these two rights, so that freedom is given the maximum scope compatible with excluding from public viewing, or from viewing by children, material deemed unacceptably offensive. In this case the freedom involved is the freedom, important to a liberal society, to have a maximum range of choice of what to see, a freedom from restriction. The board focuses on two rights, freedom and the right to protection from offensive material, and the board must do justice to their conflicting claims. If you, as a member of the board, were simply to say, "I believe in freedom" and "I believe in certain standards of public decency," and to repeat this whenever the chairperson of the board asked for your opinion about the classification of a specific film, then you would very likely find yourself omitted from the board's membership at the earliest possible opportunity, since you would be contributing very little to its crucial task. In all likelihood, all of the members of the board would believe both in freedom and public decency—their crucial disagreements would be about the demarcation between these two goods in specific cases. This is the task that concerns the board, a task to which a simple declaration of your own commitment to the general goods involved would contribute little.

If the board was successful in its work, it would formulate a number of norms. (In this case, the norms have some *legal* status through the authority of a public statutory body, whereas specifically *moral* norms derive their authority purely from the goodness of things, rather than from any human legislative authority.) These norms are rules of action, defining the relationship that should be observed between the goods of freedom and public decency. The point about these norms is that they guide moral action in concrete ways. They guide the moral person's intention to do good.

Norms, then, are *rules of moral action*, statements of what we should do, based on a consideration of the goods and rights involved in a situation or situations. Norms do not exist for their own sake, they are not given to us ready-made, and most norms are not unchanging. Rather, norms are developed in order to serve the good, to express the meaning of goods and rights in specific situations. Norms safeguard rights by ensuring that justice is done to their force and importance in specific situations. This is clear in the example we have just considered: the purpose of the board's deliberations is to ensure that two important rights are respected. The norms that the board agrees on and recommends for enforcement provide balance in community life between individual freedom and protection from offensive material. The norms do not exist for their own sake, and they are not unchanging; they will probably change in various ways when community perceptions of the relationship of these two rights change. The content of these norms is not a simple and obvious matter, but must be arrived at through a process of debate, which is the chief task of the board that recommends them.

This last point highlights the fact that *norms are formed by moral reasoning.* Moral reasoning is an engagement of our thinking powers through which we attempt to discover the concrete meaning of a good and how to realize and respect that good in specific, changing situations. Moral reasoning expresses our freedom and responsibility to make moral judgments, rather than simply to accept a system of laws. The crucial importance of moral reasoning derives from the fact that norms must be formed by us, by human beings; they are not simply given. In the discussion of freedom and responsibility in chapter 3, we reflected on the uniqueness of the human species in terms of its vocation to freely respond to the call of the good, to shape its own life and its environment in a way which is in accord with the fundamental goods that we see in it, but which can take many diverse forms.

Human beings are called to respect the goods of creation, to live in justice and freedom in fulfillment of their nature as the "image of God." Yet the concrete meaning of justice and freedom will be the concern of their own freedom and the burden of their own responsibility. The goods that we find in the world can be realized in many different ways, just as the virtues that make up human character can be expressed in many different ways of life. It is the task of moral reasoning to be morally creative, to develop norms that can best express the quality of our love through our respect for what has inherent goodness.

Kinds of Norms

The purpose of norms, then, is to give guidance for action, to put our awareness of values into the imperative mood. Yet the kinds of guidance that norms can give vary enormously. Some norms, called *formal* norms, are fundamentally a source of inspiration, a general call to perfect our character. Others, called *material* norms, give specific guidance for action.

Formal Norms

Formal norms have the purpose of putting a virtue or good into high relief. They remind us of the importance of a particular virtue or good; they encourage, admonish, or inspire us. They do not give specific guidance about what to do, but they emphasize the importance of our moral decisions. They are called "formal" because they have the imperative form of a norm, but do not have any specific or material content. They call and oblige us, but give us no specific guidance what to do.

Formal norms can apply to both virtues and goods. A crucial imperative of the teaching of Jesus is "Be merciful, just as your Father is merciful" (Luke 6:36). This norm does not tell us what a merciful person should actually do—although Jesus' teaching as a whole paints a unique picture of merciful, or compassionate, action (for example, Luke 6:27–49). It rather inspires us to live by the virtue of compassion, because in doing so we respond to the creator God of compassion. It urges us to give this virtue the highest place in our lives, to strengthen and intensify the habit of compassionate feeling and action. Similarly, the imperatives "Be just!" "Be prudent!" "Be moderate!" and so on, do not tell us what just, prudent, or moderate action is, but they do inspire us to live by these virtues and to develop the importance that they have in our lives.

In a similar way, formal norms with respect to goods help to sensitize us to the importance and value of those goods. The imperative "Respect life!" does not tell us what this respect should consist of, but it does highlight for us the value of life. When we are exhorted to "Defend freedom!" we are not told how to do this, nor what the extent or type of that freedom is, but we are reminded that freedom is a great good.

Sometimes formal norms seem to have some specific content, but in fact they simply act to reinforce the importance of a particular virtue or good. The negative norm or prohibition "Do not murder!" does prohibit a certain kind of action—murder—but it does not tell us what kind of killing is murder. Murder is unjust killing, and so this prohibition simply reinforces the fact that unjust killing is wrong, without helping us to distinguish between just and unjust killing. It acts, then, as a negative form of the formal norm "Respect life!"

The point of formal norms, then, is to highlight the importance of the moral life itself. They appeal to our conscience by emphasizing the values with which the moral life is concerned—the virtues that should shape the moral subject and the goods that make up the inherent value of the world and of the persons who live in it. Formal norms revive and encourage the moral life, bringing us back to its point and purpose.

Material Norms

Material norms, as their name suggests, give us material guidance in moral action. Rather than functioning as urgent reminders of the importance of general values, material norms oblige or prohibit specific actions. Material norms take up a specific stance about the relative importance of the goods in our lives.

Consider, for example, the prohibition "Do not murder!" If we want to develop this into a guide to action, then we must consider the good that it expresses with regard to more specific moral questions. We should not kill, but is it permissible to kill in self-defense? Is it permissible to use capital punishment? Is it permissible to kill animals? Is abortion ever permissible? Is euthanasia permissible? All of these questions—and many more—arise when we consider the ethics of preserving and respecting life; a norm capable of giving specific guidance must take account of these diverse questions.

For the Christian tradition, a reasonably specific set of material norms for both respecting and preserving life and deciding what is permissible killing might take this form: The plant life of the natural environment should be disturbed only for the sake of important human needs; animal life may be taken only for the purpose of fulfilling the basic human needs of food, clothing, and shelter; human life may be taken only in cases of self-defense, and may be taken in wartime only in the circumstances of a just war, when there is a reasonable expectation that the taking of the life of aggressors can lead to a just and peaceful conclusion.

This statement of the norms applying to the preservation of life and the permissibility of killing is, of course, still very general—but it is a long way from the simple imperative "Do not murder." This shows us that a full development of moral norms which are appropriate to the moral challenges we face is a very specific task, involving a careful consideration of a whole range of factors.

Norms and Moral Reasoning

Consideration of a range of questions of this kind impels us to use *moral reasoning* to develop more and more specific norms, norms that can do justice to the complexity of the situations with which we're faced. Moral reasoning is *practical reasoning* because it is a reflection on our practice, our actions, and because its purpose is to enhance the moral quality of those actions. The crucial role of moral reasoning is to assess the relationship between moral norms and the goods they are intended to serve. If the purpose of moral norms is to guide us in respecting and fulfilling what is good, then moral reasoning should clarify whether the moral norms we live by are adequate to this task. This is particularly important when moral situations present a clash of accepted moral norms. If we understand norms as a means of expressing the importance of different goods, then a clash of norms can be resolved by reflecting on the interrelationship of the goods that they are intended to serve.

In the last chapter, we saw that the good of human dignity can be expressed in terms of a number of rights, and moral norms are generally oriented to obliging respect for those rights. If moral norms clash, we must use moral reasoning to understand the relationship of those rights and develop a norm adequate to that relationship.

Example: Truth-Telling and Protecting the Innocent

The late Bernhard Häring, CSSR, an eminent writer on Christian ethics, cites the following case:

161

When German nuns, who were responsible for a large number of mentally and physically handicapped children, were asked by Hitler's obedient slaves how many children they had of this and that category of deficiency, they responded simply that they had none of them. Did they lie? They did not, because in the context there was no communication about children and children's sickness; the real question asked was "How many children do you have to deliver for our gas ovens?" And the only truthful and, at the same time, life-saving response was "None."[1]

A clash of the norm of truth-telling with the norm of preventing harm to the innocent is resolved by an appeal to the meaning of the good behind the norm of truth-telling, that is, the good of authentic communication, a good which would in no way have been served by giving a "correct" answer to the demands of the murderers. Authentic communication is related to the questioner's right to know, and the questioner's right to know is related to the questioner's relationship to the one being asked and what the questioner will do with the information contained in the answer to the question. In this case, the questioner has arbitrary power of life and death over the person being asked, and intends to use the answer in order to destroy innocent life; he therefore has no right to know. The purpose of the norm "Tell the truth!" is to ensure mutual communication and trust, but, in this case, revealing the children's whereabouts would simply be a matter of acquiescing in the ability of the powerful to destroy the innocent.

Example: Property Rights and the Right to Sustain Human Life

God destined the earth with everything it contains for the use of all humanity and of all peoples, so that the good

---

1. Bernhard Häring, *Free and Faithful in Christ* (Slough, UK: St. Paul Publications, 1978), vol 1, 361.

things of creation should be available equally to all, under the guidance of justice tempered by charity. Whatever the structures of property are, according to the legitimate institutions of different peoples, and in varied and changing circumstances, we must never lose sight of this universal destination of created goods....Therefore, everyone has the right to have a share in these goods that is sufficient for each and for the needs of dependents....A person in extreme need has the right to take from the riches of others what is necessary to satisfy basic needs.[2]

The norm of respecting property is not an absolute norm, but is limited by the right of all human beings to share in the fruits of the earth to satisfy their basic needs. The purpose of the norm "Do not steal!" is to respect the right of individuals or groups to own property. This right is one expression of individual human dignity, since personal property is linked with individual identity, as well as individual effort and achievement.

Yet the norm "Do not steal!" is a *formal* norm that does not tell us the extent of anyone's right to own property; it simply tells us that it is unjust to take the property of others without due reason. It therefore does not apply to the person "in extreme need" described above since he is, in his extreme necessity, taking from what others have in abundance. If some human beings possess an abundance of goods and others nothing, in a world created for the use of all, the norm "Do not steal!" applies more appropriately to those with abundance than to those with nothing.

We can see from these two examples that a clash of norms must be resolved by a use of moral reasoning to reflect on the purpose of those norms in relation to the goods they are intended to serve. If the norms are taken as absolute, they deny their own purpose, which is respect for human dignity. In the first case, making the norm of literal truth-telling absolute would pervert the purpose of that norm, which is communication of truth based on trust. In

---

2. Vatican II, *Gaudium et Spes*, §69.

the second case, an unlimited and absolute right to private property would deny the physical basis of human dignity for many, and it is human dignity that the norm of private property is intended to serve in the first place. The appeal to the interrelationship of goods and rights to resolve a clash of norms is intended to prevent norms being understood out of context in a way which would pervert their own purpose. The relationship of different norms must be considered in light of the fundamental good of human dignity in its various constitutive dimensions. And the relevance of specific norms to particular situations must be considered in light of the goods that they are intended to serve.

The Development of Norms

Material norms are norms that are developed for specific situations by moral reasoning. We saw in chapter 5 that our perceptions of the implications of human dignity have developed over time. Today we are aware of rights that were insufficiently recognized in the past, just as we are also less sensitive to some human values than past generations were. Because our perception of the meaning and implications of human dignity develops, norms can change in order to fulfill the good that they are intended to serve in new situations.

Let us consider, for example, the following commandment: "You shall not covet your neighbor's house; you shall not covet your neighbor's wife, or male or female slave, or ox, or donkey, or anything that belongs to your neighbor" (Exod 20:17). This biblical passage—usually expressed as the ninth and tenth commandments—deals with the basic value of respect for the property of the neighbor, an aspect of respect for human dignity. It is clear, however, that it is conceived in terms of the patriarchal perspective of an ancient culture: the neighbor's wife is grouped together with the rest of his property. It does not condemn coveting one's neighbor's husband! This is because the wife was understood to be the property of her husband, and not vice versa.

This norm is essentially an expression of property rights, with the neighbor's wife included in it as part of a man's property. A contemporary attempt to express this norm would firstly have to distinguish the different aspects of human dignity involved, that is, distinguish between the importance of the right to property and the importance of the marital relationship between a husband and wife (although some development in this direction is apparent in the restatement of the Ten Commandments in Deut 5:21). Norms pertaining to the marriage relationship would have to be distinguished from those relating to property, and developed as an expression of the equality of the sexes and of the nature of marriage as a free, exclusive, and permanent commitment.

Perhaps the most famous example of a norm that was changed because of a shift in circumstances is the example of the norm against usury, or charging interest on a loan. During the medieval period, the Church forbade the taking of interest on a loan, since this was understood as an act of exploitation of the needy. In the early modern period, however, loaning as investment in order to support large business ventures such as merchant voyages became more and more relevant. In these cases, interest was a charge between businessmen based on the market cost of money, in a way similar to today, and not necessarily an exploitation of the needy. The Church, however, was very reluctant to accept this and continued to ban usury long into the modern period. This is one example of a norm becoming largely irrelevant with socioeconomic change. The basic value—concern for economic justice—clearly remains relevant but must be expressed in a way carefully focused on contemporary socioeconomic conditions.

Norms, then, can change, especially those norms that attempt to express the meaning of basic values in relation to specific social situations. Clearly, the more specific a norm is, the more it is likely to change with social change. Norms concerning modesty in dress, for example, are subject to great variation in different cultures and different historical periods. There are some norms, however, that may change very little because they are very general or because they are concerned with aspects of human life that remain constant in the midst of social change. The norm, for example, against directly and deliberately killing an innocent human being has remained the same since ancient times; it concerns a fundamental human value and expresses this value in a way which is independent of social change.

The Purpose of Moral Norms

Norms act as a bridge between the virtues of the moral subject and the goods that are in the world. If we seek to live by love, it is the relevant moral norm that will guide us in knowing what the concrete meaning of love is in relation to the needs of other human beings. If we truly care for someone, we will seek the best insights into human action to guide us in helping the person, and good moral norms encapsulate these insights. Yet moral norms are often experienced as restrictive and irrelevant, rejected as a form of legalism that stifles love and imposes a set of general categories on the subtle diversities of human existence.

There are two false extremes that can distort the true and crucial role of moral norms. One of these is to take norms rather than values as the essential criterion for ethical action. To do this would be to create an ethics of law, rather than an ethics of value. As we have seen, to give norms this role would be to fly in the face of the evidence that norms are developed to give guidance in historical situations, and that social change may make change necessary to the norms that deal with social life.

At the other extreme, moral norms are sometimes rejected altogether as useless for the challenges of moral life. This point of view would argue that we can respect the goods inherent in human dignity in a unique and different way for every different situation without any guidance from norms. A person of loving and wise character, it might be argued, can express love without the need for the bridging role of moral norms; that person will know that it may be loving to hide the truth from someone in one situation and loving to tell the truth in another. There is no need for the guidance of any general norm of truth-telling.

This tension between love and moral norms sums up one of the fundamental questions of ethics. As we saw in chapter 1, it is one of the crucial disagreements between the Kantian and utilitarian traditions. For the Kantian tradition, respect for human dignity must take the form of conforming to certain general norms of action: always to act in ways which all free and equal persons could imitate, and never to treat any person purely as a means to an end. For the utilitarian tradition, in contrast, the purpose of loving action is to maximize the happiness of those involved. The meaning of love is not defined in any norm except the norm of bringing about happiness. In chapter 1, we saw this contrast between Kantian and utilitarian approaches in the different perspectives on the importance of promise keeping. For Christians, these questions are especially important since the Christian gospel is summed up in terms of love, and no ethics can be called Christian that is not based on love of neighbor. Not surprisingly, then, the relationship between love and moral norms is a major concern of the Bible and Christian tradition. The importance of this subject calls for a careful look at some of the key areas of scripture.

Christian Love and Moral Norms

Love and the Law in the Faith of Israel

In the Bible, the relationship between love and moral norms is expressed in terms of the relationship between love and *law*, especially the traditional Law of the Jews contained in the Torah or "teaching," the first five books of the Bible. (*Moral norms* were not distinguished from *legal norms* since in ancient societies morality and legality were one, in contrast to modern, pluralist societies where moral and legal norms need to be carefully distinguished.) The Torah proclaims the integral relationship between covenant and law, the gifts of God and the response of human freedom. As we saw in chapter 3, the ancient Israelites understood obedience to the Law as a response to the gift of the covenant, the relationship with the living and liberating God (Ps 1). The development of the faith of Israel shows profound reflection on the meaning of law as an expression of the moral life lived in the sight of God.

The Ten Commandments

The discussion of covenant in chapter 3 noted that the faith of ancient Israel can be described as an ethical monotheism, a faith in one personal and liberating God, fidelity to whom is demonstrated by commitment to the moral life. Nowhere is this more evident than in the most well-known element of the Law, the Ten Commandments, or *Decalogue* (from the Greek for "ten" and "word"). Some of the Ten Commandments show strong affinities to the moral laws of other ancient cultures and may well have been derived from their influence. What is unique to Israel is the union of the moral life with a profound sense of the holiness of God, a union that bears witness to the influence of Moses, the first and greatest of the prophets.

The Ten Commandments are stated in slightly different versions at two points in the Old Testament: Exodus 20:1–17 and Deuteronomy 5:6–21. In each case, they are introduced by the words "I am the LORD your God, who brought you out of the land of Egypt, out of the house of slavery" (Exod 20:2, Deut 5:6). These words put the commandments in a covenantal context, emphasizing that fidelity to them is a response to the Lord's gift of freedom. The commandments probably developed as a separate unit of oral tradition and were subsequently juxtaposed with this covenantal text by the priestly editors of the scriptures in order to express their conviction of the union of covenant and law. The compact, emphatic, and repetitive style of the commandments lent itself to memorization and recitation, and the text of the commandments was probably used in liturgical services celebrating the covenant with the Lord (Ps 50).

The first three commandments express religious obligations. The first commandment forbids idolatry, the worship of any part of the creation in place of God. Although idolatry is a religious act, an

168

act of worship, it has crucial implications for ethics. If—as was argued in chapter 4—the logical conclusion of sin is idolatry, then the commandment against idolatry is a commandment that sums up the meaning of the moral life: to worship God and to value the world, including my own self, as the creation of God rather than as a vain substitute for God. The link between the first commandment and the values that express our real priorities in life was summed up with concise insight by Martin Luther in his *Large Catechism:* "The confidence and faith of the heart alone make both God and an idol" (III, par. 1).

The second commandment forbids any manipulation of the divine in magic and curses; it emphasizes that the power of God cannot be used to serve secular purposes, nor to drive fear into the hearts of others. The third commandment, concerning the Sabbath, expresses two related values, given different emphasis in the two versions. In Exodus, the Sabbath is expressed in terms of religious worship, the necessity of balancing everyday work with worship of God (20:8–11). In Deuteronomy, the Sabbath is related to rest from labor, rest that must be granted to slaves and animals as well (5:12–15). The Sabbath, then, is a day of both rest and worship, a day of restoration and recollection. It gives shape and focus to the rhythm of human activity.

The remaining commandments relate specifically to ethical goods, aspects of human relationships. Put in modern language, they emphasize the importance of fundamental dimensions of human dignity. They mark out the moral bounds of community life, the respect for the good of others that is the minimum requirement of love.

The Book of Deuteronomy

We have noted that the Ten Commandments are presented in two versions. In Exodus, the commandments are set in the context of the dramatic narrative of the liberation from Egypt and the covenant of Mount Sinai. In Deuteronomy, they are given a new and more reflective context. The book of Deuteronomy was developed during the seventh century BC at a time of crisis in Israel's history, a time when the threat of foreign invasion and the annihilation of state and people was intense. In light of those challenges, Deuteronomy reflects on and restates the meaning of covenant and law—hence its title *Deuteronomos,* Greek for "the second law."

In the book of Deuteronomy, we see that the ancient Israelite conception of law did include an element of sheer obedience to overwhelming authority, but at the same time it had also achieved an insight into the meaning of moral law as the means for the fulfillment of human goods. Sometimes we find the reason why the law should be obeyed stated in terms like these: "The LORD your God you shall fear; him you shall serve, and by his name alone you shall swear. Do not follow other gods, any of the gods of the peoples who are all around you, because the LORD your God, who is present with you, is a jealous God. The anger of the LORD your God would be kindled against you and he would destroy you from the face of the earth" (Deut 6:13–15). Disobedience, then, is met with terrible divine punishment, and fear of this punishment is inspired as a motivation to obey. Other passages, however, emphasize that the reason why the law should be obeyed is because it will lead to human fulfillment: "Keep his statutes and his commandments, which I am commanding you today for your own well-being and that of your descendants after you, so that you may long remain in the land that the LORD your God is giving you for all time" (4:40).

The fundamental message of the book of Deuteronomy is that the Lord loves his people and desires their life and happiness. It reminds the Israelites that they owe their existence as a people to the love of God calling them out of slavery, and it evokes for them the uniqueness of their history (4:32–40). It paints a picture of the abundance and prosperity that follow from obedience to the law (6:12–15). An important purpose of the Sabbath day is rest from labor, and this rest must also be given to slaves and foreigners: "Remember that you were a slave in the land of Egypt, and the LORD your God brought you out from there with a mighty hand and an outstretched arm" (5:15). Sympathy for others through imaginative identification with their lot is a motive for obedience to the

Sabbath law. The choice for or against obedience to the law is a choice between life and death, because what the law commands is life-giving and what it forbids is the path to destruction (30:15–20). The greatest commandment of the Law is the love of God, a love that calls on all the resources of the human person since only love is a fitting response to love (6:4–9).

The Two Great Commandments

The law of ancient Israel was a developing and complex reality, covering all aspects of religious, moral, and civil life. Part of this development was the insight that an obedience worthy of the covenantal relationship with the Lord could not be purely external; it must be an obedience of conscience, an obedience that expressed the moral person's desire to fulfill the will of God. As we saw in the discussion of conscience in chapter 3, this insight was characteristic of the prophetic movement, especially of the prophet Jeremiah (Jer 31:33–34). The development of the Law led also to the questions whether some laws were more important than others, and whether the meaning of the Law could be expressed in a few great commandments. As we have seen, the book of Deuteronomy gives first place to the commandment to love God. By the time of Jesus, leading Jewish rabbis summed up the Law in two great commandments, love of God (Deut 6:4–9) and love of neighbor (Lev 19:18). Here are both passages:

> Hear, O Israel: The LORD is our God, the LORD alone. You shall love the LORD your God with all your heart, and with all your soul, and with all your might. Keep these words that I am commanding you today in your heart. Recite them to your children and talk about them when you are at home and when you are away, when you lie down and when you rise. Bind them as a sign on your hand, fix them as an emblem on your forehead, and write them on the doorposts of your house and on your gates. (Deut 6:4–9)

171

You shall not hate in your heart anyone of your kin; you shall reprove your neighbor, or you will incur guilt yourself. You shall not take vengeance or bear a grudge against any of your people, but you shall love your neighbor as yourself: I am the LORD. (Lev 19:17–18)

A story about the great rabbi Hillel has it that when he was challenged to recite the Law standing on one leg, he easily did so by reciting these two great commandments, concluding with the judgment "all the rest is commentary."

Different schools of thought within Judaism also debated the question of the changeability and adaptability of the Law. For the priestly class, the Sadducees, the Law could not be changed in either its religious or moral aspects. They therefore rejected the doctrine of the resurrection of the dead since this was not directly stated in the Torah and affirmed a particularly strict attitude on the ban on Sabbath work. The Pharisees, members of a lay movement that was much closer to the common people, were open to the development of religious teaching and also attempted to interpret the Law in ways which would be accessible and practicable for ordinary people. Rather than simply banning all forms of human exertion on the Sabbath, they attempted to formulate a list of prohibited activities so that people of humble and despised pursuits could be assisted to know and live by the Law. By their own exemplary obedience to the Law, the Pharisees sought to atone for the sins of Israel and prepare for the coming of the Messiah.

The Teaching of Jesus in the Sermon on the Mount

The teaching of Jesus radicalized those tendencies that saw true obedience to the Law as inspired by an informed conscience, and that summed up the Law in terms of its purpose and values. On the basis of his own experience of the love of the Father, Jesus approached the traditional Law with great respect but at the same time with sovereign freedom. He affirms the expression of the Law in terms of the two great commandments (Mark 12:28–34; Luke

10:25–29). He respects the sacred value of the Sabbath day, but insists that its meaning should not be understood in a way which runs contrary to urgent human need (Mark 2:23–28; Luke 6:6–10). The Law's concern for ritual cleanliness is rejected by Jesus in favor of inner cleanliness of the heart (Mark 7:18–21). And in Jesus' teaching on divorce, he argues that a law that allows a man to divorce a woman does not express the fullness of the union in equality between man and woman in the story of creation (Mark 10:1–12).

Jesus did not reject the Law itself, since it was the sacred bond between God and Israel. It was the religious tradition that had nourished the experience of the love of the Father, which was the essence of his own ministry. The gospels give ample evidence that Jesus identified with the religious traditions of his own people; he is steeped in the scriptures and celebrates the feasts with his disciples. The gospels also portray Jesus' respect for the Law in relation to his own ministry. For example, when Jesus heals a leper, he instructs him to show himself to the priest so that he can be declared clean and so he can offer sacrifice for his healing in accordance with the Law (Mark 1:44; cf. Lev 14).

Like the prophets, however, and like other great Jewish teachers, Jesus criticized a certain attitude to the Law. Legalism is an attitude that displaces law from its proper role as the guardian of moral values and makes it the sole and literal criterion of right action. For Jesus, obedience to the will of the Father was not obedience to a set of laws but rather faithfulness to a relationship; the gift of the kingdom demanded the response of the whole person. The inherent weakness of legalism is its incompleteness and externality. A law, by its nature, is limited since it requires or forbids specific actions. The temptation of legalism is to observe the law where the law is explicit and to ignore the spirit of the law where the law is silent. Further, a law is concerned with observable obedience, not with internal response and attitude. Obedience to a law is necessarily limited obedience since a law can only demand a specific action. Legalism therefore encourages self-righteousness since a person who sees the law as self-sufficient will then be convinced that obedience to the letter of the law is all that can be expected of him.

Jesus' rejection of legalistic interpretations of the traditional Law emphasized both the interior aspect of true obedience and its unlimited scope. Legalism represented a reduction of obedience to specific actions and external behavior. For Jesus, however, in continuity with the prophetic tradition, the source of obedience was "the heart"—in modern language, personal conscience. Only a conscience sincerely committed to fulfilling the meaning and intention of the Law could be said to be rendering obedience to God.

In the Sermon on the Mount, Jesus radicalized the demands of the Law by emphasizing the origin of sin in thoughts and intentions; gross acts of wrongdoing have their source in the heart's malice, self-centeredness, and contempt for others (Matt 5—7). The obedient heart cannot rest content with fulfilling the specific actions demanded by the letter of the law; it seeks to fulfill the intention of the law by enacting the spirit of the ancient commandment to "love thy neighbor as yourself" (Lev 19:18). Jesus' rejection of all legalistic self-satisfaction is expressed against the background of the social conditions of the time in a typically apt and challenging parable:

> "Who among you would say to your slave who has just come in from plowing or tending sheep in the field, 'Come here at once and take your place at the table'? Would you not rather say to him, 'Prepare supper for me, put on your apron and serve me while I eat and drink; later you may eat and drink'? Do you thank the slave for doing what was commanded? So you also, when you have done all that you were ordered to do, say, 'We are worthless slaves; we have done only what we ought to have done!'" (Luke 17:7–10)

The two great commandments, then, expressed the essence of the Law. In Jesus' teaching, a fitting response to the gift of the kingdom is summed up in obedience to these commandments. The meaning of love of neighbor cannot be summed up in any set of laws since any legal expression of it would restrict its scope. In his teaching on the meaning of love of neighbor, Jesus describes a way of life that constantly transcends the limits of our willingness to give, to reconcile, and to care (Luke 6:27–42). The extent of love of neighbor must be defined by the extent of the neighbor's needs, rather than by a code of limited and defined responsibility for our neighbor. Jesus' answer to the question "Who is my neighbor?" (Luke 10:29) made clear that the neighbor is anyone in need of help. The concept of neighbor cannot be defined in any terms that restrict concern to any group and thereby excludes others, even one's enemies.

For Jesus, such a radical concept of love of neighbor was the only response worthy of the kingdom because it was a response that attempted to imitate the universal and indiscriminate quality of the love of God. Only a love of neighbor that extends to all can emulate the love of the Father who "makes his sun rise on the evil and on the good, and sends rain on the righteous and on the unrighteous" (Matt 5:45). Love of neighbor, then, is a love that can give without expecting or depending on a response. It is a love that seeks the good of others, and that will not fail for lack of acknowledgement. Love of neighbor, in this sense, is different from love of personal friends and "loved ones." Personal friendship and sexual love are based on reciprocity and mutuality. They enrich and affirm the individual person's sense of being cherished for their own uniqueness. They involve both giving and receiving. "Love of neighbor," in contrast, is a concern directed to all purely for the sake of the needs of the other, someone with whom I may have no personal relationship.

How can someone be capable of this love? How can we give without response? This question touches on the essence of the teaching of Jesus, which always situates our love for others in the context of the Father's prior love for us. A love that gives without response is in danger of exhaustion and resentment. Only those who know themselves to be truly and securely loved will be able to give to this extent. The teaching of Jesus is an affirmation of our blessedness, of the

Father's love for us: it makes no demands without first offering the conditions for their fulfillment. For Jesus, those who have faith in the blessings of the Father, who know themselves to be cared for, will be capable of giving with the Father's generosity (Luke 12:22–34). Those who know themselves to be worth loving will be able to give a love worth giving. To love one's neighbor as oneself is to love in the security of being loved.

The Letters of Paul

Apart from the gospels, the most important Christian teaching on the relationship between love and law is contained in the letters of Paul. After his own conversion to the Christian faith, Paul proclaimed salvation for all nations through the death and resurrection of Jesus. Paul's sense of identity as an apostle was rooted in his conviction that, though he was himself a Jew, he was called by the risen Christ to proclaim salvation to the Gentiles, the non-Jews. The relationship between the Jewish Law and Christian life was thus a central concern of many of his writings.

For Paul, the Jewish Law had its immeasurable value and significance as a response to the blessings of God in the history of Israel. The Law was "holy and just and good" (Rom 7:12) because it was the authentic response of the chosen people to the covenant freely given them by God. It had been a unique path to salvation for the people of Israel, and it was from this people that the Savior of the world had come. But this Law—the Law of Moses—was an expression of the particular religious, moral, and liturgical tradition of the Jews. The life, death, and resurrection of Jesus had created a new and different situation: in Jesus, God had reconciled himself with the whole world. The salvation offered to the Jews—an offer which God would never revoke (Rom 9–11)—was now offered to all nations. All nations could know and love God in Christ according to their own ways and culture. For Paul, this meant that the Gentiles, people of non-Jewish religion and culture, did not need to become Jews in order to become Christians. Christian identity was to be marked out by baptism and Eucharist, rather than by circumcision.

The Jewish Law in all its liturgical and ritual particularity need not apply to Gentiles.

The gospel that Paul preached, then, proclaimed salvation in Christ while freeing the Gentiles from the specific obligations of the Mosaic Law, symbolized by the ritual of circumcision. The new Gentile Christians need not live according to the ancient Jewish traditions. (During the early decades of the history of the Church, Christians of Jewish origin, including Paul himself, tended to continue living according to Jewish tradition.) But if the Jewish Law did not apply to Gentile Christians, what would their moral life consist of? If they were freed from the obligations of traditional Jewish law, were they thereby freed from all law? The Jews had responded to the blessings of the Sinai covenant by living in fidelity to the Law of Moses. How would Christians respond to God's gift of salvation in Jesus? What would be the sources and substance of the moral life of Christians?

Paul found that his gospel of freedom was both rejected and misunderstood. It was rejected by those who insisted that the traditional religious culture of the Jews should also be imposed on Gentile Christians. Rather than attempt to develop an understanding of the moral life that could apply to Christians of all cultures, many opponents of Paul argued that one legal tradition should be normative for all. It was misunderstood by those who interpreted his gospel of freedom as an abolition of all moral norms, by those who understood freedom from Jewish Law as freedom from moral obligation as such. Some came to the conclusion that if they were saved in Christ, then they were above morality—they no longer had any need for it.

Paul's answer to this misunderstanding of the gospel of freedom was to insist that, although the detailed obligations of the Jewish Law did not apply to Gentiles, the fundamental moral values that inspired the Mosaic Law remained of central importance for all Christians. The Law was not crucial to the *religious* identity of Christians, since that identity was founded in the paschal mystery of Jesus of Nazareth (whose life and teaching could only be understood in the context of the faith of Israel); but this did not mean that the fundamental ethical content of the Law was rendered irrelevant. Christians were free to express this *ethical* content in new ways, and they need not give any particular code of laws a special sacred status, but they must remain faithful to the insights that were the hallmark of the Jewish ethical tradition. One expression of this was to be the importance of the Ten Commandments in the history of Christianity.

For Paul, as a disciple of Jesus, it was the value of love that could sum up the moral life best of all. Jewish tradition had put the commandment to "love one's neighbor as oneself" in high relief, and it had been the foundation of the moral teaching of Jesus. For Paul, the only fitting response to the saving love of God, revealed in Jesus, was a love of neighbor inspired by the teaching and example of Jesus himself. In his teaching on the meaning of love, Paul showed that to live by love was a higher and more demanding task than any set of laws. Love was not merely a generalized sentiment, but a commitment of attitude and behavior to others in specific and practical ways.

Both the freedom and the demand implicit in Paul's understanding of love and the moral life is evident in the advice he offers the Corinthian Christians on the question of whether they may eat meat that had been offered to idols. The context of this particular moral question was the sacrifice of animals to the many and varied deities of the Hellenistic religions. After sacrifice was offered, most of the carcass of the animal was sold in public markets. For Gentiles who had recently become Christians there was a very real fear that consumption of such meat might mean that they were implicitly taking part in worship of the old gods. This fear was particularly acute for those whose family members were still devotees of other religions and so were sharing meals with them.

In the fifteenth chapter of the book of Acts we learn of one of the responses of the early Church to this problem. There, Christians are declared free of the detailed prescriptions of the Jewish Law except for a number of points, including abstention from meat sacrificed to idols (15:29). Clearly, many Christians of Jewish origin felt this was a point that could not allow compromise. For Paul, however, who was also of Jewish tradition, there was no reason in principle why such meat could not be eaten. Since all things in this world were the creation of a good God, and since the meat was not polluted by being sacrificed to deities who did not exist, there was nothing wrong with the meat in itself. Christians were free to eat it. This freedom must, however, be exercised with sensitivity. Love of neighbor means that I will consider my neighbor's conscience and avoid doing something that could be a source of scandal. A Christian might be robust in his conviction that meat offered to an idol presents no problem in principle. But if he is aware that eating it in the presence of someone whose Christian identity is still fragile might offend that person's conscience, then he should refrain from eating it. The fact that we are free to do something does not mean that we should do it if the demands of love of neighbor are otherwise (1 Cor 8, 10:23–33).

In the thirteenth chapter of the same letter, Paul wrote a hymn to love that can be compared only with the Sermon on the Mount in the depth and power of its evocation of love's meaning. Greek literature had placed great emphasis on *eros*, the love of desire, and *phile*, the love of friendship. The word *agape* had had little significance in Greek literature until it was taken up by Greek-speaking Jews in their translation of the scriptures into Greek. Paul gives it pride of place in the proclamation of the Christian gospel. *Agape*, which was translated into Latin as *caritas* (hence the English "charity"), is the love that reflects the indiscriminate love of God, the love that can give without expecting a response. In the Sermon on the Mount, Jesus talks of love of neighbor by describing the lengths love will go to in order to help someone in need. In his hymn to *agape*, Paul personifies it and gives it all the virtues that make up the portrait of someone truly dedicated to serving what is good.

> If I speak in the tongues of mortals and of angels, but do
> not have love, I am a noisy gong or a clanging cymbal. And
> if I have prophetic powers, and understand all mysteries
> and all knowledge, and if I have all faith, so as to remove

179

mountains, but do not have love, I am nothing. If I give away all my possessions, and if I hand over my body so that I may boast, but do not have love, I gain nothing.

Love is patient; love is kind; love is not envious or boastful or arrogant or rude. It does not insist on its own way; it is not irritable or resentful; it does not rejoice in wrongdoing, but rejoices in the truth. It bears all things, believes all things, hopes all things, endures all things. (1 Cor 13:1–7)

Love, Justice, and Moral Norms

This consideration of the relationship between law and love in the Bible indicates that the relationship between love and moral norms is characterized by both harmony and tension. The harmony between norms and love is based on the fact that the purpose of norms is to guide love in doing good, to indicate what the true needs of our neighbor are, and to remind us of our obligation to assist in their fulfillment. Norms give love guidance and direction, helping it to focus on what is really at stake. The tension between love and norms is evident in that the guidance they seek to give can become irrelevant and restrictive, ceasing to be guidance and becoming rigid and stifling, an obstacle to the fulfillment of love's desire to do good.

The teaching of the Bible does not resolve this relationship of harmony and tension. It highlights both the supreme value of love as the summation of the ethical life, and the importance of the fundamental goods of creation, which moral norms should identify and safeguard. An ethics informed by the Bible will resist both the reduction of the meaning of love to a set of norms and an interpretation of love that claims no need for the guidance that norms can provide.

The relationship between love and moral norms can be expressed in terms of the relationship between love and justice. An ancient definition says that justice means "to give each his own."

Justice means to give due recognition to what is good, to treat things according to their value. In particular, justice means to recognize the good of human dignity and the rights that are relevant to it. To act with justice is to respect and cherish the rights of those who are affected by our actions. The purpose of moral norms is to identify those rights, to guide us in respect for them, and to prohibit actions that ignore them.

Love is a commitment of our self to others, a commitment which recognizes and affirms the value of others, seeking to understand their needs and situations and acting for their good. It is a commitment of internal motivation, which gives our external actions a particular quality of care and responsiveness. If justice recognizes and protects the good of others, and love is committed to affirming that good, then love and justice can support each other. Further, the norms that express justice can act as concrete expressions of the meaning of love. A justice without love might be simply a matter of obedience to a set of regulations: a justice not tempered by mercy. A love without justice might be a love that is blind to the goods of the real world. The norms that seek to express the meaning of justice can never be fully adequate to express the quality of committed love, just as a love that ignores the guidance of norms can harm the goods to which those norms draw attention. Because love is a quality of the moral *subject*, it needs guidance about its *object*, the moral world. Because it is a quality of the moral subject, it must be characterized by *freedom* so that its full scope and intensity cannot be externally defined.

The Servant Functions of Moral Norms

The purpose of moral norms, then, is to indicate those actions which will in fact respect and enhance the good, especially the good of persons. Norms serve the moral life by mediating between loving intentions and the complex world of interrelating goods.

Norms can serve the moral life in the followings ways:

- *They express the force of fundamental and inalienable rights,* such as the right of an innocent person to life.
- *They express the accumulated moral experience of humanity.* Consider the norm, characteristic of the Christian and many other ethical traditions, that sexual intercourse should take place within the mutually committed context of marriage. This norm expresses the human experience that sexual intercourse outside marriage is intrinsically unsatisfying because it lacks commitment. If sexual intercourse is to be a genuine mutual exchange, rather than a purely genital act, then it involves the vulnerability of giving. To give oneself to another at this level, without any commitment to fidelity, is to risk grave hurt. The norm that restricts sexual intercourse to the committed context of marriage seeks to express that experience and to make the wisdom which is the fruit of experience available to later generations.
- *They guide individuals in complex and unfamiliar situations.* In situations when we may be unable to untangle the web of different factors, moral norms can represent the present state of moral wisdom. They can help us to act while we devise more sophisticated norms that apply more precisely to given situations. An example of this is the relation between moral norms and the developing fields of medical and biotechnology;
- *They help individuals to avoid self-deception.* Sticking to the norm of truth-telling, for example, may help us avoid the self-deception that might be involved when we say, for example, "I do respect this person, but I just won't tell him the truth this time";
- *They give a community a common code of behavior.* This applies in particular to legal norms. Common norms play a crucial role in making a just and stable community life possible so that "justice is done and seen to be done."

The Role of Norms and Consequences

We have seen that the fundamental ethical good is human dignity, expressed in terms of the basic rights of the person, and that the purpose of norms is to serve this good. Norms describe certain actions that embody respect for others, actions which serve the good. The norm "tell the truth," for example, obliges us to communicate the truth to others since such communication respects others' right to know. Yet we are all aware of situations when telling the truth, revealing all the facts, can cause a great deal of harm, and one of those situations was discussed earlier in this chapter. In discussing that situation, we noted that the norm of truth-telling could not be considered to apply to that situation in a literal sense since those asking the question had no right to the truth. Because telling them the truth would have had massively destructive *consequences*—the killing of many innocent children—the norm of truth-telling was subordinated to the norm of protection of innocent life.

This raises the very important question of the general relationship between *norms* and *consequences* in moral action. Are moral actions those actions that are in accord with right norms or rather those actions that have the best possible consequences? We saw in chapter 1 that this debate has been very important in the history of ethics. While Kant and his followers insisted that moral action was action in accordance with universal norms or principles of freedom and reason, the utilitarians argued that the whole purpose of morality was to maximize human happiness, and therefore positive consequences were what moral action is all about. In chapter 5, we developed an approach to human dignity emphasizing its expression in terms of various rights that implied prohibitions and obligations. This approach reflects a central emphasis on Kant's moral philosophy, that is, his emphasis on the human person as characterized by an inalienable dignity, an emphasis expressed in his principle that we should never treat others purely as means to an end. Concretely, when we relate to others with our own purposes in mind, we must always respect their own rights as well.

183

A critical question that the utilitarian tradition poses to an understanding of ethics in terms of rights is whether or not rights can be overridden for the sake of bringing about good consequences. I have, for example, a right to freedom of speech. But if exercising my freedom of speech by telling malicious lies damages the reputation of others, then it can be overridden. I have a right to own property, but if my accumulation of property threatens the livelihood of multitudes of people, my rights as an owner can be overridden. But if rights can be overridden, should we talk of morality in terms of rights at all, or should we rather understand morality as the attempt to maximize good consequences for as many people as possible? Is an action good or bad because it respects or ignores rights, or rather because it does or does not lead to good consequences?

Context and Intention

In order to answer these questions we must first emphasize the importance of putting moral actions into their *context*. We cannot know the moral meaning of an action when we consider it in isolation from the context of circumstances that are associated with it. For example, we see someone breaking a window and jump to the conclusion that a burglar is breaking into a home. In fact, it is the householder who has lost his keys and must get in immediately because he can hear the fire alarm. The action of someone breaking a window is in itself morally neutral; we can only know whether it is a morally good or bad action when we know something about its context.

A part of that context is the *intention* of the person doing the action. The burglar's intention is to steal goods from the home—a morally bad action. The householder's intention is to save his home from fire—a morally good action. The intention informing an action indicates the context in which it should be considered. That does not mean, however, that good intention will always make an action good. As we have seen, we must distinguish between the subjective sincerity of the moral agent and the objective moral quality of the

184

action. Someone can be of sincerely good intention, but still be engaged in morally bad action. For example, a terrorist may act with good subjective intention because he believes in the ideology of the cause that he serves. He acts for the sake of purposes that he believes are good, such as the independence of an ethnic minority group. Yet his actions are morally wrong because the means that he uses are evil. A good subjective intention is in itself no sure indication of the good or bad quality of an action, since the premises on which the intention is based may be quite mistaken. The intention of the action must, therefore, be considered in light of the wider objective context.[3]

Consequences and Rights

Context, then, is crucial to understanding the meaning of a moral action. But what part do consequences play in forming the context and deciding the meaning of moral actions? Consequences are clearly an important part of that context. One of the primary purposes of moral action is to bring about good consequences. As we have seen, the intention of bringing about good consequences is sufficient to override some rights. This might suggest that understanding ethics in terms of respecting rights should give way to understanding a moral action in terms of intending to bring about good consequences. Yet if we consider cases where rights are overridden for the sake of good consequences, we can observe that these consequences involve the preservation of more fundamental rights. The fact that a right is overridden does not mean that we should cease thinking in terms of rights at all, but rather that we are aware of the relationship of rights to each other and to the good of the human person.

This relationship between rights was noted in chapter 5. In wartime, for example, censorship may be applied for the sake of the

---

3. The traditional term for this combination of factors in appraising an action is the *three font principle*. The objective character of the action, the intention of the agent, and the circumstances or context are the three "fonts" or "sources" of the action.

survival of a nation's population in the face of dire threat. The right to freedom of public information is overridden by the right to life, provided that the context of this suspension of freedom includes an intention to restore it as soon as it is safe to do so. Human beings have a right to freedom of movement, but this right can be forfeited, if there is good reason to think that a person's freedom of movement may gravely threaten the safety of others. The act of imprisoning a human being may be morally right, if it is for the sake of the fundamental right of others to physical security.

In most contexts, then, acting to respect rights and to bring about the best consequences can be in harmony. Some rights can be overridden if the consequences are that the basic rights of others are thereby protected. The point of moral action is to respect and fulfill the good or dignity of human persons. In most cases, by respecting the rights of others, we also do good for as many people as possible.

Let us consider the institution of promise-keeping. By keeping a promise, we respect the rights of those to whom we made the promise. If we freely promise something to someone, they have made an act of trust in us, an act which obliges respect for that trust. By respecting that trust, we respect the rights of our partner in this relationship of promise. But we also bring about good consequences for others. We contribute to the maintenance of the extremely useful institution of promise-keeping. If people can trust each other's word, then everyone can benefit from a climate of trust. In many spheres of life, whether in personal or business relationships, a well-grounded confidence in the promises of others contributes to the ease and stability of human agreements. The alternative is a climate of suspicion and of constant insistence on legal guarantees and sanctions.

Respect for rights, in this case the right to have trustworthy relationships, brings about the best consequences for all. Actions that respect the rights of individuals will also contribute to the good of all because they contribute to a moral climate in which the good of all can flourish.

Respect for individual rights, then, and concern for the good consequences of our actions are generally in harmony. Usually neither form of moral thinking need give way to the other. Yet situations arise where they can clash, and these situations mark out the difference between an ethics based on rights and an ethics based on a concern for consequences. We have seen that some rights can be overridden for the sake of respect for the more basic rights of others. But if we are committed to respect for persons, we cannot override the most basic rights of a person because of an intention to bring about good consequences for many others. In chapter 5, we noted that there are some actions, such as judicial murder, torture, sexual assault, and brainwashing, that are direct attacks on the dignity of persons. Are there situations where such actions could be justified if good consequences for many people might result?

The following example is often considered in discussing this ethical issue: A judge in a small town is faced with the choice of sentencing an innocent man to death or risking a murderous riot in which many people will be killed. What is the relationship between rights and consequences here? By killing an innocent man, we are making a direct attack on his most basic rights. Yet if we do not do so in this case, we have every reason to think that many other innocent human beings will be killed, including the wrongly accused man himself. Normally there would be a powerful argument, on utilitarian grounds, that if the judge's decision to hang an innocent man were to become known, the public knowledge of this deliberate, although benevolent, miscarriage of justice would undermine the institutions of justice in such a serious way that the original purpose of avoiding the deaths of many innocent people could no longer be considered equally weighty. Purely from the point of view of general consequences, then, he should not be sentenced to death. Yet we can, without much difficulty, imagine situations where such a decision could be kept secret, where essential evidence might be known only to the judge himself, or a completely trustworthy confidant, evidence which would never become public knowledge.

It could also be argued that the death by execution of the innocent man is much more certain than the bad consequences it is supposed to prevent, the loss of life of innocent people from the riot that would ensue were he not to be hanged. Since these bad consequences are uncertain and his death certain, utilitarian reasoning might also indicate that he should not be killed. Yet we can easily imagine situations of mob passion, inflamed by demagogues, where a "not guilty" verdict would act as a surefire trigger to dreadful violence, and where those concerned could know this with virtual certainty.

Such cases are, no doubt, relatively rare. In general, actions that respect individual innocent life are also those that have the best consequences in terms of increasing respect for human life as such, or of saving the lives of many innocent people. Yet cases such as this can arise, and their possibility obliges us to focus on a fundamental question of ethics: is it our responsibility to act in a way which respects the worth of individual persons, most fundamentally, the principle of the sanctity of innocent human life, which we believe to be binding on us in all circumstances; or is it rather our responsibility to act in ways which are oriented to maximizing the good for the benefit of as many people as possible, even, if necessary, by deliberately taking innocent human life? For the Christian tradition, if the fundamental ethical good is the good of human persons, then any action that deliberately takes innocent life denies the basis of ethics itself. We may override some rights for the sake of more basic rights, but we cannot override the most basic right of all—the right of an innocent person to life—without destroying what gives ethics its point and purpose.

For the utilitarian, such an approach can be irresponsible since it denies that we sometimes have it in our power to do a great deal of good for humanity by causing harm to one individual. The premise of utilitarianism is that there are no overriding principles of action except general benevolence: to seek the greatest good for the greatest number of people. From this point of view, there is no reason why individual human life has a value that can never be overridden for the sake of the great good that may come to many people. This is especially true if, as in the example discussed above, the innocent man himself would be highly likely to die anyway in the ensuing chaos. For the utilitarian, human beings have a responsibility to act in a way which will be best for their fellow men and women. They are responsible for the consequences of their actions, and therefore for acting in a way which will bring about the best consequences. To deny this by insisting on nonnegotiable principles such as the sanctity of innocent human life is to deny human responsibility for the future.

Yet to observe the principle of the sanctity of innocent human life is not to deny our responsibility for the future of humanity, but rather to argue that our responsibility cannot be exercised in a way which deliberately ignores the most basic ethical goods, since if we ignore these goods we lose a fundamental sense of what the moral life is about. Our responsibility is precisely to human persons, because the meaning of a moral action is an action that is informed by respect for persons. Any action that destroys an innocent person destroys morality itself because morality has its roots in respect for the fundamental created good of human life. If our responsibility to respect this good in our own actions is denied, then our moral life loses its orientation to what gives it its overriding importance in defining the quality of our humanity.

The Principle of Double Effect

The meaning of morality, then, is to act responsibly in relation to the human good that I encounter. I am responsible for what I intend, for what I wish to happen as a result of my actions. Sometimes, however, I may act in ways which also have consequences that I do not intend. Am I equally responsible for these consequences of my actions? Is there a real distinction between my responsibility for what I intend and for the unintended, although perhaps foreseen, consequences of my actions? If it is always wrong to deliberately (intentionally) take innocent human life, is it possible to countenance the taking of human life as an unintended, although foreseen, consequence of my action?

In response to these questions, the Catholic tradition in ethics has developed what is called "the principle of double effect," a principle that attempts to reconcile our best efforts to save life with respect for the inviolability of innocent human life. The principle of double effect states that an action with an unwanted and unintended evil effect may be morally permissible if the following four conditions are met:

(a) the action is itself good, or at least morally neutral;
(b) the evil effect follows or is simultaneous with the good effect;
(c) the evil effect is not directly intended; and
(d) there is a good reason for the action as a whole: the good effect outweighs the bad effect.

Condition (a) lays down that the action itself, with its direct and intended effect, should be morally unobjectionable. Condition (b) requires that the evil effect may not be the first and direct effect of my action since otherwise I would in fact intend the evil effect by using it as a means. Rather the direct effect of my action must be good, although it may have evil and unintended indirect effects. Condition (c) emphasizes the link between responsibility and intention: if I intend the evil effect then I am morally responsible for it. Condition (d) emphasizes that the quality of the good effect must be such as to justify the occurrence of the evil but unintended effects, that is, that there must be a *proportionate reason* for the action as a whole.

The most well-known example for the principle of double effect is the removal of a cancerous uterus from a pregnant mother, as a result of which the fetus dies. In harmony with condition (a), the removal of the cancerous uterus is in itself good since it is intended to save the life of the mother. In accordance with condition (b), the fetus is not killed as a prerequisite for the removal of the uterus; rather the removal of the uterus leads to the death of the fetus.

Following condition (c), the death of the fetus is not intended but is the unintended consequence of the removal of the uterus. Finally, in relation to condition (d), the action as a whole is justified since the cancerous condition of the uterus would have caused the death of the fetus in any case, and the mother's life is saved by the operation.

Contemporary critique of the principle of double effect has focused on the relationship between condition (a) and condition (d). Condition (a) assumes that we can know whether or not our action is a good, or at least morally unobjectionable, action independently of condition (d), which assesses whether or not the overall effect of the action, taking both good and bad effects into account, is good. In other words, the principle of double effect is based on the assumption that the goodness or badness of an action can be determined apart from its consequences. This principle was developed against the background of a theory of ethics that put considerable emphasis on acts that were evil in themselves, regardless of consequences. Deliberately telling an untruth, for example, was often held to be evil in itself, regardless of the consequences for human welfare.

In our discussion of rights, we have seen that there are many actions that do override or limit certain rights for the sake of good consequences in terms of more fundamental rights. Truth-telling, for example, is related to a right to know, which is not unlimited; the rights and wrongs of truth-telling must be considered in the context of the right to know, which is affected by the fundamental rights of all those involved. So if we are asked whether a particular case of truth-telling or suppression of the facts is right or wrong in itself, as condition (a) of the principle of double effect asks us to do, we cannot give an answer without considering condition (d), the relationship of our telling the truth, imparting relevant information, to the consequences that it may well have for the rights of others. In many cases, then, the answer to condition (a) can only be given by assessing condition (d). For the great majority of actions, then, the principle of double effect is no longer relevant in its traditional form.

If, however, there are actions that are always wrong in themselves, because they represent a direct and deliberate attack on the core dimensions of human dignity, then the principle of double effect retains its relevance, because in these cases condition (a) is asking something that is important and that is different from the answer to condition (d), because it is asking whether the action in question is an action that is wrong in itself. We have seen that the taking of innocent life is one such action. We cannot deliberately and directly take innocent human life, but it may be the unintended and indirect result of our actions, actions that are oriented to saving life and relieving pain. A doctor, for example, may administer a pain-killing drug, aware that it may have the unintended effect of suppressing vital functions. For situations such as these, the principle of double effect retains its relevance as a way of guiding responsible human action that is inspired both by respect for human life and by the benevolent desire to reduce human suffering.

Love and Self-Sacrifice

We should not conclude a chapter entitled "Love, Rights, and Moral Norms" without reflecting on the meaning of actions that express love, but that cannot be expressed in norms and that seem to represent the voluntary abandonment of rights! Traditional Catholic ethics spoke of "works of supererogation," actions that could not be prescribed by moral norms and that expressed love in ways that were "above and beyond the call of duty." Citing Jesus' parable of the servant referred to earlier ("We have done only what we ought to have done!" Luke 17:7–10). Protestant writers rejected this concept, arguing that we can never exceed the fulfillment of our duties to God. This dispute among Christians centered on the difficulty of developing an understanding of acts of love that have great moral value yet cannot reasonably be expected of everyone, and that therefore cannot be expressed as a moral norm.

Such acts often represent a voluntary sacrifice of one's personal rights. Someone might, for example, forego a prosperous career in order to offer professional services to those who need but cannot pay for them and whose place in society is anything but prestigious. The person in question has every right to continue in his or her chosen career but voluntarily relinquishes that right and the benefits attached to it for the sake of others. We cannot legitimately develop a moral norm out of this, to the effect that "Everyone should relinquish his or her right to a career for the sake of the welfare of the most needy," since it is by no means clear that everyone should do this nor how the needy would be assisted if every professional career was abandoned.

Such acts might best be understood in terms of the individual character of our response to the good. We are all bound by the moral norms that express the crucial dimensions of the dignity of persons. These norms define our moral duty. Yet, as we have seen, the extent to which love can respond to the call of goodness cannot be defined by these norms, which are a statement of the minimum respect due to the good. The extent to which we can offer a love that exceeds this minimum, and the way we will do so, is a matter of individual vocation. Some may express an abundance of love for the needy by abandoning a successful career; others demonstrate their love of their fellow human beings by pursuing that career in ways that express a concern for justice, honesty, and generosity. Each must decide on the basis of individual circumstances on what each can give. The gospels do not prescribe what lifestyle our love should be expressed in; they simply ask of us that the love we give will be worthy of the love we have received.

Summary of Chapter 6

1. Moral norms are rules of moral action. They answer the question "What should I do?"—which is different from the questions "What sort of person should I be?" and "What is the good?"

2. Norms are formed by moral reasoning, which is an expression of our freedom and responsibility.

3. A distinction should be made between formal norms, which remind us of the importance of virtues and goods, and material norms, which provide concrete guidance for action.

4. Moral reasoning is of particular importance in resolving a clash of norms by judging the relationships of the goods that they are intended to serve.

5. Moral norms are characterized by historical development, and not all moral norms retain their relevance in new historical and social situations.

6. The purpose of moral norms is to act as a bridge between the virtues of the moral subject and the goods that are in the world.

7. The relationship between love and moral norms is a fundamental concern of biblical ethics. Old Testament ethics gives great importance to the norms that guide the moral life, recorded in the Law of Moses, as well as to the love that inspires and sums up obedience to the Law. The teaching of Jesus is a radical statement of those currents of Jewish ethics that saw true obedience to the Law as inspired by an informed conscience and that summed up the Law in terms of love of God and of neighbor. The epistles of Paul express a critique of all forms of legalism as well as an emphasis on the meaning of Christian freedom as a practical commitment of love for our neighbor. An ethics informed by the Bible will resist both the reduction of the meaning of love to a set of norms and an interpretation of love that claims no need for the guidance that norms can provide.

8. Norms have a number of servant functions:

   - They express the force of fundamental and inalienable rights.
   - They express the accumulated experience of humanity.
   - They guide individuals in complex and unfamiliar situations.
   - They help to avoid self-deception.
   - They give a community a common code of behavior.

9. The meaning of moral actions should be understood in light of their context and of the intention of the agent.

10. The relationship of norms and consequences is a crucial ethical question and is a matter of dispute between the Kantian and utilitarian ethical philosophies. The relationship between norms and consequences should be resolved in terms of the goods and rights involved. Normally, respect for moral norms and concern for consequences will be in harmony. Some rights can be overridden for the sake of achieving the consequence of protecting more fundamental rights. However, the most fundamental rights, such as the right of an innocent person to life, cannot be overridden for the sake of consequences since this would be to override the dignity of the individual person, which is the fundamental ethical good.

11. The principle of double effect attempts to maintain respect both for the principle of never deliberately and directly taking innocent life and for the benevolent desire to reduce human suffering, by making a distinction between direct and indirect, intended and unintended, effects of an action.

12. The ways in which individuals will express love is a matter of personal vocation, and so there are actions—especially acts of self-sacrifice—that cannot be expressed in terms of universal moral norms.

Questions for Discussion

1. Consider the case of the film-censorship board discussed at the beginning of this chapter. Using some specific examples, develop a moral argument in relation to the question of film censorship that would reconcile the goods of freedom and public decency in what you think is an appropriate way.

2. The example quoted from Bernhard Häring suggested that the imperative to tell the truth is linked to authentic communication, related to the right to know the truth. What are situations where there is no "right to know," and what are situations where we may falsely deny someone's "right to know" out of self-interest?

3. If property rights are limited by the right to sustain life, on the principle of the universal destination of created goods, what implications does this have for our lives and the life of our nation?

4. Are there other cases of moral norms that have lost their relevance? Make a list of new moral norms that have become relevant because of social or technological change.

5. What relevance does the first commandment against idolatry have to contemporary moral life? What aspects of human dignity are safeguarded in commandments four to ten?

6. What do you think should be the place of the Ten Commandments in Christian moral education?

7. Read Deuteronomy 4—6. How are the moral life and the covenant with God linked? What motivation is given in these chapters for living the moral life?

8. Read Matthew 5:21–48 (included in the Appendix), an extract from the Sermon on the Mount. In what ways does the Sermon on the Mount proclaim a vision of the moral life that goes beyond law to the prompting and motivations of the heart? What is the meaning of "love of neighbor" for the Sermon on the Mount?

9. Read 1 Corinthians 8 and 10:23–33. How does Paul give *agape* a practical and specific meaning for the Corinthian community?

10. Read 1 Corinthians 13. Consider a moral situation that you are aware of from the media or some other source. How do you think the loving person described by St Paul would act in that situation?

11. Consider the case of the innocent man who may be executed to prevent mob violence. Do you think our responsibility obliges us primarily to refrain from taking innocent life, or rather to act in such a way that our actions have the consequence of saving as many lives as possible?

12. Discuss the contemporary relevance of the principle of double effect, considering some examples other than those presented.

13. Is there such a thing as a morality of personal vocation? Do we have moral obligations that are uniquely our own?

7

The Task of Moral Reasoning

We have seen that moral norms play a crucial role in the moral life by guiding our respect for the good. Moral norms are developed by moral reasoning to do justice to the claims of the good, to express love of neighbor in effective and relevant ways. Because our moral existence is based on reason and freedom, we have the task of reasoning how to respond to the good in the varying circumstances of our history. Moral reasoning is particularly important in modern societies since they are involved in a constant process of change. This chapter will be concerned with that task, the process of moral reasoning. We will consider the basic elements of moral reasoning and apply them to a particular ethical issue.

Before we look at the elements of moral reasoning, however, we should pause to consider two important points: first, the person actually doing the moral reasoning, and second, the purpose of moral reasoning.

A Person of Moral Wisdom

We recall that the question "What sort of person am I?" is a question about character and virtue. The quality of moral reasoning will depend on the character of the person engaged in it. To develop moral norms that are truly responsive to the good of human persons, and that reveal insight into the demands and complexities of moral situations, is an art requiring commitment and dedication. It requires moral wisdom, or *prudence*. While modern philosophy has interpreted prudence as a rational concern for one's own benefit, rather than as a moral virtue, its original meaning in the philosophy of

Aristotle was in terms of practical wisdom. For Aristotle, prudence was the virtue which enables us to discern moral situations and judge them wisely.

The great contribution of the understanding of ethics in terms of virtue is that it gives us a description of persons who can make good moral decisions because they live the moral life well. Kantianism emphasizes the importance of fundamental norms that respect the dignity of the human person. Utilitarianism emphasizes that moral reasoning must be informed by benevolence. An ethic of virtue, however, paints a picture of a person of moral wisdom, someone who is able to make good moral judgments because good judgment and action become part of their own character, a habit which shapes their lives. These are people who will act morally with spontaneity because they know the moral life to be fulfilling. This approach complements the best features of the others; a virtuous person's judging and acting is informed by moral wisdom, respecting the inviolable dignity of the human person, with a benevolence that seeks the best consequences for all concerned.

The best preparation for the task of moral reasoning, then, is a life which has been formed by good moral judgment and action. Although we may well feel that this is more of an ideal than a reality in our own lives, moral reasoning is certainly not the preserve of some kind of moral elite, but something that everyone is called to through their uniquely human gifts of freedom, reason, and conscience.

The Purpose of Moral Reasoning

It was emphasized at the beginning of chapter 6 that the purpose of moral norms is not to answer the questions "What sort of person should I be?" nor "What is the good?" Rather, the purpose of moral norms is to answer "What should I do?" and to develop moral norms that give guidance for action. Because of this, moral reasoning must attempt a conclusion that also answers the question "What should I do?" We have not completed the task of moral reasoning if we simply state what goods are involved in an issue, nor if we simply give a description of a loving person. The task we have is to state what a loving person would do in order to do justice to the goods involved. Moral reasoning, then, must have as its conclusion a norm that could be put into practice. Without this, moral reasoning falls short of the task of providing guidance for the moral life.

This is not to deny that there are many problems arising today that may have no readily apparent solution or that may suggest a number of alternative courses of action. The contemporary debate about organ donation, for example, is characterized by strong arguments for donation because of its lifesaving potential and strong arguments against donation related to the ways in which the death of the donor is defined. In its attempt to develop a norm that can guide action, moral reasoning cannot go beyond the evidence and insight available to it. Yet even in situations of this kind, we need to note the various possible conclusions, judging that responsible moral action could take different paths in the present state of moral debate.

Elements of the Process of Moral Reasoning

1. Definition

Moral reasoning begins with a careful definition of the question to be considered. Without clear definition, we do not know what problem we are tackling, and we can waste our energy by considering a range of issues not really relevant to the problem we originally intended to focus on. If we are considering the moral problem of the distribution of wealth in society, for example, we need to define our terms: Are we considering the ways in which wealth is created, in terms of private or public ownership of the means of production; or are we considering equality of opportunity to have access to wealth by participation in well-paid work; or are we considering the appropriate tax or welfare system for the redistribution of wealth? Moral questions usually involve a range of different issues, which do need to be distinguished from each other in order to be effectively treated.

2. Knowledge

Once we have achieved some clarity about which question we are attempting to answer, we must inform ourselves about it. However loving a person we are, we must know the world in order to act well in it! We cannot develop a relevant moral norm unless we have detailed and specific knowledge of the situations in which this norm is intended to guide us. Moral reasoning draws on the social and natural sciences in order to know the contexts within which the good of human persons must be expressed and fulfilled. Because we live in a society characterized by both technological and social change, the task of acquiring relevant knowledge is a constant one. Medical and bioethics, for example, is that field of moral reasoning which focuses on the good of human persons in relation to constantly developing medical and biotechnology.

3. Empathy

Detailed factual knowledge about moral situations is crucial to the process of moral reasoning, but there is another kind of knowledge that must complement it. We may know the facts of a situation, but our moral reasoning lacks credibility unless it is informed by empathy for those involved; empathy is the knowledge that springs from involvement. Empathy is a crucial element in the process of moral reasoning since without empathy we do not consider the situation with moral seriousness. The word *empathy* derives from the Greek words for *in* and *suffering*—when we empathize, we "suffer in" the situation of others (compassion, a word of similar meaning, derives from the Latin *com-passio*, or *suffering with*). Moral situations are not merely of theoretical interest but involve decisions of conscience. They can only be effectively reasoned about if such reasoning is done on the basis of a commitment of the whole person to understanding and feeling for the moral quality of the situation at hand. Empathy, then, is not merely a particular stage in the moral reasoning process, but is rather the

201

commitment of the moral subject that inspires and energizes the process as a whole.

Art and literature have a special power to arouse our empathy for moral situations. A work of visual art can portray human experiences to us in ways that bring us to new awareness of their meaning, expanding the horizons of our feeling and insight. The countless paintings of the crucifixion of Jesus portray the suffering of one man and can at the same time convey to us the universal pathos of the suffering of the innocent. A good work of literature can reveal to us the meaning of moral situations that we might otherwise be tempted to disregard altogether or to consider only in a detached and distanced way. *The Diary of Anne Frank,* for example, enables us to "suffer in" the situation of a young Jewish girl striving to embrace life in an environment haunted by the fear of extermination, a girl whose story can help us to realize the precious uniqueness of the story of every individual of the millions who suffered her fate. Alexander Solzhenitsyn's novel *One Day in the Life of Ivan Denisovich* portrays the dogged integrity of the life of an ordinary man facing the daily round of privations and obstacles in a Soviet labor camp, a man whose story brings to life for us the story of the countless inhabitants of the Gulag.

Our empathy for contemporary moral situations can also be evoked by photography, by news reports and by the contact we may have with those who are involved. All of these means can bring home to us the human urgency of the situations we are attempting to reason about. It is of great importance that moral empathy truly embrace a situation as a whole, attempting to understand the position of all those involved in a question. A partisan identification with the feelings of only one partner in a moral dispute prevents good moral reasoning, not because it is empathetic but because it is not empathetic enough, selecting only one aspect of the question as worthy of our sympathy. By empathy with the whole of a human situation, we enable our own reasoning to be disinterested without being uninterested, to be impartial without being detached.

4. Tradition

Whoever we are, we do not come to moral questions cold. Whether we are aware of it or not, our moral perspectives have been formed by the culture we live in and by the traditions that have formed that culture. Moral traditions can be of enormous benefit in developing our moral awareness and guiding our moral life, yet they can also narrow our moral horizons and lessen our readiness to appreciate the true meaning of new moral situations. When we approach moral questions, we need to ask ourselves how the traditions that influence us see these questions, both in order to learn from tradition and to criticize its limitations.

An important part of Western cultural tradition, for example, is the notion that diligence, regular hard work, is a virtue. Sociologists of religion have argued that this traditional Western value has its origin in the religious ideas of some Protestant groups in early modern Europe, who understood the call to holiness in their daily lives in terms of thrift and diligence. These ideas led to economic success and achievement and gained great prestige in Western society. They led, however, to painful clashes with the understanding of life characteristic of indigenous peoples in the countries that Western Europeans colonized. Indigenous peoples were often condemned as lazy simply because they did not share a particular cultural attitude to regular daily work. Colonizers often identified their own attitude to daily work as a virtue, rather than realizing that it was a particular attitude to life, involving both benefit and harm. An explicit consciousness that our values are formed by a tradition can help us to learn from that tradition in a more critical and discerning way, distinguishing its permanent value from the prejudices that can accompany it.

As we saw in chapter 2, tradition is of particular importance to Christian ethics since Christian faith itself is a tradition, a tradition based on the community that remembers and celebrates the person of Jesus of Nazareth and attempts to live as his disciples. Since Christians believe that Jesus of Nazareth reveals the creator God of love, they believe that their tradition offers something of value for all humanity. At the same time they must recognize that many individual elements of their tradition need to be subjected to critique and enriched by the insights of other traditions. For all Christians, the Bible is the principal written source of their faith tradition. All Christians also give some role to the teaching tradition of their own church. For Catholics, the role of the teaching tradition of the Church is of particular importance because of the general Catholic understanding of the nature of the Church and of authority within it. How, then, is the Christian tradition relevant to the task of moral reasoning?

The Bible and the teaching tradition of the Church are relevant to moral reasoning on two levels: first, in terms of the contribution they can make to our reflection on the moral goods involved, to our consideration of morally relevant features of situations; and second, through the contribution that they make in terms of proposing specific moral norms as guidance for the Christian community. These two levels need to be distinguished and considered in turn.

Moral Goods

In chapter 5, the attempt was made to sum up the outstanding features of the Bible's testimony to the universal and inalienable worth of the human person. The Bible's affirmation of human dignity gives the rights of the person particular importance since it roots them in the providential love of God. In addition to this, the Bible offers a portrait of human existence that can enrich our reasoning about human situations. Some key aspects of a biblical understanding of human existence were presented in chapter 2. Church teaching over the centuries has also contributed to moral reflection on the worth of persons by emphasizing the goods that are morally relevant and significant in human situations. Since the influence of Christian tradition on ethics is principally in terms of enriching and informing our vision of the meaning of human existence, its relevance for the process of moral reasoning is greatest at the level of our reflection on the meaning and importance of the human goods involved in moral situations.

The Bible and Moral Norms

It is important to note that the Bible's rich evocation of human dignity, with the picture of human existence it offers, does not of itself give us specific moral norms. Rather, it gives us the moral insight that is invaluable in the process of moral reasoning, leading to the formulation of relevant moral norms. At some points, however, the Bible does propose moral norms. How should a contemporary Christian evaluate these? First, we should distinguish whether the Bible is proposing formal or material norms. The Ten Commandments themselves are essentially formal norms; they remind us of the importance of certain fundamental goods and virtues, rather than giving us specific guidance on how to act.

The Bible does, however, propose many material norms. Some of these are clearly related to the conditions of life in ancient Israel or the earliest Christian communities. The prophet Samuel, for example, insisted that it was the will of the Lord that the defeated enemies of Israel be put to the sword and all their goods destroyed—they were under the ban of holy war (1 Sam 15). The earliest Christians saw no fundamental conflict between Christianity and the institution of slavery (Eph 6:5–9). The fact that a moral norm is proposed in the Bible cannot in itself be the reason for accepting it. Critical biblical studies must be employed to understand why certain moral teachings were made by the biblical communities, and theological reflection must distinguish those teachings that simply reflect the cultural limitations of those communities from teachings that are a part of the continuing message of the Bible. And we must always ask whether a moral norm expresses the spirit of the teaching of Jesus since, for Christians, the final test of the meaning and coherence of the Bible is the person of Jesus.

The Bible does propose some moral norms that are both relatively specific and of continuing relevance. Jesus himself, for example, in response to a question posed to him about divorce, answers that the Torah's allowance for divorce runs counter to the original purpose of creation, and that man should not separate what God has joined (Mark 10:2–12). In Catholic tradition, this has been interpreted as a specific prohibition of divorce. However, we should note two things about this: First, the saying of Jesus does not attempt to define the meaning of divorce, and so it was the task of the Church's moral reasoning to interpret divorce as a breach of a free and full commitment to marriage, while allowing for the annulment of marriages that, for various reasons, were not believed to be based on the free and full commitment of partners capable of marriage. Second, the Catholic Church has understood this teaching of Jesus to be a prohibition of divorce in light of its understanding of marriage as a whole. Because the Catholic Church believes marriage to be sacramental, it interprets this teaching of Jesus more strictly than other Christian churches, who understand it as a statement of an ideal, rather than as a specific prohibition.

No moral norm proposed in the Bible, then, should be simply accepted as a direct and explicit statement of the will of God. It must be interpreted both in terms of the teaching of Jesus as a whole and in terms of our own human experience. We saw in chapter 2 that Christian ethics is based on a unified understanding of God as the source of both creation and revelation. God as the creator of the good world within which we live our moral lives cannot be opposed to the God who reveals himself in the testimony of the Bible. The ancient conundrum about God and goodness can be answered: God is the creator of goodness, so the revelation of his will cannot run counter to the inherent meaning of the world he has created, and God's revelation of himself to humanity enriches and enlarges our insight into that same inherent meaning. This means both that the moral teaching of the Bible must be interpreted in light of our own best efforts to know this created world, and that our own sense of values must be open to the judgment of the teaching of the Bible, in particular the teaching of Jesus. Only in this way can we avoid both the legalism and authoritarianism that stem from treating the Bible as a source of unchallengeable and unambiguous moral norms, and the complacent self-satisfaction with our own world of values that resists the Bible's prophetic and liberating challenge.

The *teaching of the Church and moral norms* will be the specific concern of the next chapter, so this discussion of the process of Christian moral reasoning should be studied in light of that chapter. The Catholic Church has made many teachings on specific moral norms, which need to be taken into serious account by someone engaged in the task of moral reasoning within the Catholic tradition. The Church's contemporary moral teaching can be found in the documents of the Second Vatican Council and in many post-conciliar documents, including papal encyclicals, documents from Vatican Congregations and Councils, and documents from national bishops' conferences.

5. Reasoning

The above elements all inspire and inform the act of moral reasoning itself, which can be considered under these headings.

Identification of Goods and Rights Involved

If we have studied a moral question and attempted to appreciate its seriousness as a human situation, we must then identify the goods that are involved in this question. We must ask ourselves what dimensions of personal existence are at stake and what human rights are crucial features of the situation. This reflection on goods is essential because it points out the *morally relevant* aspects of the question under discussion. It is these morally relevant aspects that can guide us in formulating a relevant norm. Consideration of the human rights and obligations involved needs to include reflection on the relationship of these rights in situations where they conflict with each other. We therefore need to draw on a picture of the overall good of human persons, in order to be able to have some sense of an appropriate hierarchy of rights. This reflection on goods provides the basic premises of our moral argument, since it expresses our convictions about what is at stake in a moral situation.

If we are considering, for example, the question of the immigration of refugees into a country, there are a number of different human rights that need to be considered to develop an appreciation of the moral question as a whole. We need to consider the importance of the rights of conscience, of freedom of worship, and of political freedom, and situate the question of refugees in relation to these rights. We will need to consider the relative claims of political and economic refugees. The rights of the citizens of the country offering asylum are also morally relevant, in terms of their ability to offer accommodation, welfare services, and employment and still maintain reasonable conditions of life for themselves. Our understanding of the human person will indicate whether we consider that any of these rights override the others, whether, for example, we consider the right to freedom of worship or freedom from political persecution to be so important that we offer refugees in this category priority over all others and impose no limit on the number of such refugees entering our country.

Aspects of Moral Reasoning

Once we have clarified the goods and rights involved in a particular question, we can reason about it and formulate a conclusion in terms of a moral norm. This involves the following different aspects of moral reasoning:

Analytical: Reason involves analyzing situations by asking the questions characteristic of a good investigator. We have informed ourselves about the situation, but in order to grasp it we must ask questions that bring out its significant features; we must distinguish the relevant from the irrelevant, the important from the unimportant, and the essential from the inessential. What are the decisive points, the crucial items of information, that will have a bearing on the key human goods that we have identified as constituting the morally relevant features of the situation?

Let us imagine, for example, that we are considering whether or not a country's participation in a particular armed conflict could be considered justified on the basis of the traditional concept of the just war. Assuming that we accept the traditional criteria for a just war—which emphasize self-defense, war as last resort, and the reasonable expectation of the conflict leading to a just conclusion—we must analyze the particular conflict we have chosen and discern which features of it are relevant for the criteria of the moral argument. We must be able to make clear what is meant by aggression, last resort, and the prospect of a just conclusion and point out which features of the situation correspond to these points in our argument. Without this, we cannot apply the criteria to the situation at hand, so the factual information that we have gathered cannot be deployed to good effect.

Analysis includes a consideration of the *relationship of different goods and rights* to each other, as well as the *relationship between norms and consequences*. The reflection on goods has identified the morally relevant features of the situation, providing the premises of our moral argument, but it is an analytical task to clarify their relationship to each other. Reasoning must also consider the likely consequences of an action, and the bearing that these consequences have on the adequacy of the norm which is being proposed.

The analytical role of reason also involves *conceptual analysis,* the analysis of the concepts that are relevant to identifying actions and distinguishing them from each other. If we are considering the question of the relationship between medical treatment and terminal illness in relation to the euthanasia debate, we must analyze the relevant concepts in order to clarify what we are talking about. Euthanasia (from the Greek words for *well* and *death*) is ending someone's life with the benevolent intent of ending his or her pain. Life can be ended either by *commission* of an act (that is, a lethal injection) or *omission* of necessary life support.

From the point of view of Catholic teaching, analytical reasoning must make two careful distinctions here: The first, in terms of *commission,* is in the difference between administering an injection with the intention of bringing about death, and administering an injection with the intention of lessening pain or distress, in the knowledge that this might also have the unintended consequence of hastening death. As noted in the discussion of the principle of double effect above, the latter action is considered acceptable in Catholic teaching. The second distinction, in terms of *omission,* is the difference between ordinary and extraordinary means of medical care. While the cessation of ordinary means of preserving life, with the intention of hastening death, is considered by Church teaching to be euthanasia, the cessation of extraordinary or burdensome means is not since the teaching argues that there is no moral obligation to prolong life at all costs.

Critical: Reason's critical function is to ask for and examine the grounds for received ideas and opinions on moral questions. This critical function is crucial to moral progress, since it does not simply take for granted that accepted ideas are adequate, but rather raises the possibility that they can be improved or superseded. The Israelite prophets exercised this critical function of reason, informed by their faith in the Sinai covenant, by questioning the moral basis of the institutions of their own day. This critical function includes the critique of ideology, of ideas that purport to be based on good argument, but that on critical examination may be seen to be attempts to offer a justification for unjustifiable relationships of power and privilege.

Imaginative: By critically testing the validity of established ideas and analyzing moral situations and the concepts that are used to grasp them, reason can make a judgment on the adequacy and relevance of a specific moral norm. Yet, at its best, moral reasoning will involve more than this: it will be informed by imagination, an imagination that seeks out positive and creative solutions to moral questions, an imagination that discovers new ways to allow human goods to flourish. Moral reasoning should be imaginative reasoning, as well as analytical and critical. The imaginative use of reason is inspired by empathy; the more we "suffer in" the situations of others, the more likely we are to develop moral norms that reflect a search for positive and creative options. Communities have often been led out of a moral impasse by leaders who had the moral imagination to see problems in a new light and propose solutions that could recognize what was of positive value in the different positions of contending parties.

The example of abortion can illustrate the contribution of imaginative reasoning. On the basis of a reflection on goods in light of the Christian vision of life, the Catholic tradition argues that abortion is morally wrong since a fetus is a human being and the direct and deliberate killing of an innocent human being is always wrong. In developing this argument, the analytical role of reason is expressed in the analysis of relevant situations and in the distinction between direct and indirect, and innocent and non-innocent. Reason's critical role can be expressed in testing whether this norm is relevant in the context of contemporary medical technology and in the critique of arguments in favor of abortion. The reasoning which opposes abortion must develop arguments showing that the critiques stemming from other positions have been taken into account.

It is the imaginative role of reason that proposes moral solutions that attempt to do justice to all the goods involved in creative ways. Proponents of women's right to an abortion often contend that social institutions offer scant help to the young unmarried mothers who might seek abortions. Those who are opposed to abortion can develop imaginative responses to this situation. One such response, adopted by a number of Christian groups, is to offer a guarantee of financial and social support to any woman who wishes to carry her child to term but who lacks the support to do so. In general terms, church communities can develop ways that provide a context of support and affirmation for those bearing children outside traditional marital relationships, as well as for married couples. In this way, moral reasoning can supplement the affirmation of a moral norm prohibiting abortion with imaginative solutions that affirm the worth of both mother and child.

6. Judgment

Finally, the process of moral reasoning must come to a conclusion by making a moral judgment. A moral judgment proposes a norm that expresses our moral obligation in relation to a particular moral question. The point of all the elements that have been considered above is to enable us to come to a moral judgment, to develop a relevant moral norm. Unless we do so, we cannot give guidance to ourselves or others, or test the continuing validity and relevance of the norms characteristic of our tradition. In making a moral judgment, a person exercises freedom and responsibility: the freedom to reason about human life, and the responsibility implicit in committing oneself to a particular judgment. (The moral judgment involved in concluding a process of moral reasoning or formulating a moral norm should, of course, be distinguished from the attempt to judge the state of someone's subjective conscience, that implicit form of relationship with God which is beyond the power and authority of any human being to judge.)

An Example of Moral Reasoning:
The Question of Capital Punishment

1. Definition

The question of capital punishment concerns the moral legitimacy of a public authority killing someone who has been convicted of a grievous criminal offense or offenses in a fair and public trial. In order to define the question sufficiently, we must state as a premise that the public authority is a legitimate authority that recognizes the rule of law and that does not interfere with the judicial process.[1] "Grievous criminal offense" can be taken to mean murder, particularly in association with other crimes of violence, such as sexual

---

1. The major country fitting this description is the United States, in a number of its state jurisdictions. Capital punishment statistics in the United States can be found at www.ojp.usdoj.gov/bjs/cp.htm, Bureau of Justice Statistics: Capital Punishment Statistics.

assault. Capital punishment by dictatorships or systems of arbitrary rule is ruled out in advance as illegitimate.

2. Knowledge

Since capital punishment is generally imposed in relation to the crime of murder, knowledge of the relevant situation must include a study of the criminology of murder.

The consensus of available research informs us that most murders are committed in moments of unpremeditated violence, largely within families or between people who know each other. Some are planned and committed in the context of organized crime, and some are unprovoked attacks by strangers, for example, the rape and murder of a woman by a man or group of men unknown to her.

Study of the life histories of murderers, especially those guilty of unprovoked attacks on strangers, shows that many murderers have been childhood victims of prolonged abuse and that they have rarely experienced normal human relationships.

Relevant records reveal that, if capital punishment had continued in certain countries, then individuals who were imprisoned for murder and subsequently acquitted would have been executed following their original sentence.[2]

Those countries that have abolished capital punishment do not report an increase in murders since abolition. This may be related to the fact that the fear of capital punishment may have little deterrent effect on the majority of murders, which are committed in moments of unpremeditated violence.

> Scientific studies have consistently failed to find convincing evidence that the death penalty deters crime more effectively than other punishments. The most recent survey of research findings on the relation between the death penalty and homicide rates, conducted for the United

---

2. For a presentation and discussion of the research of Hugo Adam Bedau and Michael L. Radelet on the execution of the innocent, see, for example, http://www.pbs.org/wgbh/pages/frontline/shows/case/failure.

Nations in 1988 and updated in 2002, concluded that "it is not prudent to accept the hypothesis that capital punishment deters murder to a marginally greater extent than does the threat and application of the supposedly lesser punishment of life imprisonment."[3]

3. Empathy

Empathy for the victims of violent crimes and their families should involve an attempt to recognize and understand the fear and anguish of those who have suffered unprovoked and traumatic violence. Empathy for those who have committed murder should involve reflection on their life histories and the degrading and brutalized environment that may be a factor contributing to their criminality.

The rape and murder of Sydney nurse Anita Cobby in 1986 was one of the most notorious murders in Australia in recent history. These words of her father, Garry Lynch, are an extraordinary testimony by a bereaved parent. His words are prefaced by a brief description of his own life

> As a young ex-serviceman, Garry worked in different parts of the country, doing a variety of jobs from heavy manual labor to skilled draftsmanship for the Navy.
>
> A religious quest for truth and meaning accompanied his travels. This spiritual search led Garry to believe in the power of Christ in his life. He also came to meditation, a way of praying and an approach to life which enabled him and his wife to endure what seemed unendurable.
>
> "*An acceptance of whatever happens, whatever happens. It will be there for a time and then it will go. It might be a terrible time, as when we lost our daughter— that was a terrible, terrible time, but I had the sense that it was going to go. I know when—and when we went*

---

3. Roger Hood, *The Death Penalty: A Worldwide Perspective* (Oxford University Press, 3rd ed., 2002), 230, quoted on the Amnesty International Website: Against the Death Penalty at http://www.amnesty.org.

through the agonies, and Peg will agree with me on this, there was a fire; we had to walk through the fire, but once we were out the other side we had endured and we were then able to get on with our lives."

Garry was also concerned to help others get on with their lives. He tells how he made a gesture of conciliation toward the families of Anita's murderers.

"Well, I did. I thought I knew the father. He was at the Blacktown Returned Soldiers League Club, and still is, doing a good job. And he was very well liked there, and they gave him all the support in the world once this thing had happened; he wanted to just run forever and they held on to him. They said, 'No you don't; you're staying with us and we're going to back you up.' Now, this was a wonderful thing to have happened, and I heard this and went in a couple of times but he just wasn't there, and then one night he came up. He was working down below and he came up and I just held my hand out and I said, 'Look, I want to say to you that we hold no responsibility on you whatsoever for what your sons did.' And he just grabbed my hand in his two...(in tears)...and there was just a silent interchange. And I felt good and I'm pretty sure he did, too, about that. So yes, I did that. I felt I had to do that because I knew he'd be going through a pretty terrible hell."[4]

4. Tradition

Moral Goods

The Bible: The Bible affirms the reality of human responsibility for wrongdoing and condemns the taking of innocent human life. It also affirms the importance of forgiveness and mercy, emphasizing

---

4. Interview with Garry Lynch from *The Search for Meaning: Conversations with Caroline Jones* (ABC Publications/Collins Dove, 1992), quoted, with commentary, in Hidden in Pain, Risen in Love, Sydney Archdiocesan Lenten Programme, 1996 (Sydney, AUS: Catholic Adult Education Centre, 1996), 47.

that forgiveness can bring new life both to the forgiver and the one forgiven. The teaching of Jesus warns against making any ultimate judgment about someone's guilt (John 8:1–11), emphasizing that God is sovereign over life and death. Actions motivated by vengeance are wrong because they usurp the judgment of God, who alone knows the secrets of conscience (Heb 10:30–31; Matt 7:1–5). The life of Jesus demonstrated a concern to communicate with wrongdoers, rather than shun them, even those who collaborated with the violence of the Roman oppressors by exploiting the poor with a crushing burden of taxation (Mark 2:13–17).

Moral Norms

The Bible: There is no explicit teaching on capital punishment in the Bible that can be associated with the authority of Jesus. Clearly capital punishment is accepted in the Bible as a social fact, and it is not explicitly challenged or condemned. The Bible was written at a time when capital punishment was commonplace, and its lack of critique of it may indicate nothing more than that it was taken for granted. The New Testament communities did not exercise state power, and so the question of capital punishment is not one they could exercise any decisive influence over. Many passages of the Old Testament affirm the righteousness of capital punishment (for example, Gen 9:6), but this cannot be associated with the teaching of Jesus, which is the fundamental criterion of judgment for all other biblical material.

Church teaching: In previous centuries, the institutions of the Catholic Church actively participated in capital punishment and, in many cases, encouraged state authorities to impose it. At the same time, many members of the Church were active in seeking clemency for prisoners in various situations, and since ancient times, the Church has offered the grace of the sacraments to those condemned to death.

Until very recently, capital punishment was accepted by the Church as a legitimate measure in some circumstances. In recent decades, Church hierarchies in many countries have expressed criticism of it, and many groups within the Catholic Church are active in their opposition to capital punishment. Pope John Paul II has introduced an important change in the Church's teaching on capital punishment, a change evident in the difference between the statement in the first English edition of the *Catechism of the Catholic Church* in 1994 and the Encyclical *Evangelium Vitae (The Gospel of Life)* in 1995, both given below. His emphasis is that the circumstances which warrant capital punishment, as the only means of serving the legitimate purposes of punishment, "are very rare, if not practically non-existent."

> Preserving the common good of society requires rendering the aggressor unable to inflict harm. For this reason the traditional teaching of the Church has acknowledged as well-founded the right and duty of legitimate public authority to punish malefactors by means of penalties commensurate with the gravity of the crime, not excluding, in cases of extreme gravity, the death penalty.
>
> If bloodless means are sufficient to defend human lives against an aggressor and to protect public order and the safety of persons, public authority should limit itself to such means, because they better correspond to the concrete conditions of the common good and are more in conformity to the dignity of the human person. (*Catechism of the Catholic Church*, 1994, §2266–67)

> On this matter [the death penalty], there is a growing tendency, both in the Church and in civil society, to demand that it be applied in a very limited way or even that it be abolished completely. The problem must be viewed in the context of a system of penal justice ever more in line with human dignity and thus, in the end, with God's plan for man and society. The primary purpose of the punishment which society inflicts is to "redress the disorder caused by the offence" (*Catechism* 2266). Public authority must redress the violation of personal and social rights by impos-

ing on the offender an adequate punishment for the crime, as a condition for the offender to regain the exercise of his or her freedom. In this way authority also fulfils the purpose of defending public order and ensuring people's safety, while at the same time offering the offender an incentive and help to change his or her behavior and be rehabilitated.

It is clear that, for these purposes to be achieved, the nature and extent of the punishment must be carefully evaluated and decided upon, and ought not go to the extreme of executing the offender except in cases of absolute necessity: in other words, when it would not be possible otherwise to defend society. Today however, as a result of steady improvements in the organization of the penal system, such cases are very rare, if not practically non-existent. (John Paul II, *The Gospel of Life*, 1995, §56)

5. Reasoning

The relevant moral features of the situation include the following three rights:

(a) *The rights of the criminal.* The criminal's human dignity is not abolished by his or her commission of the crime. The question is whether or not the criminal has forfeited the right to life by taking the lives of others without justification.

(b) *The rights of the community.* The community has the fundamental right to physical security of person and the right to live in a society characterized by respect for the law, which involves the enforcement of law by appropriate and just punishments.

(c) *The rights of the authorities.* The jury that must reach a verdict in cases likely to culminate in execution, the judge who must pass sentence under the authority of laws for capital punishment, the prison personnel who must guard and supervise prisoners condemned to death, and the executioners who administer capital punishment—all these individuals have particularly heavy responsibilities placed on them by societies that endorse capital punishment. The question whether these responsibilities can legitimately be given to them is a morally relevant feature of this situation.

Crucial to this part of the process is a *critical conceptual analysis* of the notion of punishment. Ethical discussion has distinguished a number of purposes of punishment:

(a) *Retribution.* A retributive understanding of punishment sees it as a penalty incurred by the criminal for the crime; this retribution is deserved by the criminal since the crime was a conscious commitment of freedom and responsibility against the law and thus against the rights and interests of other members of society. Retributive punishment restores the imbalance between good and evil caused by crime. It upholds the law and the values it expresses by punishing those who treat such values with disregard. Those in favor of capital punishment contend that it is a retributive punishment appropriate to violent crimes, especially multiple murders.

(b) *Prevention.* One purpose of punishment is to prevent future crime, and especially to protect victims of crime from repeated attacks on their person. This is particularly important with crimes of violence.

(c) *Reform.* A further purpose of punishment is to reform the criminal by depriving him of his liberty and subjecting him to situations and educational processes that may change his self-esteem, personal habits, and attitude to society so that he is no longer likely to commit crime once released. Clearly, capital punishment has no reforming element. (The thought of one's own imminent death may be a stimulus to repentance and remorse, but capital punishment means that this remorse cannot be expressed in a changed way of life.)

(d) *Deterrence.* A final purpose of punishment is to deter others from committing crime from fear of the punishment that they will thereby incur. Capital punishment, since it is the ultimate penalty, is often believed to have a deterrent effect. Whether it does so or not is therefore an important question. Since most murders are unpremeditated, involving minimal consideration of the consequences, deterrents are irrelevant to most murders. There is also evidence to suggest that the deterrent effect of capital punishment is irrelevant to premeditated murders, such as those characteristic of gang violence, since the internal sanctions of such gangs are at least as fearsome as capital punishment.

However, even if capital punishment did have a strong deterrent effect, the question can still be raised whether it is thereby justified. There are many effective deterrents that are quite unjustified because their severity is out of all proportion to the scale of the offense. A teacher, for example, may punish a boy for talking in class by giving him detention every day for a month: this may very well be an effective deterrent, in the sense that it may result in silence on the part of the other pupils, but its severity is out of all proportion to the disturbance caused by the boy talking.

If a harsh punishment is justified principally by its deterrent effect rather than as deserved retribution or as reform, that is, when the severity of the punishment is out of proportion to the gravity of the offense, then it becomes a case of using a human person as a means to an end, since that person is being inflicted with an undeservedly severe punishment for the sake of deterring others. To be justified as a deterrent, then, a punishment must be shown to be in proportion to the crime; that is, it must be deserved retribution. This means that the deterrent effect of the punishment can only be given as a relevant additional justification if the punishment is already deserved by the individual concerned; if capital punishment is to be justified, it must be in terms of deserved retribution.

An *imaginative* use of moral reasoning, which attempts to be informed by empathy, would seek moral solutions that recognize violent crime's affront to life and at the same time the humanity of violent criminals. If a society desists from capital punishment, it must offer possibilities for the reform of violent murderers, while recognizing that a person who has a deeply ingrained attitude of contempt for the lives of others, often associated with a brutalized upbringing, will have great difficulty in ridding himself of this. Church and other voluntary groups can offer violent criminals assistance in their search for repentance and reconciliation. Victims' support groups can also help to provide the mutual support essential to the bereaved.

The work of Garry Lynch, who was quoted earlier, is an impressive example of this ministry. Today Garry, with his wife, Peg,

> spends time with others who have lost a child by violent crime. His acceptance of an appointment with the New South Wales Department of Corrective Services brings him into contact with prisoners who have committed the most vicious crimes, men like those who took his daughter's life. Garry does not offer explanations to the victims of crime, nor does he preach to the perpetrators of crime. He comes to each carrying the fruit of his pain and his love. He simply tries to be present, attempting to listen, seeking to understand.[5]

6. Judgment

In my judgment, capital punishment is morally unjustifiable. The most important argument for capital punishment is that it is deserved retribution for very grievous crime; its deterrent effect is probably minimal and would not be sufficient justification on its own in any case. Punishment does have an important retributive element; it redresses the wrong that has been done to human

---

5. *Hidden in Pain, Risen in Love*, 48.

values. Because human beings are free and responsible, punishment can be deserved.

Yet the fact that retributive punishment can be deserved does not mean that capital punishment is legitimate. Capital punishment is a particular form of retribution that destroys the person being punished; it therefore must be based on the premise that the person is totally responsible for the crime committed. A court of law can establish responsibility and can establish that a criminal is of sound mind, but it cannot establish *total* responsibility. The imposition of capital punishment rules out giving any mitigating role whatsoever to the factors limiting responsibility in a criminal's upbringing because it subjects the criminal to the ultimate penalty. The possibility of capital punishment also means that a judge has to sit in judgment over the life and death of another human being, a judgment that can only be justified by the power to judge a person's guilt in some ultimate sense of the word. Yet this is not a power that human beings should claim. Capital punishment also prevents the redress of a miscarriage of justice at some future time.

While retribution is one justification for punishment, punishment should not take a retributive form that excludes all other justifications and purposes of punishment. Capital punishment does this since it prevents any possibility of repentance and reform of the criminal or reconciliation with the victim or the victim's family. Yet repentance and reconciliation are very great goods, goods which are at the center of the Christian understanding of human existence. Even though capital punishment may be associated with certain rituals that indicate respect for the human dignity of the sentenced criminal (such as the ministry of chaplains and respect for last wishes), the execution of criminals degrades human dignity in a fundamental sense; it is a social act that totally disowns a human being, affirming that *that* human being is beyond the scope of our concern and not worthy of any more attention from his or her fellows.

It was noted above that one of the purposes of punishment is prevention, and that the physical security of other members of society is a fundamental right that forms of punishment must consider. Deprivation of liberty through secure methods of imprisonment, which include opportunities for personal reform, is a sufficient retribution for violent crimes and can also serve the purpose of prevention of future crimes. The period of deprivation of liberty can only be decided by competent authorities in relation to individual cases.

Moral Reasoning and the Range of Ethical Debate

The above is an example of a discussion of a specific ethical question. Most of this book is concerned with general or foundational principles in Christian ethics, rather than with such specific questions. Yet if ethics is going to assist people in actually coming to terms with the questions that face them in their common life, such general principles must be put to use by focusing on these questions. The task of moral reasoning is the task of reflecting on the morally significant questions that arise in our lives and the life of our community, whether local, national, or global, and of developing an answer that can guide our freedom.

There is a vast literature that deals with the areas of *applied ethics*, that is, with ethical discussion of a great range of morally significant questions in particular areas of life. We will conclude this chapter by giving a brief overview of them. Not surprisingly, these areas relate in general ways to the dimensions of the human person discussed in chapter 5. There is no one way of classifying these areas; the reader will find that the literature is characterized by different ways of dividing and subdividing the great range of contemporary ethical issues, with much overlap between the areas.

Social Ethics

Social ethics is concerned in general terms with the ethical content and implications of social and economic relationships. Questions that are subjects of inquiry in social ethics include the following:

Economic Relationships

—ownership of property
—means of producing and acquiring wealth
—distribution of wealth
—extent and causes of poverty
—industrial relations
—"social wage" in relation to "user pays"
—financial institutions, loans, and interest
—meaning of the common good
—forms and amount of taxation

Work

—work and personal fulfillment
—working conditions
—work opportunities, employment, and unemployment
—strikes and withdrawal of labor
—work and technological change

Relations between Social Groups

—ethical rights of different social groups, such as the aged, children, or the handicapped; relationship of these groups to society
—relations between men and women
—questions of sexual harassment and assault
—relationships between different socioeconomic groups
—race relations

Family Ethics

—role and significance of the family for its members and for society
—family relationships, such as husband-wife, parent-children
—marriage
—divorce and remarriage

Cultural Ethics

—maintenance and development of specific cultures
—cultural and religious rights of indigenous peoples, including the question of land rights

Political Ethics

Political ethics is concerned with the ethical character of political institutions and processes, and the relationship between the citizen and the state. It includes such questions as these:

—ethical character of public life
—vocation of politics in a free society
—freedom of information
—truth and propaganda in political communication
—ethical responsibilities of public institutions
—education for democracy
—effectiveness of political institutions and processes in relation to fundamental political rights
—legal institutions
—citizens' rights and obligations, including jury duty, military service, conscription, and conscientious objection
—ethics of civil disobedience; peaceful noncooperation
—civil rights

International Ethics

Many economic, political, and social questions that have international scope can be grouped under this heading:

—human rights in the international context
—international distribution of wealth and resources
—trade relationships
—scope and character of international responsibility
—purpose and effectiveness of international institutions
—peace between nations
—war, and the debate about the possibility of and conditions for a just war
—disarmament
—forms of weaponry, especially nuclear, biological, and chemical weaponry
—immigration
—refugees and asylum seekers
—nationality rights
—population growth

The Ethics of Life

This area is concerned with ethical questions associated with preserving or taking human life, and with the ways in which human life is understood:

—war
—capital punishment
—abortion
—euthanasia
—ethics of procreation: artificial insemination, IVF, surrogacy
—experimentation on human tissue
—genetic engineering
—cloning
—use of the human body in experimental or medical contexts
—organ donation
—use of drugs

Bioethics is the ethical field that deals with life issues in the context of medical technology, as well as various forms of biotechnology. The issues that bioethics is concerned with are as many and varied as the ways in which these technologies can be used in relation to human life.

Medical ethics is concerned with issues arising in medical care, including the relationship between the patient and medical and nursing personnel, and the various ethical issues associated with medical treatment.

Environmental or Ecological Ethics

This area concerns questions related to the natural environment. Animal ethics may also be grouped under this heading, which would include points such as these:

—relationship between economic and environmental values
—breeding and killing of animals for human use and consumption
—use of animals in scientific experiments
—use of animals in product testing
—endangered ecologies, endangered species
—our obligations to future generations

Media Ethics

Ethical questions associated with the role and activities of the media include the following:

—media ownership
—media censorship
—media standards
—extent of the public's right to know
—privacy and the media
—advertising

Sexual Ethics

Ethical questions associated with the meaning and purpose of human sexuality and the human procreative faculty cover a wide range:

—sexual dimension of the human person

—meaning and relational context of sexual intercourse

—marriage

—relationship between the unitive and procreative aspects of sexual intercourse

—regulation of births; contraception

—sterilization

—homosexuality

—sexual abuse

—pornography

Summary of Chapter 7

1. Moral reasoning is best engaged in by a person of moral wisdom or prudence, and the best preparation for moral reasoning is a life that has been formed by good moral judgment and action.

2. The purpose of moral reasoning is to develop specific moral norms that can give guidance in concrete situations. This is particularly important in a society characterized by rapid and constant change.

3. Moral reasoning has a number of elements, which together make up a process of moral reasoning: a definition of the question, knowledge, empathy, tradition, reasoning, and judgment.

4. Knowledge: moral reasoning must draw on the natural and social sciences in order to know the contexts within which the good of persons can be fulfilled.

5. Empathy: unless we empathize or "suffer in" the situations of others we cannot reason about them with moral seriousness. Works of art and literature play a crucial role in evoking our empathy for moral situations.

6. Tradition: tradition contributes to moral reasoning in terms of its enrichment of our reflection on moral goods and in terms of the norms that express the accumulated wisdom of that tradition.

7. For Christian moral reasoning, the Bible contributes to a reflection on goods in terms of its affirmation of human dignity and its portrait of the meaning of human existence. It also proposes specific moral norms, which need to be interpreted in light of the life and teaching of Jesus and the meaning of the Bible as a whole, with the aid of the tools of biblical criticism.

8. Reasoning about moral situations has different aspects: an identification of the goods that constitute the morally relevant and significant features of a situation; analytical reasoning, which seeks to understand situations and the concepts we use to grasp them, by dividing them into their parts and distinguishing their different meanings; critical reasoning, which asks for the grounds for received ideas and opinions, especially in relation to ideology; and imaginative reasoning, which attempts to develop positive and creative solutions to moral problems.

9. The judgment that concludes a process of moral reasoning proposes a specific norm that is relevant to a given situation and that can give guidance for action.

Questions for Discussion

1. What do you think characterizes a morally wise person? What virtues does such a person have? What is it that makes their decisions good decisions?

2. Name a work of art (visual, literary, film, etc.) that you think is capable of evoking moral empathy. What difference do

you think this work of art can make to our appreciation of and insight into a moral situation?

3. Consider a moral question. In developing moral norms in relation to it, what role would you give to the analytical, critical, and imaginative aspects of moral reasoning?

4. In recent years, there have been many cases of elderly war criminals being put on trial. Most of the individuals concerned now live orderly and respectable lives, and there is no likelihood that they will ever repeat the crimes that they did commit during wartime. A trial may well be divisive, legally difficult, and extremely expensive; it may also involve painful recollections for the victims of war crimes. Should such trials proceed? Develop a moral argument to answer this question, clarifying what conception of punishment is involved.

An Exercise of the Process of Moral Reasoning

Consider the list of ethical issues presented at the end of this chapter. Choose one issue and develop a moral norm in relation to it, taking the content of this chapter as your guide.

Your standpoint on the question you have chosen should be based on the following:

—detailed factual research on the topic;
—a clear process of moral reasoning;
—a study of biblical material and Church teaching relevant to the topic.

(A careful reading of chapter 8 is important as preparation for using Church documents on moral issues.)

Remember that when you are developing a moral norm on a particular issue, you are not focusing on the question "What sort of person should I be?"—although the answer to that question will inform your approach to moral reflection. Neither are you focusing on the question "What is the good?"—although the answer to that question will be crucial to identifying the morally significant aspects of the issue. Rather, you are focusing on the question "What should I (or we) do?"—in other words, you are asked to develop and propose a specific norm, a guide for action. If, for example, you are considering an issue in ecological ethics, it is not sufficient to stress the importance of the environment and of an attitude of respect to it. Ethical reasoning needs to develop an *argument*, to proceed to the point where it can recommend a specific course of action, for example, in the attempt to reconcile economic and ecological needs in a specific case.

8

Christian Ethics and the Teaching Authority of the Church

The approach to Christian ethics developed in this book has emphasized the contribution made to ethics by the Christian faith tradition, a tradition based on the story of Jesus of Nazareth. It has argued with equal emphasis that Christian ethics also draws on all other sources of moral truth in common with other secular and religious ethical traditions. As we saw at the end of chapter 1, the Catholic Church traditionally emphasized the common sources of moral truth by speaking of fundamental ethical norms being based on "natural law," that is, on moral truths commonly recognized by people of many different traditions. Christian ethics, then, draws on specifically Christian sources, such as scripture and Church tradition, as well as on sources common to all, such as reasoning, experience, and scientific knowledge. Christians attempt to relate the story of God revealed in Jesus to the knowledge of human life and human values that they have in common with other human beings.

Christian Life as Community Life

By identifying him- or herself as a Christian, a person belongs to a community of faith, a community that shares common beliefs and practices and that has as its reason for existence a call to live as disciples of and witnesses to Jesus of Nazareth. By being part of this community, a Christian inherits a tradition of moral life and reflection. The common life of the community can guide the individual in developing a personal moral understanding, his or her own attempt to respond to what is good. The community's tradition is the context within which the individual can grow in personal judgment and commitment, sometimes by taking up a critical stance to aspects of that tradition.

Whatever tradition or community we belong to, our own moral responses are not purely an individual matter. They are developed in some kind of relationship with the tradition that has been influential in our own personal formation. In pluralist societies, of course, Christians are freely exposed to a great range of ideas and values, rather than exclusively to their own tradition. Yet if membership in the community that attempts to witness to Jesus of Nazareth is crucial to their identity, Christians will regard its traditions as an indispensable guide in living their own moral lives in freedom and responsibility.

Revelation and the Teaching Authority of the Church

Since the life of Christians is a community life, Christian ethics is a community reflection. If Christians are called by Jesus to be one body and to live a life of witness, then they have a common responsibility to seek and live by the truth in moral matters. For the Catholic tradition in particular, this community, the Church, has a teaching authority in relation to moral truth. This claim of the Church to teach with authority is based on the nature of revelation. The theological concept of revelation expresses the conviction of Christian faith that God has given himself to the human race by involving himself in its own history, in the history of human freedom. God is not known only through the created, natural world, nor only in the experience of the spiritual dimension of life that we can have through meditation and contemplation: God became human and shares in human existence.

If God's involvement with the human race encompasses such total commitment, to the point of becoming human, then God's communication of himself to us is necessarily *historical;* that is, it occurred at a particular time and place. If God's revelation were not historical, then there would be no reason why any figure in the past need be of any special religious significance. Yet since God shows himself to us within the history of our freedom, then there are times and places in human history when the saving and loving presence of God was experienced in special ways and to a special degree. For Christians, this definitive and total commitment of God to the human race was experienced in the history of ancient Israel, culminating in the life of Jesus of Nazareth. In his witness in word and deed to the unlimited compassion of the Father, in his commitment to freedom and justice to the point of death, and in his free self-sacrifice for the sake of others, Jesus revealed God as he really is. This conviction of faith is summed up in the Gospel of John's witness to Jesus: "Whoever has seen me has seen the Father" (14:9).

It is in the life of Jesus, then, that Christians of all ages find a definitive and unsurpassable story of God. The authority of the Church as teacher is based on nothing except the power and uniqueness of this story, a story based not on human wishes and imaginings, but on events that happened within the space and time of history—the story of a man born of a woman and crucified by a Roman governor. Through the experience of the resurrection of Jesus and the gift of the Holy Spirit at Pentecost, the disciples of Jesus received a mission to teach in his name, to proclaim the meaning of his life, death, and resurrection to all nations and all ages. It is the revelation of God in Jesus that gives the Christian Church its existence and its teaching authority.

The Teaching Authority of the Church and Morality

If the teaching authority of the Church is based on its witness to the revelation of God in Jesus, what does it have to do with morality? This is a particularly important question, since morality draws heavily on sources of moral truth that are independent of Christian revelation. Morality draws on the nature, reason, and experience that human beings share, regardless of religious tradition. Yet, as we have seen, the human values that we are aware of from these sources are both *affirmed* and *intensified* by Christian revelation. The Golden Rule, for example, is taught in many ancient traditions and affirmed in the Christian gospels. At the same time, the gospel intensifies the teaching of the Golden Rule by grounding its message of respect for persons in the love and providence of God that Jesus proclaimed. This relationship between the gospel and other sources of moral truth reflects the relationship between creation and revelation. Human beings have knowledge of what is good through reflection on the created world, the world that a good God has made. Whether they believe in God or not, all human beings are made in the image of God and have reason and freedom. They can achieve some knowledge of what is good and act on it. Revelation, the Christian gospel, affirms and intensifies that awareness of good that we have from reflection on creation.

Because the Christian gospel both affirms and intensifies *all* moral truth from all sources, it is part of the responsibility of the Christian Church to teach on moral matters. Human dignity, the value of human persons, is a fundamental part of the teaching of the gospels. The ministry of Jesus was dedicated to a reconciled and fulfilled humanity in God's care, and this must be the concern of the Church that his disciples founded. The Christian Church proclaims the value of human dignity not only on the authority of human sources of moral truth, but also on the authority of Jesus, the revelation of God. It is the mission and responsibility of the Church to reflect on and teach what it believes will advance the cause of human dignity and to condemn what harms it. Since the Church believes that the gospel offers something of great value for all human beings, its moral teaching is offered to all humanity, not simply to its own members. Christian ethics is an ethics of humanity, a reflection on human existence in light of the story of Jesus, rather than an ethics for a particular group. However, the moral teaching of the Church is clearly of particular relevance to its own members, who are a part of the same community of disciples of Jesus, a discipleship that has at its heart a commitment to living according to his

teaching and to reflecting on the meaning of that teaching in different times and contexts.

The fundamental relevance of the gospel for morality, then, is
in its affirmation and intensification of the fundamental good of
human dignity, the worth of persons as existing in the providence of
God, destined to share in the resurrection of Jesus. It is the importance of human dignity to the gospel that gives the Church its
teaching authority in moral questions since it teaches in the name
of the gospel. The relevance of the gospel to ethics, and hence the
teaching authority of the Church in moral matters, is preeminently
at this level of our awareness of and insight into the good. Yet if the
Church was simply to proclaim the good of human dignity only in
the most general terms, its teaching would be of little direct relevance and would have little effectiveness in actually realizing
human dignity in concrete situations. A development and statement
of moral norms is required to do this.

As we have seen, the purpose of moral norms is to serve the
good: to express, protect, and preserve it. At the beginning of chapter 6 we considered the example of a member of a film-censorship
board whose contributions to debate were confined to professing
commitment to the goods of freedom and public decency; thus
these contributions were of little value to the task of the board. The
Church's teaching must include moral norms for the same reason:
only moral norms can express the meaning of values in concrete situations, situations which do call for a moral judgment that
Christians believe is in harmony with the gospel.

The Church, then, claims authority to teach moral norms as
well as to proclaim the importance of fundamental goods and
virtues, since moral norms give the values of the gospel practical
effect. In doing so, however, it faces the difficult task of finding the
right level of generality for its moral teaching. It must teach at a
level specific enough to give the values of the gospel a concrete and
challenging meaning in different social contexts, but at the same
time avoid committing itself to norms that are so specific that they
exceed the Church's competence, which is based on the authority of

the gospel alone. This has been a particularly important issue in the Church's social teaching, where Church leaders face the difficult task of achieving a balance between stating bland generalities and pronouncing on detailed matters that exceed their competence.

How Is the Teaching Authority
of the Church Defined?

Since the teaching authority of the Church is based on revelation, the scope and degree of its teaching authority is defined in terms of revelation. The Church believes it has been given authority by Jesus to teach on matters of faith and morals, that is, on the content of Christian faith and on its implications for the moral life. If it had authority to teach on faith alone, and not on morals, then this would imply that Christianity was purely a cognitive affair rather than a way of life. The Church's authority to teach both faith and morals emphasizes the unity of faith and life in the gospel and in the life of the individual Christian.

The teaching authority of the Church has its highest form when it is teaching *matters that are essential to the gospel,* matters that it believes are part of the content of divine revelation. When teaching on such matters, the Church believes that it is *infallible.* To say that the Church is infallible is not to say that it is omniscient, that it knows everything, but rather to say that when proclaiming truths that it judges to be part of the gospel of Jesus Christ, it is protected by the Holy Spirit from error. The doctrine of the Church's infallibility is based on the promise of Jesus that he will be always with his disciples, that the Church founded by his disciples will be inspired by him to remain faithful to his gospel for all time, and that the Church will continue to teach the truth about him for all coming generations. The doctrine of infallibility expresses the Church's faith that its teaching will never so distort the meaning of the gospel that the truth that Jesus proclaimed will disappear from the face of the earth. Truths that the Church believes are crucial to the gospel, and that are therefore taught infallibly, are called dogmas.

It is important to note that the primary meaning of infallibility is the infallibility of the Church, the community of disciples of Jesus *as a whole*. The Roman Catholic Church, however, also teaches the doctrine of papal infallibility. This doctrine was defined as an article of faith in the First Vatican Council (1870), following much controversy. The doctrine of papal infallibility is itself defined in terms of the infallibility of the Church, rather than in any dichotomy between itself and the faith of the Church as a whole. The teaching of the First Vatican Council was that the pope is infallible when he deliberately intends to teach as head of the Church about matters that are part of divine revelation. Papal infallibility is thus not the infallibility of the pope as a private person, but rather a conscious expression of his teaching office to the universal Church. The doctrine of papal infallibility expresses the faith of the Roman Catholic Church that Jesus promised Peter, the leader of the apostles, that he would strengthen him in the truth (Luke 22:31–32), and that the popes exercise this ministry of Peter for the Church from generation to generation.

Papal infallibility has, however, only been invoked once since it was formally defined, in the definition of the Dogma of the Assumption by Pius XII in 1950. Despite the great significance attached to it by its proponents in 1870, popes since that time have—with the exception mentioned—seen no need to invoke it. Normally, the dogmas of the Roman Catholic Church have been defined by Church councils, presided over by the pope.

The pope and bishops of the whole Church together exercise what is called the *magisterium,* or official teaching office of the Church. Through their baptism, all Christians can share in the teaching or prophetic role of Jesus. It is the Church's magisterium that exercises this role in a way which has official and authoritative status for the whole Church. Papal or conciliar teachings that claim infallibility, because they express part of the content of revelation, are expressions of what is called the extraordinary magisterium. A much greater number of teachings, however, are in the category of what is called ordinary teaching. This includes papal encyclicals, documents issued by Vatican congregations with papal authority, and so on. Ordinary teachings with papal authority are directed to the Church as a whole. Bishops of particular dioceses, or groups of bishops from a particular country, can also teach in relation to matters of faith or morals affecting their own countries or dioceses.

The Magisterium's Teaching Authority on Moral Questions

It is important to be aware of these differences in the exercise of the teaching authority of the magisterium since they are crucial to understanding what claims to authority it is making when teaching on moral questions. The first point to make is that the Church's magisterium has never issued an infallible teaching on a moral question. This is not because moral goods are not important to the gospel; the good of persons is at the heart of the gospel, and any denial of this value would be a denial of Christian faith. The magisterium of the Church could, if it was felt to be necessary, teach infallibly that this value is part of Christian faith, that all human persons have value because they are all created by and exist in relationship with a loving God.

But there is a very good reason why even this value has not been made an infallible teaching: such a teaching would be so general, and without any clear application to any specific issue, that it would contribute little to the solution of any particular moral problem. The exercise of the Church's infallible magisterium has traditionally been reserved for issues that demand resolution, that need to be clarified for the sake of the unity of the Church, and that pertain to the very meaning of the gospel. The good of human dignity is at the heart of the gospel, but defining it in very general terms would be unlikely to offer a resolution to concrete problems.

As we have seen, it is only when values are expressed in terms of moral norms, prescribing specific kinds of action, that any degree of concrete application is indicated. The magisterium of the Church has made many teachings on moral norms, but none of these teachings has made any claim to infallibility. The reason for this is the converse of why no infallible teaching has been made about the most fundamental and general goods. An infallible teaching that simply proclaimed the worth of persons would be too general to be of concrete guidance, but teaching on specific norms would be too specific to be able to make a direct claim for the authority of divine revelation, the authority of the gospel. This is because the development of a specific norm involves a process of moral reasoning, and this process includes elements that cannot directly claim the authority of the gospel.

The Magisterium and the Processes of Moral Reasoning

The degree of teaching authority of the magisterium on moral norms can be understood by reflecting on the elements of the process of moral reasoning, considered in the previous chapter. First, moral reasoning requires detailed *knowledge* of human affairs, knowledge that can only be drawn from specific disciplines, whether the natural or social sciences. Although it has a very considerable body of knowledge at its disposal, the magisterium has no unique competence or authority in the detailed knowledge required for developing specific moral norms.

Second, moral reasoning requires *empathy,* the development of moral imagination, and a commitment to the moral seriousness of human situations. Despite all the sins committed by members of the Church in its name, the Church's life shows that it is a community dedicated to human values, and striving over many centuries to live in discipleship to the one who embodied the compassion of God. Yet clearly the magisterium, and the Church that it is spokesperson for, has no exclusive claim on moral empathy. This commitment of the heart to the needs and sufferings of others is common to all people of good will.

The final element, *reason,* is also clearly not exclusive to the Church or its magisterium, but is shared by all those who have a commitment to using their reasoning powers to develop moral norms that are marked by relevance, consistency, and clarity. Yet a key aspect of moral reasoning is a discernment of the goods at stake, an insight into what are the truly important features of moral situations. As we have seen, *tradition* is a key element in moral reasoning, and the Christian faith tradition makes a fundamental contribution to this discernment. The Christian vision of the meaning of life, expressed in the key beliefs noted in chapter 2, can give a particular sensitivity to the moral realities of our human condition. It is here, as we have seen, that the magisterium attempts to express the meaning of the gospel for the cause of human dignity.

All of this means that the degree of teaching authority that the magisterium has in moral matters is dependent on the degree to which a particular teaching is related to the fundamental and unchanging values of the gospel, which in turn affirm and intensify the values of creation. Because of these considerations, the magisterium of the Church has not invoked infallibility in relation to specific moral questions. On many moral issues, the magisterium of the Church has made no authoritative teaching at all, leaving it for members of the Church to decide in the light of Christian values and on the basis of their own process of moral reasoning.

The magisterium has not, then, made the claim of infallibility for teaching on specific moral norms since moral norms are developed by a process of reasoning that includes elements which do not have the infallible authority of the gospel. The Church's magisterium must use human reason and human knowledge to develop moral norms for specific situations, and it has no unique or infallible competence in moral reasoning. It does, however, make a serious claim to authority for such teaching, which is a part of the ordinary magisterium of the Church and a key part of its mission of proclaiming the gospel. This claim is particularly weighty when the teaching is directly concerned with fundamental aspects of human dignity, such as the good of innocent human life.[1] The magisterium

---

1. As in the papal teaching on abortion and euthanasia in the encyclical *Evangelium Vitae* (1995), §§62 and 65.

brings to bear a long tradition of reflection on moral questions, and a commitment to the moral life as a life inspired by the values of the gospel. These values have given the magisterium of the Church a powerful and inspiring basis for teaching moral norms that enhance human dignity in individual and social life.

The Church's tradition has also drawn on the resources of philosophy and the sciences in powerful ways. It has been informed by the knowledge and commitment of many Catholics expert in specific areas of life, who have put their knowledge at the disposal of the magisterium for the sake of developing Catholic moral teaching.

The magisterium's use of such expertise highlights the fact that good moral reasoning must draw on detailed knowledge and experience in the areas of life it is concerned with. Thus the moral teaching of the magisterium can derive added strength from the cooperation of members of the Church drawn from those groups who have expertise in, or who are most affected by, the teaching concerned. In recent times, conferences of bishops in various countries have developed their own teaching on social questions on the basis of a wide process of consultation, inviting members of the Church holding many different views to contribute to the process. Such processes do justice to an understanding of the Church as a community of faith, whose faith and insight the magisterium attempts to express.

Without such a process of consultation and dialogue, the magisterium runs the risk of teaching moral norms that do not take sufficient account of the knowledge and life experience of many members of the Church community. Such lack of broad consultation with a range of views can result in teaching that is not informed by all relevant knowledge or that is not readily intelligible. This is one reason for the tension between the moral teaching of the magisterium and broad sections of the Church in the present day, particularly in the areas of sexual and reproductive ethics.

The Moral Teaching of the Magisterium and the Conscience of the Catholic

The magisterium's moral teaching, then, is an exercise of its ordinary teaching authority, the normal form of magisterial teaching authority. Though non-infallible, this teaching must carry considerable weight for the Catholic; it is a serious and significant contribution to human reflection on the moral life, made in the light of the gospel. As such, it makes a serious claim on the conscience of the Catholic, who is a member of a community of faith that recognizes the pope and bishops as its authoritative teachers, those who have the responsibility of guiding the members of the Church in the life of discipleship. Because of this, the moral teaching of the Church is a key source of Catholic identity, the way of life as a member of a community that bears witness to Jesus of Nazareth.

What kind of claim on conscience is made by such teaching? Catholic theology distinguishes between two levels of assent to Church teaching. The first, known as the "assent of faith," is the assent appropriate to dogma, to what the Church, through its magisterium, teaches infallibly. This assent is fundamental to Catholic identity since it pertains to those teachings that define the identity of the faith itself; this is why it is called the "assent of faith." Moral teachings fall into the category of ordinary teaching, assent to which is defined in another way, in terms of a "religious submission of intellect and will" (Vatican II, *Lumen Gentium,* Dogmatic Constitution on the Church, §25).

A "religious submission of intellect and will" is a technical term in theology and Church law meaning an attitude of respect toward Church teaching. A Catholic should regard such teaching with respect and deference, departing from it only after serious personal consideration. It does not mean that a Catholic should abandon his or her own conscience, which is the highest subjective criterion for a human being. Nor does it mean that someone is no longer a Catholic if they do not follow some aspects of the Church's teaching on some specific moral norms, since, as noted, the assent

243

of faith is not required for teaching of this category.[2] It is the assent of faith to the dogmas of the Church, which define the meaning of Catholic faith, that is constitutive of the creedal dimension of Catholic identity. What "religious submission of intellect and will" does mean is that a Catholic must include a serious consideration of the teaching of the magisterium in his or her own process of formation of conscience, departing from it only on the basis of a sincerely and self-critically developed contrary judgment, grounded in careful examination of all the evidence that is reasonably available.

Public Dissent from the Church's Moral Teaching

A conscientious decision not to follow a particular aspect of the Church's teaching in one's own private life should be distinguished from public dissent. Public dissent is not simply a matter of not following a teaching in one's own life, but rather of expressing disagreement with or critique of this teaching in some kind of public forum. The two are distinct both because private dissent or noncompliance presents no public challenge to a teaching and because those publicly dissenting from a teaching may in fact continue to adhere to it in private, since they may believe it is their duty to do so as long as it is taught by the Church's magisterium.

Private and public dissent have different effects on the life of the Church. Private dissent on a large scale creates a situation where the magisterium's teaching is neither followed nor publicly challenged. There is simply a gap between the official teaching of the Church and the private lives of Catholics, a gap which demonstrates either the irrelevance of the magisterium's teaching to the experience of many Catholics or the refusal of many Catholics to

---

2. This is not to deny that a disregard for fundamental moral principles is destructive of Christian identity. If this disregard has a public effect, the Church sometimes has the right and the duty to defend the integrity of the Gospel by excommunicating those who claim to be Catholic yet engage in practices, such as torture, that ignore fundamental moral principles. This has been a question of great urgency in, for example, the recent history of the Church in Latin America.

seriously consider what the magisterium's teaching has to offer them in terms of a challenge to live by the gospel.

The history of the Church offers examples of both of these phenomena. During the nineteenth century, the magisterium of the Church repeatedly affirmed its teaching that the state should give special privileges to the Catholic Church because it was the true religion, while many Catholics gave their allegiance to the liberal political principle that all churches should have equal political rights. Eventually, the magisterium of the Church accepted the validity of the liberal state. In our own times, the Church's magisterium has often affirmed the importance of a commitment to social justice on the basis of the gospel, a challenge which, it would appear, many Catholics have given little serious consideration to. A gap of this kind between the teaching of the magisterium and the views of many Catholics has profoundly detrimental effects on the morale of the Church community and must be overcome by a commitment to genuine dialogue among all groups within the Church.

Public dissent, in contrast, voices critique of the teaching of the magisterium in the public forum. This public forum could be the secular media or the Church's own public forums, such as teaching situations, Church media, theological journals, or Church synods. Public dissent necessarily carries a different burden of responsibility as opposed to private dissent; while private dissent is essentially private noncompliance, with immediate significance only for the individual's private sphere of life, public dissent is an attempt to change opinion in the Church by voicing critique. Public dissent claims a hearing within the life of the Church and carries the appropriate responsibility.

Since the moral teaching of the Church on specific moral norms makes no claim to infallibility, and since the process by which these moral norms are developed shares the common human elements of moral reasoning, public dissent from Church teaching can make a real contribution to progress in the Church's moral teaching and reasoning. History provides us with a number of examples of changes in the magisterium's teaching, which retrospectively recognized the validity of the insights of those who dissented from earlier teaching. Members of liberal societies know from their own experience that the possibility of dissent and critique can be of great benefit to progress in insight.

Although the teaching of the Church gives no explicit recognition to the contribution that responsible dissent can make to the life of the Church, it has often given credit to the insights of those whose views were previously condemned. In the opinion of the present author, public dissent from non-infallible Church teaching can contribute to progress in the Church's understanding and can be an expression of the Christian's responsibility to conscience. Such public dissent should, however, be critically aware of its own responsibilities. These responsibilities are related to the forum in which dissent is expressed. The expression of dissent must always bear in mind the degree of maturity, theological understanding, and general commitment to the Church of the audience in question.

These considerations of context are particularly important for those who have accepted the responsibilities of Catholic religious education. In school situations, the religious educator is in *loco parentis* ("in the place of the parent"), a term meaning that the teacher has accepted the responsibility of representing the religious tradition in which parents wish their child to be brought up. Because of this, the teacher has a responsibility to present and explain the Church's teachings clearly and accurately, while at the same time encouraging his or her pupils to engage with the values and reasoning that inform this teaching in light of their own experience.

Public dissent should demonstrate its own commitment to the unity of the Church and its respect for its teaching authority by being oriented toward the constructive development of the Church's teaching as a service to the Church's search for truth. Someone who dissents from Church teaching on the basis of a conscientious and critical examination of the evidence has a responsibility to clearly distinguish between his or her own views and the official teaching of the Church. Dissent that fulfils these criteria can make an important contribution to the life of the Church since it attempts to express, with freedom and responsibility, a Christian commitment to truth by pointing out the limitations and inadequacies of attempts to express the meaning of the gospel for contemporary human beings.

Summary of Chapter 8

1. Christian life is community life since Christians are called to live in union with Jesus and each other. Christian moral reasoning, therefore, has a community character.

2. The teaching authority of the Church is based on revelation. The concept of revelation expresses the belief that God communicated himself in a definitive way in certain historical events, centered in the life, death, and resurrection of Jesus. It is the mission of the Church to proclaim the truth and meaning of these events.

3. Moral reasoning draws on many sources that are independent of Christian revelation. Because of the harmony of creation and revelation, the truths which we are aware of from these sources are affirmed and intensified by Christian revelation.

4. The Church proclaims the value of human dignity not only on the authority of human sources of moral truth, but also on the authority of the gospel. Its teaching on moral questions is therefore part of its attempt to proclaim the meaning of the gospel.

5. Since moral norms are required to express the meaning of human dignity in concrete situations and contexts, the moral teaching of the Church includes teaching on moral norms. In doing so, it must discern what level of specificity is appropriate in terms of the importance of the goods at stake and its own competence to give specific guidance.

6. The official teaching authority of the Church is called the magisterium, which is exercised by the pope and bishops in communion with each other. The Church believes that it is infallible, or protected from error, when teaching truths that define part of the meaning of the gospel. The First Vatican Council declared that the pope can express the infallibility of the Church in certain circumstances.

7. The magisterium of the Church has never made a moral teaching claiming infallibility since any specific moral teaching includes elements of knowledge and reasoning that cannot claim the direct authority of the gospel.

8. The magisterium of the Church develops its moral teaching by a process of moral reasoning in the light of the gospel. This process is best fulfilled by drawing on the experience, knowledge, and reasoning of all members of the community of the Church who are willing to contribute to it.

9. The moral teaching of the magisterium calls for respect and serious reflection by members of the Church and should only be departed from after conscientious and self-critical consideration of the relevant question. It does not require the "assent of faith," which is the assent appropriate to what the Church teaches infallibly.

10. Public dissent from the magisterium's moral teaching can assist the Church in developing this teaching, but should be engaged in only in the appropriate manner and forum.

Questions for Discussion

1. To what extent do you think that belonging to a community of faith can assist someone in the moral life and in the development of moral judgment?

2. On what grounds does the Catholic Church claim the authority to teach in the name of Jesus? Why does this authority extend to moral questions? Why has the Church never invoked infallibility when teaching on a moral question?

3. How specific do you think the Church's moral teaching should be? Consider some concrete examples of moral issues and give reasons why you think the teaching authority of the Church should or should not take up an official stance on them.

4. What claim does the Church's moral teaching have on the conscience of a Catholic? To what extent is obedience to the Church's moral teaching essential to the identity of a Catholic?

5. What do you think are the advantages and disadvantages of recognizing a right to public dissent in the Church in relation to moral teachings? How far do you think this right should extend?

Appendix:
Scriptural Sources
for Select Ethical Issues

Human Dignity in Scripture

A. Fidelity and Justice in Isaiah 1:2–23

The prophet Isaiah wrote in the eighth century BC, at a time when the kingdom of Judah was being attacked by the Assyrian army. The Assyrian empire was a powerful and ruthless state centered in the cities of Nineveh and Nimrod in Mesopotamia. The Assyrians had already destroyed the Northern Kingdom of the Hebrews (called Israel). Now Judah, centered in Jerusalem, had been laid to waste as well, with most of its cities destroyed. Jerusalem, on Mount Zion, stood above its devastated surroundings. That is why the city is compared to "a shelter in a cucumber field" in v. 8: cucumbers grow on vines on the ground, and a shelter stands out above the ground-creeping vines. Jerusalem itself was besieged by the Assyrian emperor Sennacherib, but was spared when a plague broke out in the Assyrian army. (The Assyrian empire was eventually overthrown by the Babylonian empire, which in turn destroyed Jerusalem itself in 587 BC.)

For Isaiah, the royal family of Judah had brought this destruction upon themselves and their people by making foolish foreign alliances and by ignoring the covenant. The true religion had become hypocrisy. Much of the text below attacks empty ritual, practiced by those who rejected the true demands of the covenant. Isaiah emphasized that the way forward was fidelity to the covenant and justice for the marginalized. The prophets of Israel were great poets, and Isaiah's critique is expressed in magnificent, hard-hitting rhetoric.

Some questions to consider while reading:

- How does Isaiah link fidelity to the covenant and justice for the marginalized?
- Whom does he identify as the marginalized? Why those groups in particular?
- What is his critique of hypocritical religious ritual?

²Hear, O heavens, and listen, O earth;
    for the LORD has spoken:
I reared children and brought them up,
    but they have rebelled against me.
³The ox knows its owner,
    and the donkey its master's crib;
but Israel does not know,
    my people do not understand.

⁴Ah, sinful nation,
    people laden with iniquity,
offspring who do evil,
    children who deal corruptly,
who have forsaken the LORD,
    who have despised the Holy One of Israel,
    who are utterly estranged!
⁵Why do you seek further beatings?
    Why do you continue to rebel?
The whole head is sick,
    and the whole heart faint.
⁶From the sole of the foot even to the head,
    there is no soundness in it,
but bruises and sores
    and bleeding wounds;
they have not been drained, or bound up,
    or softened with oil.

⁷Your country lies desolate,
    your cities are burned with fire;

in your very presence
 aliens devour your land;
  it is desolate, as overthrown by foreigners.
⁸And daughter Zion is left
 like a booth in a vineyard,
like a shelter in a cucumber field
 like a besieged city
⁹If the LORD of hosts
 had not left us a few survivors
we would have been like Sodom
 and become like Gomorrah.
¹⁰Hear the word of the LORD,
 you rulers of Sodom!
Listen to the teaching of our God,
 you people of Gomorrah!
¹¹What to me is the multitude of your sacrifices?
 says the LORD;
I have had enough of burnt offerings of rams
 and the fat of fed beasts;
I do not delight in the blood of bulls,
 or of lambs, or of goats.

¹²When you come to appear before me,
 who asked this from your hand?
 Trample my courts no more;
¹³bringing offerings is futile;
 incense is an abomination to me.
New moon and sabbath and calling of convocation—
 I cannot endure solemn assemblies with iniquity.
¹⁴Your new moons and your appointed festivals
 my soul hates;
they have become a burden to me,
 I am weary of bearing them.
¹⁵When you stretch out your hands,
 I will hide my eyes from you;
even though you make many prayers,

I will not listen;
    your hands are full of blood.
[16]Wash yourselves; make yourselves clean;
    remove the evil of your doings
    from before my eyes;
cease to do evil,
[17] learn to do good;
seek justice,
    rescue the oppressed,
defend the orphan,
    plead for the widow.

[18]Come now, let us argue it out,
    says the LORD:
though your sins are like scarlet,
    they shall be like snow;
though they are red like crimson,
    they shall become like wool.
[19]If you are willing and obedient,
    you shall eat the good of the land;
[20]but if you refuse and rebel,
    you shall be devoured by the sword;
    for the mouth of the LORD has spoken.
[21]How the faithful city
    has become a whore!
    She that was full of justice,
righteousness lodged in her—
    but now murderers!
[22]Your silver has become dross,
    your wine is mixed with water.
[23]Your princes are rebels
    and companions of thieves.
Everyone loves a bribe
    and runs after gifts.
They do not defend the orphan,
    and the widow's cause does not come before them.

B. Three Healing Stories of Jesus in Mark 5

Chapter 5 of Mark's Gospel presents three healing stories of Jesus. The first deals with the expulsion of demons from a wretched and disturbed man, who lived in the area of Gerasa on the shores of the Lake of Galilee. For Jesus' contemporaries, living in a presci-entific culture, disease was often understood in terms of demonic possession. There is no reason why contemporary Christians should not use a more scientific explanation for the illness of this man, which is clearly a severe psychiatric trauma of some kind. (The story of the demons going into the pigs and stampeding them off the cliff need not detain us here: "It may well be...that in a seizure accom-panying the exorcism the demoniac hurled himself at the pigs, thinking that the demons who possessed him wished to enter the swine. In panic, the pigs ran down the steep hillside and were drowned.")[1]

The narrative then moves on to two intertwined healing sto-ries. Jairus, a synagogue official, implores Jesus to come and heal his critically ill daughter. On the way there, Jesus is touched by a woman suffering from a hemorrhage. This woman probably suf-fered from a gynecological condition with the symptom of a chronic show of blood. According to ancient Jewish ritual law, this made her constantly unclean.[2] She also rendered anyone she touched unclean, so she was undoubtedly anxious about going about in pub-

---

1. C. S. Mann, *Mark*, Anchor Bible (New York: Doubleday, 1986), 280.

2. Leviticus 15:25–30: "If a woman has a discharge of blood for many days, not at the time of her impurity, or if she has a discharge beyond the time of her impu-rity, all the days of the discharge she shall continue in uncleanness; as in the days of her impurity, she shall be unclean. Every bed on which she lies during all the days of her discharge shall be treated as the bed of her impurity; and everything on which she sits shall be unclean, as in the uncleanness of her impurity. Whoever touches these things shall be unclean, and shall wash his clothes, and bathe in water, and be unclean until the evening. If she is cleansed of her discharge, she shall count seven days, and after that she shall be clean. On the eighth day she shall take two turtledoves or two pigeons and bring them to the priest at the entrance of the tent of meeting. The priest shall offer one for a sin offering and the other for a burnt offering; and the priest shall make atonement on her behalf before the LORD for her unclean discharge."

lic and had summoned up all her courage to approach Jesus and touch him in the hope of cure.

The story then moves back to the daughter of Jairus. In ancient Israelite society, the death of children was all too common, and boys were valued more than girls. Yet clearly her family grieves for her deeply, and Jesus shares in this.

Some questions to consider while reading:

- What details in these healing stories bring out the unique worth of the sick person?
- How does the compassion of Jesus emphasize each person's dignity in the sight of God?

1 They came to the other side of the sea, to the country of the Gerasenes. ²And when he had stepped out of the boat, immediately a man out of the tombs with an unclean spirit met him. ³He lived among the tombs; and no one could restrain him any more, even with a chain; ⁴for he had often been restrained with shackles and chains, but the chains he wrenched apart, and the shackles he broke in pieces; and no one had the strength to subdue him. ⁵Night and day among the tombs and on the mountains he was always howling and bruising himself with stones. ⁶When he saw Jesus from a distance, he ran and bowed down before him; ⁷and he shouted at the top of his voice, "What have you to do with me, Jesus, Son of the Most High God? I adjure you by God, do not torment me." ⁸For he had said to him, "Come out of the man, you unclean spirit!" ⁹Then Jesus asked him, "What is your name?" He replied, "My name is Legion; for we are many." ¹⁰He begged him earnestly not to send them out of the country. ¹¹Now there on the hillside a great herd of swine was feeding; ¹²and the unclean spirits begged him, "Send us into the swine; let us enter them." ¹³So he gave them permission. And the unclean spirits came out and entered the swine; and the herd, number-

ing about two thousand, rushed down the steep bank into the sea, and were drowned in the sea.

14 The swineherds ran off and told it in the city and in the country. Then people came to see what it was that had happened. ¹⁵They came to Jesus and saw the demoniac sitting there, clothed and in his right mind, the very man who had had the legion; and they were afraid. ¹⁶Those who had seen what had happened to the demoniac and to the swine reported it. ¹⁷Then they began to beg Jesus to leave their neighborhood. ¹⁸As he was getting into the boat, the man who had been possessed by demons begged him that he might be with him. ¹⁹But Jesus refused, and said to him, "Go home to your friends, and tell them how much the Lord has done for you, and what mercy he has shown you." ²⁰And he went away and began to proclaim in the Decapolis how much Jesus had done for him; and everyone was amazed.

21 When Jesus had crossed again in the boat to the other side, a great crowd gathered around him; and he was by the sea. ²²Then one of the leaders of the synagogue named Jairus came and, when he saw him, fell at his feet ²³and begged him repeatedly, "My little daughter is at the point of death. Come and lay your hands on her, so that she may be made well, and live." ²⁴So he went with him.

And a large crowd followed him and pressed in on him. ²⁵Now there was a woman who had been suffering from hemorrhages for twelve years. ²⁶She had endured much under many physicians, and had spent all that she had; and she was no better, but rather grew worse. ²⁷She had heard about Jesus, and came up behind him in the crowd and touched his cloak, ²⁸for she said, "If I but touch his clothes, I will be made well." ²⁹Immediately her hemorrhage stopped; and she felt in her body that she was healed of her disease. ³⁰Immediately aware that power had gone forth from him, Jesus turned about in the crowd and said, "Who touched my clothes?" [31]And his disciples said to him, "You see the crowd pressing in on you; how can you say, 'Who touched me?'" [32]He looked all around to see who had done it. [33]But the woman, knowing what had happened to her, came in fear and trembling, fell down before him, and told him the whole truth. [34]He said to her, "Daughter, your faith has made you well; go in peace, and be healed of your disease."

35 While he was still speaking, some people came from the leader's house to say, "Your daughter is dead. Why trouble the teacher any further?" [36]But overhearing what they said, Jesus said to the leader of the synagogue, "Do not fear, only believe." [37]He allowed no one to follow him except Peter, James, and John, the brother of James. [38]When they came to the house of the leader of the synagogue, he saw a commotion, people weeping and wailing loudly. [39]When he had entered, he said to them, "Why do you make a commotion and weep? The child is not dead but sleeping." [40]And they laughed at him. Then he put them all outside, and took the child's father and mother and those who were with him, and went in where the child was. [41]He took her by the hand and said to her, "Talitha cum," which means, "Little girl, get up!" [42]And immediately the girl got up and began to walk about (she was twelve years of age). At this they were overcome with amazement. [43]He strictly ordered them that no one should know this, and told them to give her something to eat.

Love and Moral Norms in Scripture

A. The Ten Commandments

As mentioned in chapter 6, the Ten Commandments are present in the Bible in two different versions. In Exodus, the commandments are set in the context of the dramatic narrative of the liberation from Egypt and the covenant of Mount Sinai. In Deuteronomy, the commandments are set during a time when Israel faced the threat of foreign invasion and the annihilation of state and people. In light of those challenges, Deuteronomy presents the commandments in a new and more reflective context, as they reflect on and restate the meaning of covenant and law.

In Exodus 20:1–17

1 Then God spoke all these words: ²I am the LORD your God, who brought you out of the land of Egypt, out of the house of slavery; ³you shall have no other gods before me.

4 You shall not make for yourself an idol, whether in the form of anything that is in heaven above, or that is on the earth beneath, or that is in the water under the earth. ⁵You shall not bow down to them or worship them; for I the LORD your God am a jealous God, punishing children for the iniquity of parents, to the third and the fourth generation of those who reject me, ⁶but showing steadfast love to the thousandth generation of those who love me and keep my commandments.

7 You shall not make wrongful use of the name of the LORD your God, for the LORD will not acquit anyone who misuses his name.

8 Remember the sabbath day, and keep it holy. ⁹Six days you shall labor and do all your work. ¹⁰But the seventh day is a sabbath to the LORD your God; you shall not do any work—you, your son or your daughter, your male or female slave, your livestock, or the alien resident in your towns. ¹¹For in six days the LORD made heaven and earth, the sea, and all that is in them, but rested the seventh day; therefore the LORD blessed the sabbath day and consecrated it.

12 Honor your father and your mother, so that your days may be long in the land that the LORD your God is giving you.

13 You shall not murder.

14 You shall not commit adultery.

15 You shall not steal.

16 You shall not bear false witness against your neighbor.

17 You shall not covet your neighbor's house; you shall not covet your neighbor's wife, or male or female slave, or ox, or donkey, or anything that belongs to your neighbor.

In Deuteronomy 5:6–21

6 I am the LORD your God, who brought you out of the land of Egypt, out of the house of slavery; ⁷you shall have no other gods before me.

8 You shall not make for yourself an idol, whether in the form of anything that is in heaven above, or that is on the earth beneath, or that is in the water under the earth. ⁹You shall not bow down to them or worship them; for I the LORD your God am a jealous God, punishing children for the iniquity of parents, to the third and fourth generation of those who reject me, ¹⁰but showing steadfast love to the thousandth generation of those who love me and keep my commandments.

11 You shall not make wrongful use of the name of the LORD your God, for the LORD will not acquit anyone who misuses his name.

12 Observe the sabbath day and keep it holy, as the LORD your God commanded you. ¹³Six days you shall labor and do all your work. ¹⁴But the seventh day is a sabbath to the LORD your God; you shall not do any work—you, or your son or your daughter, or your male or female slave, or your ox or your donkey, or any of your livestock,

or the resident alien in your towns, so that your male and female slave may rest as well as you. ¹⁵Remember that you were a slave in the land of Egypt, and the LORD your God brought you out from there with a mighty hand and an outstretched arm; therefore the LORD your God commanded you to keep the sabbath day.

16 Honor your father and your mother, as the LORD your God commanded you, so that your days may be long and that it may go well with you in the land that the LORD your God is giving you.

17 You shall not murder.

18 Neither shall you commit adultery.

19 Neither shall you steal.

20 Neither shall you bear false witness against your neighbor.

21 Neither shall you covet your neighbor's wife.

Neither shall you desire your neighbor's house, or field, or male or female slave, or ox, or donkey, or anything that belongs to your neighbor.

B. The Sermon on the Mount in Matthew 5:21–48

In the Sermon on the Mount, Jesus radicalized the demands of the Law. For Jesus, obedience to the will of the Father was not obedience to a set of laws but rather faithfulness to a relationship; the gift of the kingdom demanded the response of the whole person. And so the obedient heart cannot rest content with fulfilling just the specific actions demanded by the letter of the law; it seeks to fulfill the intention of the law by enacting the spirit of the ancient commandment to "love thy neighbor as yourself."

21 [Jesus said:] "You have heard that it was said to those of ancient times, 'You shall not murder'; and 'whoever murders shall be liable to judgment.' ²²But I say to you that if you are angry with a brother or sister, you will be liable to judgment; and if you insult a brother or sister,

you will be liable to the council; and if you say, 'You fool,' you will be liable to the hell of fire. [23]So when you are offering your gift at the altar, if you remember that your brother or sister has something against you, [24]leave your gift there before the altar and go; first be reconciled to your brother or sister, and then come and offer your gift. [25]Come to terms quickly with your accuser while you are on the way to court with him, or your accuser may hand you over to the judge, and the judge to the guard, and you will be thrown into prison. [26]Truly I tell you, you will never get out until you have paid the last penny.

27 "You have heard that it was said, 'You shall not commit adultery.' [28]But I say to you that everyone who looks at a woman with lust has already committed adultery with her in his heart. [29]If your right eye causes you to sin, tear it out and throw it away; it is better for you to lose one of your members than for your whole body to be thrown into hell. [30]And if your right hand causes you to sin, cut it off and throw it away; it is better for you to lose one of your members than for your whole body to go into hell.

31 It was also said, 'Whoever divorces his wife, let him give her a certificate of divorce.' [32]But I say to you that anyone who divorces his wife, except on the ground of unchastity, causes her to commit adultery; and whoever marries a divorced woman commits adultery.

33 "Again, you have heard that it was said to those of ancient times, 'You shall not swear falsely, but carry out the vows you have made to the Lord.' [34]But I say to you, Do not swear at all, either by heaven, for it is the throne of God, [35]or by the earth, for it is his footstool, or by Jerusalem, for it is the city of the great King. [36]And do not swear by your head, for you cannot make one hair white or black. [37]Let your word be 'Yes, Yes' or 'No, No'; anything more than this comes from the evil one.

38 "You have heard that it was said, 'An eye for an eye and a tooth for a tooth.' [39]But I say to you, Do not resist an evildoer. But if anyone strikes you on the right cheek, turn the other also; [40]and if anyone wants to sue you and take your coat, give your cloak as well; [41]and if anyone forces you to go one mile, go also the second mile. [42]Give to everyone who begs from you, and do not refuse anyone who wants to borrow from you.

43 "You have heard that it was said, 'You shall love your neighbor and hate your enemy.' [44]But I say to you, Love your enemies and pray for those who persecute you, [45]so that you may be children of your Father in heaven; for he makes his sun rise on the evil and on the good, and sends rain on the righteous and on the unrighteous. [46]For if you love those who love you, what reward do you have? Do not even the tax collectors do the same? [47]And if you greet only your brothers and sisters, what more are you doing than others? Do not even the Gentiles do the same? [48]Be perfect, therefore, as your heavenly Father is perfect."

Selected Bibliography

Introductions to Christian Ethics
in the Roman Catholic Tradition

Connors, Russell B., Jr., and Patrick T. McCormick. *Character, Choices and Community: The Three Faces of Christian Ethics.* Mahwah, NJ: Paulist, 1998.

Curran, Charles E. *The Catholic Moral Tradition Today: A Synthesis.* Washington, DC: Georgetown University Press, 1999.

Demmer, Klaus, MSC. *Shaping the Moral Life: An Approach to Moral Theology.* Edited by James Keenan. Washington, DC: Georgetown University Press, 2000.

Dwyer, John. *Foundations of Christian Ethics.* Mahwah, NJ: Paulist Press, 1987.

Fagan, Sean. *Does Morality Change?* Dublin: Gill and Macmillan, 1987.

Gula, Richard. *Reason Informed by Faith: Foundations of Catholic Morality.* Mahwah, NJ: Paulist Press, 1989.

Hanigan, James P. *As I Have Loved You: The Challenge of Christian Ethics.* Mahwah, NJ: Paulist Press, 1986.

Häring, Bernhard. *Free and Faithful in Christ: Moral Theology for Priests and Laity.* Vol. 1–3. New York: Seabury Press, 1978.

Hoose, Bernard, ed. *Christian Ethics: An Introduction.* London: Geoffrey Chapman, 1998.

Kelly, Kevin. *New Directions in Moral Theology: The Challenge of Being Human.* London: Geoffrey Chapman, 1992.

Macnamara, Vincent. *Love, Law and the Christian Life.* Wilmington, DE: Michael Glazier, 1988.

May, William. *An Introduction to Moral Theology*, rev. ed. Huntington, IN: Our Sunday Visitor, 1994.

O'Connell, Timothy. *Principles for a Catholic Morality*, rev. ed. New York: Harper Collins, 1990.

John Paul II's Encyclical on Fundamental Aspects of Moral Theology

John Paul II. *Veritatis Splendor:* On Certain Fundamental Questions of the Church's Moral Teaching. Vatican website, www.vatican.va.

Wilkins, John, ed. *Considering Veritatis Splendor.* Cleveland: The Pilgrim Press, 1994.

Two Outstanding Works on Christian Ethics in the Protestant Tradition

Hauerwas, Stanley. *A Community of Character: Toward a Constructive Christian Social Ethic.* Notre Dame, IN: University of Notre Dame Press, 1981.

O'Donovan, Oliver. *Resurrection and Moral Order: An Outline for Evangelical Ethics.* Grand Rapids, MI: Eerdmans, 1986.

Readers in Christian Ethics

Boulton, Wayne G., Thomas D. Kennedy, and Allen Verhey, eds. *From Christ to the World: Introductory Readings in Christian Ethics.* Grand Rapids, MI: Eerdmans, 1994.

Hamel, Ronald P., and Kenneth R. Himes, eds. *Introduction to Christian Ethics: A Reader.* New York: Paulist Press, 1989.

Dictionaries

Macquarrie, John, and James F. Childress, eds. *A New Dictionary of Christian Ethics*. London: SCM Press, 1986.

Stoeckle, Bernard, ed. *The Concise Dictionary of Christian Ethics*. New York: Seabury, 1979.

Some Books on Key Topics

On Natural Law

Porter, Jean. *Natural and Divine Law: Reclaiming the Tradition for Christian Ethics*. Grand Rapids, MI: Eerdmans, 1999.

On the Role of Christian Faith in Public Ethical Debate

Himes, Kenneth R., OFM, and Michael J. Himes, M.J. *Fullness of Faith: The Public Significance of Theology*. Mahwah, NJ: Paulist Press, 1993.

On Ethics and Interfaith Dialogue

Küng, Hans, ed. *Yes to a Global Ethic*. London: SCM, 1996.

On Conscience

Hogan, Linda. *Confronting the Truth: Conscience in the Catholic Tradition*. Mahwah, NJ: Paulist Press, 2000.

Patrick, Anne. *Liberating Conscience: Feminist Explorations in Catholic Moral Theology*. London: SCM, 1996.

On the History of Christian Ethics

Wogaman, J. Philip. *Christian Ethics: A Historical Introduction*. Louisville, KY: Westminster/John Knox Press, 1993.

On the Role of the Magisterium

Gaillardetz, Richard. *Teaching with Authority: A Theology of the Magisterium in the Church.* Collegeville, MN: Michael Glazier/Liturgical Press, 1997.

On Christian Moral and Spiritual Formation

Gula, Richard M. *The Good Life: Where Morality and Spirituality Converge.* Mahwah, NJ: Paulist Press, 1999.

O'Connell, Timothy. *Making Disciples: A Handbook of Christian Moral Formation.* New York: Crossroad, 1998.

For More Advanced Reading

New Studies in Christian Ethics, edited by Robin Gill. Cambridge, UK: Cambridge University Press. This series relates Christian ethics to an extensive range of topics in contemporary life and thought.

Readings in Moral Theology, edited by Charles Curran and Richard McCormick. Mahwah, NJ: Paulist Press. This series provides a very good selection of articles representing current debate on a range of topics.

Index